# THE
# NATIONALIZATION
# OF THE MASSES

# THE NATIONALIZATION OF THE MASSES

Political Symbolism and Mass Movements
in Germany from the Napoleonic Wars
through the Third Reich

GEORGE L. MOSSE

Cornell University Press
Ithaca and London

First published, Cornell Paperbacks, 1991.

Library of Congress Cataloging-in-Publication Data

Mosse, George L. (George Lachmann), 1918–
     The nationalization of the masses : political symbolism and
mass movements in Germany from the Napoleonic wars
through the Third Reich / George L. Mosse.
          p.  cm.
     Originally published: New York : H. Fertig, 1975.
     Includes index.
     ISBN 0-8014-9978-X (pbk.)
        1. Germany—Politics and government—1789–1900.
     2. Germany—Politics and government—20th century.
     3. Nationalism—Germany—History. 4. Mass society.
     5. National characteristics, German. I. Title.
     [DD76.M65   1991]
     320.943—dc20                                        91-55260

Typography by Albert Burkhardt
Printed in the United States of America

⊗ The paper in this book meets the minimum requirements of
the American National Standard for Information Sciences—
Permanence of Paper for Printed Library Materials,
ANSI Z39.48-1984.

The nationalization of the great masses can never take place by way of half measures, by a weak emphasis upon a so-called objective viewpoint, but by a ruthless and fanatical one-sided orientation as to the goal to be aimed at.

—ADOLF HITLER, *Mein Kampf*

# Acknowledgements

THIS BOOK is the result of a longstanding preoccupation with the dignity of the individual and its challengers, so successful during long periods of our century in stripping man of control over his destiny. Many years ago I attempted to trace how a system of moral values, Christianity, was eroded through contact with political reality during the seventeenth century. The triumph of reason of state seemed to me then to lead into a realpolitik which answered Machiavelli's eternal question of how a good man could survive in an evil world. But while I still believe that the seventeenth century was an important turning point in the absorption of Christian theology by realpolitik, the nineteenth century with the development of mass movements and mass politics seemed to transform the political process itself into a drama which further diminished the individual whose conscious actions might change the course of his own destiny. It seems to me, at least, that the creation of "mass man" was a necessary consequence of the industrialization of Europe, and that the world of myth and symbol within which such mass politics moved provided a most effective instrument of dehumanization. This in spite of the fact that men saw in the drama of politics, its myths and symbols, a fulfillment of their longings for a healthy and happy world. The flight from freedom and responsibility has never lacked appeal in our ever more complex civilization.

This book, then, seeks to understand one wellspring of modern politics by examining it within one nation during one period of its history. I believe that the method used here can be applied to other nations than Germany, and indeed some scholars are now investigating public festivals and political ritual in the Third French Republic.

Over the years I have been aided in probing these problems by friends and colleagues in Madison, London, Paris, and Jerusalem. I was able to present my findings while a visiting fellow in the History of Ideas Unit in the Research School of Social Science of the National University of Australia. I want to express my gratitude to Professor Eugene Kamenka and his colleagues for putting up with the excessive dogmatism of a scholar in the grip of new discoveries; they aided me in keeping my perspective. A preliminary summary of these findings was printed in *Nationalism: The Nature and Evolution of an Idea*, edited by Eugene Kamenka (Australian National University Press, 1973). I learned a great deal from Diplom Ing. Albert Speer, who on several occasions took the time to answer a myriad of questions and who read the manuscript of this book, keeping me from making several errors. It is not often that a historian has the opportunity to test his thesis upon a participant in the events he analyzes. Albert Speer was an important link between the earlier history of the political liturgy in Germany and its use by National Socialism which he so largely directed.

Several libraries have proved especially useful and helpful in my researches: the libraries of the University of Wisconsin, the Jewish National and Hebrew University Library in Jerusalem, the Wiener Library, London, the Bayrische Staatsbibliothek and the Architectural Library of the Technische Hochschule in Munich, as well as the Niedersächsische Landesbibliothek in Göttingen. A special word of gratitude is due to Dr. K. F. Reimers and the Institut für den Wissenschaftlichen Film in Göttingen for putting their superb collection of National Socialist films at my disposal and providing expert guidance through the maze of material as well.

The excellent editorial work of Judy Brooks Rabinbach and

Ann Adelman greatly facilitated the making of this book. I am also grateful to Howard Fertig, whose careful reading of the manuscript has contributed to such clarity of expression as this work may possess. All these debts of gratitude do not, of course, absolve me of final responsibility for the book.

G.L.M.

*Madison, Jerusalem*
*December, 1973*

# Contents

# Illustrations

11. The *Völkerschlachtdenkmal* at Leipzig (architect, Bruno Schmitz): *Monumente und Standbilder Europas* (Berlin, 1914)

12. The Tannenberg Memorial (architects, Walter and Johannes Krüger): Preussisches Archiv-Deutscher Kulturbesitz, Göttingen

13. *Thing* Theatre above Heidelberg: photograph by Bruce Finlayson

14. The Sharpshooters' Festival in Munich, 1863: Stadtarchiv, Munich

15. The Munich Workers' Gymnastic Society in 1905: Stadtarchiv, Munich

16. Festival of May 1, 1933, on the Tempelhof Airfield, Berlin, staged by Albert Speer: Rudolf Wolters, *Albert Speer* (Oldenburg, 1943)

17. Hitler Addressing a Party Day Rally at Nuremberg in 1935: Leni Riefenstahl, *Hinter den Kulissen des Reichsparteitag Films* (Munich, 1935)

18. Model of the interior of Hitler's Great Hall (architect, Albert Speer): Speer Archiv

19. Model of the Great Hall, centerpiece of Hitler's projected rebuilding of Berlin (architect, Albert Speer): Speer Archiv

# THE
# NATIONALIZATION
# OF THE MASSES

# CHAPTER ONE

# The New Politics

SITTING IN his imposing office in the Palazzo Venezia in Rome, Benito Mussolini, now eight years in power, contemplated the nature of his revolution: each revolution created new political forms, new myths and cults; it was necessary now to use old traditions and to adapt them to a new purpose. Festivals, gestures, and forms had to be newly created which, in turn, would themselves become traditional.[1] Karlheinz Schmeer has told us only recently that the invention of a new political style was the chief innovation of National Socialism; political acts became the dramatization of the new myths and cults.[2] We are still familiar with the huge mass meetings, the serried ranks, and the colorful flags so typical of European fascism. Though many of the sites where they took place were destroyed by the Second World War, enough fascist architecture remains intact to give us a feeling of the political style they symbolized.

Yet this political style was not new, and Mussolini was quite correct when he talked of adapting old traditions to new purposes. For what we call the fascist style was in reality the climax of a "new politics" based upon the emerging eighteenth-century idea of popular sovereignty. A common substance of citizenship was said to exist, of which all could partake. No longer would royal or princely dynasties take the place of popular self-expression. This concept of popular sovereignty was given precision by the "general will," as Rousseau had expressed it, by the belief that only when all are acting together as an assembled people does man's nature as a citizen come into active existence.[3] The general will became a secular religion, the people worshipping themselves, and the new politics sought to guide and formalize this worship. The unity of the people was not merely cemented by the idea of common citizenship; rather, a newly awakened national consciousness performed this function. This national consciousness had grown up alongside the ideal of popular sovereignty in many European nations. The nation in the eighteenth century was now said to be based upon the people themselves, on their general will, and was no longer symbolized solely by allegiance to established royal dynasties. The worship of the people thus became the worship of the nation, and the new politics sought to express this unity through the creation of a political style which became, in reality, a secularized religion.

How was this done? From the beginning of the nineteenth century onwards, through the use of national myths and symbols and the development of a liturgy which would enable the people themselves to participate in such worship. The concept of the general will lent itself to the creation of myths and their symbols. The new politics attempted to draw the people into active participation in the national mystique through rites and festivals, myths and symbols which gave a concrete expression to the general will. The chaotic crowd of the "people" became a mass movement which shared a belief in popular unity through a national mystique. The new politics provided an objectification of the general will; it transformed political action into a drama supposedly shared by the people themselves.

Parliamentary, representative government seemed to many men to contradict the concept of the general will, atomizing men and politics rather than creating unity. But the new politics was, from the beginning, part of the anti-parliamentary movement in Europe, advocating a secular religion as the political cement of the nation. Historians have stressed parliamentarianism as being decisive in the political formation of that age, the most important development of the past as well as the great hope for the future. As a result of the domination of this point of view, the study of the growth of a new political style connected with nationalism, mass movements, and mass politics has been neglected, not only so far as the nineteenth century is concerned but also as a necessary background to fascism.

Theories about fascism itself have tended to ignore the importance of those myths and cults which eventually provided the essence of fascist politics. For those who thought of themselves as liberals or as belonging to the left, fascism often presented an aberration of history, an "occupation" of the country by a barbaric minority. The people were held captive and when left to determine their own destiny would return either to a renewed liberalism or to Socialist ideals. Such a concept of fascism was particularly widespread among those forced to emigrate as opponents of the fascist régimes.[4] But despite the fact that some who fervently held such views in the past changed their mind,[5] this concept of fascism is still widespread. Even a more sophisticated recent historian of the movement, like Ernst Nolte, believes that the bourgeoisie turned to fascism only during a crisis, returning to their traditional liberalism once the crisis had run its course.[6]

Fascism as an actual historical movement was the product of the First World War, and this fact has been used either to deny or to underestimate its connections with a prewar past. Without the war and the peace that followed, there would have been no fascist movement and therefore, so it is argued, the prewar period did not really matter very much. Fascism thus becomes closely linked to its "epoch": the Europe between the wars. This point of view is not meant to provide an apologia for fascism, but it does endow the movement with a certain uniqueness and views it as an immediate response to a particular historical situation.

There is a large measure of truth to such an analysis, for the collapse of Europe after the war was an essential ingredient of fascism and provided much of its popular appeal. Yet, all these historians ignore fascism as a mass movement, and also mass democracy, both of which developments had a long history before Nazis and other fascists made good use of them. Indeed, the concept of totalitarianism has been misleading in this connection. For this implies terror over the population (a new version of the older occupation theory) and a confrontation of leader and people. It is based upon the presupposition that only representative government can be democratic, a historical fallacy which not only nineteenth-century mass politics but even the Greek polity should have laid to rest. For it was precisely the myths and cults of the earlier mass movements which gave fascism a base from which to work and which enabled it to present an alternative to parliamentary democracy. Millions saw in the traditions of which Mussolini spoke an expression of political participation more vital and meaningful than the "bourgeois" idea of parliamentary democracy. This could happen only because of a long previous tradition, exemplified not only by nationalist mass movements but by the workers' mass movements as well.

Though the new politics touched all of Europe, we are concerned with its growth and effect upon Germany. Within this disunited nation, the exaltation of the general will as the supreme good was stimulated by two factors once the nineteenth century opened: by the rise of nationalism, which based itself upon the Volk as an entity held together by its historical myths and symbols; and by the rise of mass movements and mass politics. Such mass movements demanded a new political style which would transform the crowd into a coherent political force, and nationalism in its use of the new politics provided the cult and liturgy which could accomplish this purpose.

The rise of nationalism and of mass democracy, the two factors which stimulated the worship of the people as a secular religion, joined hands in Germany during the nineteenth century. Nationalism defined itself as a movement of the people as it succeeded in obtaining a mass base. The masses which concern us cannot be equated with a mob. Contemporaries who witnessed the rise of nationalist mass movements by the middle of the nineteenth century believed that the mob was taking over the politics of their time. The liberal German historian Georg Gottfried Gervinus wrote with icy disapproval that the political movements of his age were supported by the instinct of the masses. At roughly the same time, in France, Comte Arthur de Gobineau attempted to analyze his own civilization, and recoiled in horror from the confrontation of élite and mass which he saw taking place everywhere.[7] The liberal and the conservative agreed on this point.

The word "mob" is usually used for men and women who stand outside society, or for those who through chaotic violence try to change it. Gobineau and many of his contemporaries perceived the masses in this way. George Rudé has attempted to show that mobs in the eighteenth century did have a purpose which informed their action, even if this purpose was not always rationally expressed.[8] The German masses with whom we are presently concerned also constituted a movement with definite goals and presuppositions. To be sure, at times such a movement lasted only for a few years or even days, but despite this, the masses always reconstituted themselves within a definite framework and according to lasting goals. Many people drifted in and out of the festivals and rituals of the nationalist movement, but its framework remained intact.

This movement had taken on the form of a secular religion long before the First World War. While mass movements and mass democracy were opposed to representative institutions as the mediating element between government and governed, they could not, in fact, dispense with such devices. "Totalitarianism" was never a system of government in which a charismatic leader beguiled his followers like the Pied Piper of Hamelin. To be sure, the official party of the one-party state could and did act as mediator between leader and followers.

But this was never satisfactory enough. New and different institutions came to the fore as part of a secular religion which bound leader and people together, while at the same time providing an instrument of social control over the masses. The secular religion which grew up in the nineteenth century has often been analyzed in terms of men and movements whose influence was confined to an intellectual élite: for example, Saint Simonism (influential in France and Germany). Our concern must be that secular and nationalist religion which became operative in German political life as part of mass movements, and which accompanied the entrance of the masses of the German population into the politics of their time.

This religion relied upon a variety of myths and symbols which were based on the longing to escape from the consequences of industrialization. The atomization of traditional world views and the destruction of traditional and personal bonds were penetrating into the consciousness of a large element of the population. The myths, which formed the basis of the new national consciousness whether of a Germanic or classical past, stood outside the present flow of history. They were meant to make the world whole again and to restore a sense of community to the fragmented nation. The "longing for myth" in Germany was noticed by many contemporaries from the French Revolution to the Second World War.[9] Its roots lay deeply embedded in history. We shall illustrate once again those characteristics which Huizinga thought were typical of the fifteenth century: "having once attributed a real existence to an idea, the mind wants to see it alive and can effect this only by personalizing it."[10] If, in that bygone age, "the mere presence of a visible image of things holy sufficed to establish their truth,"[11] this would remain the appeal of modern German national symbolism as well. Such myths had ties with religious and Christian world views, but they became secularized both through the heathen past to which they referred and through the instant happiness they promised to those who accepted them.

These myths did not stand in isolation, but were made operative through the use of symbols. Symbols were visible, concrete objectifications of the myths in which people could participate. "The community lays hold of some part of its world, apprehends the totality in it, and derives from it and through it that totality and its content."[12] This world view expressed in a specific way the mythology of a people; a mythology which, as Friedrich Wilhelm Schelling put it in 1802–3, was the "universe in a festive garb, in its primeval state, the true universe itself . . . already become poetry." Symbolism was the only adequate way to express this universe, and such symbolism must incorporate the aesthetic and artistic, for not only was this universe poetic, it was also the very font of creativity.[13]

The urge toward symbols which Schelling exemplified was typical of German romanticism. Symbols, the objectification of popular myths, give a people their identity. Gershom Scholem has told us how the Star of David as a Jewish symbol became disseminated only in the nineteenth century. He is, no doubt, correct when he explains this new urge as the search for identification with a Judaism which, after emancipation in the early nineteenth century, had become merely an "Israelite persuasion." The "Symbol of Judaism" must match the "Symbol of Christianity."[14] But Jews may have felt the same urge for symbolism as the Romantic movement did. They reflected, at times, the culture in which they lived. Nationalism, which at its beginning coincided with romanticism, made symbols the essence of its style of politics. These had always played a cardinal role in Christianity and now in a secularized form they become part and parcel of German national worship.

Public festivals had become cultic rites during the French Revolution and this tradition foreshadowed German concern with the new politics a few decades later. Various groups within Germany created their own festive and liturgical forms within a political context; the most important of these, the male choir societies, the sharpshooting societies, and the gymnasts, were to add significant elements to the new politics. These groups, important and widespread in Germany, provided the pillars for the most significant early public festivals. And permanent symbols helped to condition the population to the new politics: not only holy flames, flags, and songs but, above all, national monuments in stone and mortar. The national monument as a means of self-expression served to anchor the national myths and symbols in the consciousness of the people, and some have retained their effectiveness to the present day.

These were tangible expressions of a new political style. But "style" in this context denotes more than a political device destined to replace the liberal concept of parliamentary government or to illustrate the reality of myth. Such "style" was based upon artistic presuppositions, on an aesthetic essential to the unity of the symbolism. Friedrich Nietzsche aptly described what was involved here:

To think objectively . . . of history is the work of the dramatist: to think one thing with another and weave the elements into a single whole, with the presumption that the unity of plan must be put into the objects if it be not already there. So man veils and subdues the past, and expresses his impulse to art—but not his impulse to truth and justice.[15]

This veiling and subduing of the past was accomplished through myth and symbol, and the artistic thus became essential to such a view of the world. So did the dramatic, which will preoccupy us constantly throughout this study, for the idea of the new politics was to transform political action into a drama.

Aesthetic criteria not only informed the festivals already mentioned, but also determined the form and structure of national monuments. The direct involvement of masses of people forced politics to become a drama based upon myths and their symbols, a drama that was given coherence by means of a predetermined ideal of beauty. Political acts were often described as particularly effective because they were beautiful, and this whether German nationalists were describing their festivals and monuments, or German workers were talking about their own May Day parades.

The religious tradition played a large role here, the idea that acts of devotion must take place within a "beautiful" context. Here we are close to the theatrical and dramatic tradition of the Baroque as exemplified by the Baroque churches, though this tradition was rejected by nineteenth-century nationalists as frivolous. For the beauty which unified politics could not be playful; it had to symbolize order, hierarchy, and the restoration of a "world made whole again."

These, then, were the traditions which National Socialism eventually adopted and, in fact, changed but little in practice. As a mass movement, National Socialism successfully adapted a tradition which had presented an alternative to parliamentary democracy for over a century before the fascist movements themselves became a political reality.

Fascist and National Socialist political thought cannot be judged in terms of traditional political theory. It has little in common with rational, logically constructed systems such as those of Hegel or Marx. This fact has bothered many commentators who have looked at fascist political thought and condemned its vagueness and ambiguities. But the fascists themselves described their political thought as an "attitude" rather than a system; it was, in fact, a theology which provided the framework for national worship. As such, its rites and liturgies were central, an integral part of a political theory which was not dependent on the appeal of the written word. Nazi and other fascist leaders stressed the spoken word, but even here, speeches fulfilled a liturgical function rather than presenting a didactic exposition of the ideology. The spoken word itself was integrated into the cultic rites, and what was

actually said was, in the end, of less importance than the setting and the rites which surrounded such speeches.

To be sure, Hitler and Mussolini wrote theoretical works.
Within the Nazi movement Alfred Rosenberg's standing depended to a large extent upon books like *Der Mythus des 20.
Jahrhunderts (The Myth of the Twentieth Century.)* But in
practice it was different. No doubt millions read these works,
yet even among them the importance of the spoken over the
written expression of the ideology was emphasized. As in any
traditional cult, the cultic action itself took the place of theoretical works. Even *Mein Kampf* never became a bible for
the Nazi movement in the same sense that the writings of
Marx and Engels became fundamental to the Socialist world.
There was no need for this, for the ideas of *Mein Kampf* had
been translated into liturgical forms and left the printed page
to become mass rites of national, Aryan worship.

To term such dissemination "propaganda" is singularly in-
appropriate here, for it denotes something artificially created,
attempting to capture the minds of men by means of deliberate "selling" techniques. This is to misunderstand the organic
development of the Nazi cult and its essentially religious nature. Typically enough, even as acute an observer as Theodor
Heuss, who was to become the first president of the German
Federal Republic, believed in 1932 that the dissemination of
Nazi propaganda was influenced solely by considerations of
success or failure. It was the results which counted.[16] Moreover, such pragmatism was considered proven by the fact that
this propaganda excluded discussion with its enemies and their
point of view. There is some truth in this observation, for no
deeply held religious faith is open to rational dialogue. But the
very success of the propaganda which Heuss acknowledged
should have given him pause. It was not, after all, created for a
specific political purpose only in 1932, but constituted the
adoption of a political style which in Germany had already
passed through its necessary stages of organic growth. The
"religious instruction" given by the party was for Heuss

merely an example of bad taste. While he realized that Hitler valued the written less than the spoken word, this understanding did not lead him to connect this fact with the cultic nature of the Nazi movement. Instead, he ascribed Hitler's preference for the spoken word to the Führer's insight into his own limitations.[17] Heuss's attitude is typical of civilized and liberal people when they are faced with the phenomenon of the new politics. Many historians who now have the advantage of hindsight have followed in these footsteps.

The accusation that through propaganda the Nazis attempted to erect a terrorist world of illusions can be upheld only in part. No one would deny the presence of terror, but enough evidence has accumulated to account for the genuine popularity of Nazi literature and art which did not need the stimulus of terrorism to become effective.[18] This is true for the Nazi political style as well; it was popular because it was built upon a familiar and congenial tradition.

For those of the left, even today, the fascist appeal to irrationality was due to the supposed fact that late capitalist society could only defend itself by such a regression.[19] But if the Nazi political style was a specific phenomenon of late monopoly capitalism, then such capitalism must be read back into the time of the French Revolution and the early nineteenth century. For it was at that point that the new politics really began and was developed as an act of mass participation. But for Karl Marx that age was precisely the time when capitalism made its positive contribution to society. As we shall see, the German workers' movement itself attempted, however reluctantly, to adopt and, in fact, contribute to the new political style. Recently, however, some Marxist analyses of fascism have no longer seen that movement as merely an instrument of capitalism, but instead as a spontaneous mass movement exploiting crisis conditions. The emphasis on spontaneity still disconnects fascism from the course of history and endows it with unique qualities. In the final analysis, the left's concept of fascism with its emphasis on propaganda and manipulation is, in this case, similar to the liberal attitudes described above. How misleading these points of view actually are, this book hopes to demonstrate.

As we have stated, German mass politics and mass democracy moved in a world of myth and symbol, and defined political participation by means of cultic rites and settings. The appeal was directed to activating men's emotions, their own subconscious drives. This is hardly a new insight, nor one confined to Germany. Toward the end of the nineteenth century, when mass movements came to be more frequent and dominant, both Gustave Le Bon and Georges Sorel in France had already formulated theories similar to those we are discussing, designed to direct and control mass movements.

Le Bon stated as a fact in 1889 that the "substitution of the unconscious actions of crowds for the conscious activities of individuals is one of the principal characteristics of the present age."[20] After observing the masses in action during the movement headed by General Boulanger, Le Bon said that he was impressed with what he called the "conservatism of crowds," and the importance inherited ideas seemed to have for them. These ideas he believed were expressed through myths, and his contemporary, Georges Sorel, held that workers could not be led into a general strike without appealing to the ancient myth of heroism in battle.[21] However ambivalent Le Bon and Sorel may have been about the results of their observations, both believed that political institutions no longer mattered, but that instead a new "magic" determined the nature of politics.

Hitler and Mussolini were both influenced by Le Bon's analysis. However, Le Bon only summarized a trend which already existed before his time, and which was much more complex than the "magical" relationship between leader and led upon which he concentrated. Politics was a drama within which liturgical rites took a place, a concept which has been aptly defined by Erik Erikson: "Ceremonial permits a group to behave in a symbolically ornamental way so that it seems to present an ordered universe; each particle achieves an identity by its mere interdependence with all the others."[22] But this interdependence is cemented by symbolic action: episodic, as in public festivals; and more permanent, as in the formation of special groups like the gymnasts or in the construction of national monuments.

The French Revolution was the first modern movement where the people sought to worship themselves outside any Christian or dynastic framework. Honoré Gabriel de Mirabeau, one of the leaders of the revolution, summarized the purpose of the revolutionary cult: as in Greece and Rome, civic festivals must lead people step by step to envisage a unity between their faith and the government.[23] The "cult of reason" was supposed to replace Catholic ceremonial. But this cult of reason abandoned rationalism; it tended to substitute the Goddess of Reason for the Virgin Mary and infuse its cult with hymns, prayers, and responses modeled on the Christian liturgy. The festivals of the revolution and their symbols attempted to transform everyone into active participants. The mere creation of a worshipful mood was not considered good enough. Typically, Joseph Chénier's drama, *Triomphe de la République*, brought everyone to the stage: women and infants, old men and young, magistrates and military. Choirs and processions gave Republican ceremonies a religious cast.[24] Indeed, Goddesses of Reason replaced the Virgin Mary in churches which themselves were transformed into temples devoted to the cult of the revolution. The Cathedral of Notre Dame became known as the Temple of Reason. Nature, too, was certainly not forgotten; the revolution even endowed the early morning rays of the sun with symbolic and political importance.[25] The "general will" became a new religion.

Though the cults of the revolution dominated Paris for barely one year, they provided a dress rehearsal for the new politics of nineteenth- and twentieth-century Germany. For the mass movements of modern times also sought to worship the "general will," whether it was that of the people who formed a nation or those who formed the proletariat. The symbols would change, the concept of a sacred cult become more elaborate, but the example of the revolution was to provide a continuous inspiration. Even the classicism which an artist like Jacques-Louis David annexed to revolutionary propaganda, later, in Germany, determined much of the sense of beauty and form of the new political style.

Within the new politics, however, the de-Christianization of the worship of the people was never to become an accomplished fact. The religious and patriotic ideas of German Pietism had a profound effect upon the development of German nationalism, and therefore upon the cult and liturgy of that movement. Originally, in the seventeenth century, Pietism was a completely inner-directed movement within which state and nation vanished. Only in the eighteenth century did Pietists begin to include visions of the nation within their ideal of the spirit and Christian love. In 1784, for example, Friedrich Carl von Moser connected "Pia Desideria" (true piety) with the sanctification of service on behalf of truth and the fatherland.[26] Pietism managed to forge a unity between religion and patriotism, and fill love of the nation with Christian faith. "He who does not love the fatherland which he can see, how can he love the heavenly Jerusalem which he does not see?" (1774).[27] The nation now was not only a Christian nation, but was filled with a mystical Christianity which was constantly equated with the inner spirit. "The fatherland is within you," a "sacred space" within every man's soul.[28]

This Pietism infused the German heritage with a dynamic and emotional content of great importance in creating the kind of brotherly community, based on love, that Pietists desired. Pietism, for all its inwardness, did not discard liturgical forms. For Count Zinzendorf, a central figure in eighteenth-century German Pietism, Christian liturgy expressed the unity of the Christian community better than mere words. Christianity both through piety and liturgy unified this community, and it is small wonder that in Germany Christian liturgical form and the national cult were to exist in close proximity. Ernst Moritz Arndt, the poet of German unity, said in 1814 that Christian prayer should accompany national festivals,[29] but even when such obvious linkage vanished the national cult retained not only the forms of Christian liturgy intact, but also the ideal of beauty: the "beauty of holiness" which was exemplified by Christian churches. This tradition, fused with classicism, led to such artistic forms as could inspire political action. Both in the French Revolution and in Pietism, the ideal of inner-directed creative activity had already pushed outward into the political realm.

The artistic and the political had fused. Against the problems of industrialization, German nationalism defined itself as truly creative; the artistic became political. The parallel with Christianity was once again present. Christian art was the visible expression of Christian theology and the beauty of the liturgy aided in disciplining the congregation. Artistic creativity for the German nationalist movement was not merely an expression of man's inner nature, but helped also to give form to the shapeless mass through symbols and public festivals. In the choice of "sacred places" in which festivals and national monuments were set, a similar emphasis was placed upon emotions that were fostered by the proper environment, which was also the function that Church architecture fulfilled in Christianity.

The pragmatism of daily politics lay within this cultic framework and for most people was disguised by it. But "disguise" is perhaps the wrong term in this context, for any disguise which utilizes regular liturgic and cultic forms becomes a "magic" believed by both leaders and people, and it is the reality of this magic with which we are concerned. The politics of German national unification, its economic and social basis, these have often been investigated by historians. But they have forgotten that nationalism was a mass movement and as such embraced many different classes in propagating a fervent belief which became a major force of its own. The climax of this magic came during the Nazi period, but it was of importance long before that time.

We may not agree with the psychologist William Mc-Dougall's contention that nationalism, because it exalts character and conduct in a higher degree than any other form of group spirit, is psychologically justified. But nationalism did provide an object for mental activity which McDougall quite correctly saw as a prerequisite for the group spirit.[30] Nationalism proved most successful in creating the new politics in part because it was based on emotion. But this emotion did not produce a "crowd in ecstasy" simply because reason and logic were missing.[31] Rather, the careful efforts of nationalist movements were directed toward disciplining and directing the masses in order to avoid that chaos which defeats the creation of a meaningful mass movement.

Fascists and National Socialists have only been the most recent mass movements to make the theories of men like Le Bon come alive. It would have been more pleasant to describe the new politics as a failure. But tracing its course over so long a period, we cannot do so. Surely, if unfortunately, we have touched upon one of the principal dynamics of politics in a mass age. It would have been much more satisfactory to repeat the dialogue in one of the 1920's plays of the poet Ernst Toller: "The masses, not man himself, are the only effective force. No, the individual is supreme!"[32] Toller believed that both the masses and patriotism were surrogates for naked egoism. They stood in the way of the power which the individual should possess. If only Toller's ideal could have been transformed into historical reality! Instead, the conjunction of masses and nationalism was not manipulated by but in fact shaped much of modern German history. The voices of intellectuals like Ernst Toller were lost in the crowd.

This book is concerned with the growth of a secular religion. As in any religion, the theology expressed itself through a liturgy: festivals, rites, and symbols which remained constant in an ever-changing world. National Socialism, without doubt, illustrates the climax of the uses of the new politics. Fascist Italy also had its festivals and symbols, but Mussolini did not give them the key importance which Hitler saw in their application. We cannot claim to give a complete history of the growth and development of the new politics in Germany here; we shall merely try to analyze its nature and to demonstrate its development through the use of the most important and significant examples. Nor can we give detailed explanations of the political developments which accompanied the growth of the new politics in Germany. Yet it is useful to sketch the principal periods of German history within which the nationalization of the masses took place.

The first such period stretches from the "wars of liberation" (1813–14) against Napoleon to the attainment of German unity in 1871. The very beginning of the nineteenth century witnessed a feeling of disappointment with the disunity of Germany and the nature of its fragmented government. The German Confederation, founded at the Congress of Vienna in 1815, was unsatisfactory because princes instead of the people continued to rule; and instead of bringing national unity, the Congress created a loose confederation of thirty-nine states. This situation led to a glorification of the past "wars of liberation" against the French, when Germans had fought side by side against the intruders. The systems of government enforced by the reaction which followed the Congress of Vienna and its suspicion of nationalism gave the new politics its starting point: democratic and nationalist, opposed to the Establishment. The revolutions of 1848, important as they were as a part of German history, are of less consequence in the history of myth, symbols, and mass movements. To be sure, the 1860's saw an intensification of nationalism and its use of the new politics. But this took place under the spell of Italian national unification and as a long-range reaction to the failure to gain national unity in 1848.

The Second Reich, 1871–1918, was the fulfillment of many hopes for unity, yet that period was one of crisis for the new politics. Bismarck dominated Germany until his fall from power in 1890. The "Iron Chancellor" created a Reich in accordance with his view of *Realpolitik*, stressing the power of the state rather than the kind of spiritual unity that nationalists had thought important. The new Germany was unified only to the extent that was absolutely necessary: minorities were left alone, the individual states retained many of their powers,[33] and Bismarck's conservatism seemed unable to check the social divisions which were threatening to divide the nation at a time of rapid industrialization and urbanization. The state attempted to annex the nationalist dynamic and tame it into respectability, thus endangering its dynamic and democratic potential. Emperor William II (1888–1918) from the nationalist point of view continued these conservative policies, in spite of the high hopes first placed in the "people's Emperor." The German Republic, which followed the Second Reich and the lost war, gave the new politics a new impetus. The beginning of the Weimar Republic in 1918 ushered in the true age of sustained mass politics: as an expression of revolutionary ferment, left or right, and as a political necessity in a state based upon the ballot box. The very weakness of the Weimar Republic transformed it into a forum where each group could fight out its own vision of Germany's future, provided it could attract enough following. It was no longer Bismarck's Germany, where the emperor had held most of the threads of government in his own hands. In 1933 the triumph of National Socialism liquidated parliamentary government, but retained those techniques of mass politics that had been developing for over a century before the actual seizure of power.

Within this historical development we can see a certain rhythm which determined the growth of the new politics. From the beginning of the nineteenth century until the unification of Germany, it arose for the most part outside the framework of the German states, directed rather against the governments. The urge toward national unity did not find favor in the eyes of most kings and princes who ruled the nation. But after 1871 and until the birth of the Weimar Republic, the new German state attempted to manipulate the liturgy, to bend it toward an officially sanctioned nationalism. This attempt seemed to stifle the liturgical impulse which had been in the forefront during the earlier period. We shall see this reflected in the development of national monuments, as well as in the fate of those organizations which had proved crucial in the history of the national cult before unification. But protests against this imposition of a liturgy from above became important, and, for example, found their expression in new theatrical forms as well as in the "festivals" devised by Richard Wagner at Bayreuth. Finally, in the Weimar Republic, when all politics became mass politics, something of the earlier dynamic of the national liturgy would be restored.

Though this political style had a force of its own long before National Socialism appeared, it has seemed useful throughout this book to look forward from time to time in order that we may not lose touch with the climax of this political development. For in spite of all the problems which the new politics faced, we can detect a basic continuity that extends from the struggle for national liberation against Napoleon to the political liturgy of the Third Reich. Such continuity is not to be confused with a search for the origins of the Third Reich. Rather, we are concerned with the growth and evolution of a political style which National Socialism perfected. The aesthetics of politics, which is our concern, its objectification in art and architecture, did form Adolf Hitler's mind to a large extent. But this does not mean that it led to National Socialism or that it caused the German dictatorship. Such an assertion would be simplistic, given the complexity of history. The new politics stood on its own two feet; those attracted to it were not only National Socialists, but also members of other movements which found this style attractive and useful for their particular purposes. However attractive this political style proved to be for much of the population, however important a function it fulfilled in an age of mass politics, it provided merely one among a great variety of factors which went into the making of the Third Reich.

In analyzing a political style which was eventually used for such ugly ends, it may seem odd to begin with a discussion of beauty. But the "aesthetics of politics" was the force which linked myths, symbols, and the feeling of the masses; it was a sense of beauty and form that determined the nature of the new political style. The ugly ends to which this style was eventually used were masked by the appeal of the new politics for a large section of the population, by its usefulness in capturing their longings and their dreams. A concept of beauty objectified the dream world of happiness and order while it enabled men to contact those supposedly immutable forces which stand outside the flow of daily life.

# CHAPTER TWO

# The Aesthetics of Politics

A RECENT French writer has coined the phrase, "le snobisme de l'absolu,"[1] describing a literary and intellectual snobbishness that looks for heroes to worship and for the exceptional in life. To be sure, such an attitude had existed in the past and it eventually led many intellectuals into the arms of fascism, where they sought their heroes and a life removed from the ordinary drabness of bourgeois existence. But this kind of snobbery was also basic to the new politics, and appealed to the masses as it did to intellectuals. For the cult of politically charged myths and symbols was based on their exceptionality, on the fact that they stood outside the ordinary course of history and could be truly understood only by those who heroically defended them. The longing for experiences outside daily life, experiences which "uplift," is basic to all religious cults and was continually transferred to the secular religion of politics. Even the bourgeoisie liked to infuse their ordered lives with the extraordinary and the uplifting. An examination of the European novel around the turn of the last century has shown that the mystique of "living life to the full" had become a secularized myth in which domestic or public festivals symbolized the high point of existence.[2] Through such festive occasions the banal was transformed into a closer unity between men and nature, into a community among men.

An occasion was considered festive because, through symbols, it brought to light another world, that of wholeness, cohesion, and, above all, beauty. The German popular novel of the later nineteenth century shows constant preoccupation with the problem of beauty: a beauty which must exist in order to give life its proper meaning.[3] But what was this concept of beauty which infused not only novels read by the hundred thousands but also the new style of politics? Before we attempt to analyze it we must grasp the function it was meant to fulfill. For many Germans during the eighteenth century—Friedrich Schiller, for example—beauty was the unifying element in society.[4] It related what was common to all members of society, for beauty was considered a timeless absolute that could bring out the capacity for perfection in all men. The beautiful could unite opposites in human nature: strength and passivity, freedom and law. "Beauty," then, was an ideal type arising from that which endures in a man's character and, through this, penetrating his condition in life and ennobling it.[5] This functional element of beauty was well understood by the start of the nineteenth century.

The most important nineteenth-century attempt to create an aesthetic of the beautiful has as its theme the elimination of the merely accidental; the aim is to give man a consciousness of higher existence which will reconcile him to the reality of life. Friedrich Theodor Vischer's six-volume *Ästhetik, oder die Wissenschaft des Schönen* (*Aesthetic, or the Science of the Beautiful*) was written between 1846 and 1857 in order to prove that life in this world can be transformed into something beautiful and healthy. This could be achieved by what he first called man's fantasy, and then man's soul. Man is capable of idealization, claimed Vischer, for if our eye were like a microscope we would see not the beauty of nature and man, but the lice on the leaves of a tree and the imperfections in even the tenderest human skin. Further, beauty is a way of looking at things and at life which brings to light the "absolute idea" basic to all existence. This idea is obscured by a fragmented and atomized world, yet it is always within us.

Vischer believed that the present was unpalatable, a bour-

geois world of disorder and chaos, and that beauty had re-
treated into men's souls and could only be projected outward
through symbols. The soul infused an object with its mood; in
this way, ideals of beauty could break through and end man's
alienation from the world in which he had to live.[6] It is typical of a more general intellectual development that after 1857,
as he entered the second half of the nineteenth century,
Vischer placed increased emphasis upon the human need for
myth and religion.[7] The human soul had felt the need to
transform this world by infusing it with a beauty which stood
beyond the rational bounds of consciousness.

Vischer's ideal of beauty was functional, and he never really
defined the ideal type to which all aesthetic should relate itself. The sense of beauty was supposed to make men feel at
home in this world by providing them with a reality other
than that of daily life in an industrializing society.

As a committed liberal, Vischer had taken part in the
Frankfurt Parliament of 1848, where he advocated an extension of the franchise. But for him as for many others in the
second half of the nineteenth century, parliamentary political
activity played little part in the quest for beauty which was so
widely shared. The historian Heinrich von Treitschke was
correct when he wrote that almost everyone used Vischer's
aesthetic without giving credit to the author.[8]

Contemporary popular literature reflected Vischer's ideas.
For novelists like Marlitt, whose stories sold in the hundred
thousands around the turn of the century, the ideal of beauty
gave a unity and purpose to life, opposed to and transcending
modern materialism. The appreciation of beauty led to a definition of the truly sensitive human soul, which in the novels
then projected this ideal upon the world. Typically enough,
such a soul would also love order and harmony. A world of
beauty was a world where "everything was in its appointed
place"; a world where one was "at home."[9] For popular writers like Marlitt, at the end of the nineteenth century this
meant a harmonious and cohesive bourgeois world. For

Vischer, beauty was an intrinsic part of order, and he in-
veighed against "chaotic art." It is no accident that in the novels of the time, descriptions of beautiful objects take up much
room. The long descriptions which fill the works of a famous
writer like Paul Heyse can serve as an example. In his case, the
content of such beauty was linked to bourgeois taste: to opulence and the combination of comfort and order. But for all
these writers, the concept of beauty was related mainly to its
healing function. This was important not only for literature
and art but also for politics. Vischer described the functional-
ism of beauty as it was conceived by the national cult both
before and after his time. What was the content of this
beauty, and to what models did it refer?

The most important ideal of the beautiful was derived from
antiquity and, specifically, from Greece. Johann Joachin
Winckelmann's works played a key role here; he rediscovered
the beauty of Greek art for the later part of the eighteenth
century. Throughout the nineteenth and twentieth centuries
an important segment of German intellectual society agreed
with him that the "good taste which is increasingly spreading
through the world was first formed under the Greek skies."[10]
In order to grasp true beauty, artists were now compelled to
imitate Greek models.

What, then, is the essence of the Greek ideal of beauty?
Winckelmann attempted to describe it in his *Geschichte der
Kunst des Altertums* (*History of Ancient Art*, 1776). He
maintained that beauty resides both in the proportions and in
the structure of Greek art. The proportions had to be sym-
metrical, but this was not the principal consideration leading
to true beauty. Rather, beauty consisted in a unity of form
which encompassed all individual variety. As Winckelmann
put it, if we have an unrelated series of beautiful forms in a
nude sculpture, we cannot grasp its beauty. Therefore, a
sculpture must possess the unity of an ocean which appears
smooth ·as a mirror, although constantly in motion.[11] Beauty
had always to be grasped as a whole and must combine in one

harmony the detailed proportions of the ideal human form. Unity of form could not be described merely through points or lines drawn on the sculpture. On the other hand, nothing that was merely accidental or unique was allowed to mar its "ideal form." Not the individual, but "beautiful humanity," found expression in Greek art.[12] Beauty fulfilled a function which we have already analyzed: it stressed harmony and order, the "ideal type" of humanity, and strictness of form. These functions of beauty could be claimed only by Greek art, as symbolizing "noble simplicity and quiet greatness."[13]

The German concept of beauty in the nineteenth century was opposed to an excess of movement or decorative detail. Laocoön, strangled by snakes, Winckelmann tells us, despite all his passion represents a great and quiet soul.[14] Too much movement in sculpture represented an imprisoned and violent soul, the very opposite of the "idealistic beauty of true nobility." The Greeks were a harmonious people living under their blue skies, reconciling men with their troubled world; true passion, as Winckelmann defined it, consisted of a "quiet restfulness" through which the passion shines without disturbing the harmony of the human personality. He rejected all artistic representations of violent emotion, and his chief aversion, naturally enough, was to the art of Baroque.[15]

"The inevitable effect of the beautiful is freedom from passion," said Friedrich Schiller, echoing Winckelmann, who made the poet see Greek art through his eyes. For Schiller, too, beauty united opposites and dissolved them into one harmony. This did not mean that turbulence could not exist within the individual parts, but that the overall effect must combine "utter rest and extreme movement" in such a way that man himself did not become passionately and restlessly involved. For Schiller, man must always remain free and inviolate.[16] Beauty was never chaotic but, for Schiller as for Vischer, had laws and principles of order. This image of beauty was well equipped to influence the organization of masses and festivals. As such, we shall meet it often, adopted without giving credit to aesthetic theory, but still tied to it in its ideal of beauty which was based ultimately on these aesthetic principles.

The proper proportions of beauty, which could be mathematically expressed in the geometry of a beautiful face, were only a part of the harmonious whole. Here art must surpass nature. Beautiful nature exists, Winckelmann held, but only in bits and pieces, while the artist creates a perfect beauty in which there can be no admixture of ugliness.[17] These general principles were then illustrated through detailed descriptions of Greek sculpture and Greek buildings. His *History of Ancient Art* combined theory with concrete examples, and the theory itself was often expressed through pithy phrases which stuck in the reader's mind.

This concept of the beautiful concretized and gave meaning to the ideal of "classical form." Shortly after Winckelmann, Friedrich von Schlegel in 1794 voiced this longing for Greek examples in contrast to modernity: "When the consistence of the ancients is contrasted with our own dismemberment, their broad masses with our interminable mixtures, their simple decision with our paltry embarrassment and confusion, we are indeed impressed with the conviction that they were men of the loftiest stamp." Schlegel believed that his contemporaries might discover a still greater perfection of beauty.[18] Nevertheless, the ancients had succeeded at one time and the moderns still had to try.

The art of the ancients, through its beauty, could solve the dilemmas of modernity. The living examples were statues and temples which still impressed the beholder. Their outward form was important because it personified the functioning of the human soul. Outward appearance was linked to the state of the soul, a linkage which Vischer also stressed. For the beholder, the outward appearance must evoke the ideal type. Beauty, the highest concept of which man is capable, would in this manner transmit itself to other men. The total harmony of the figure, and all parts within it, projects what is noblest in man.

"In the formation of the human face the so-called Greek profile is the most telling part of an uplifting beauty."[19] This judgment, passed by Winckelmann in 1776, was to retain its validity during the nineteenth and twentieth centuries. It served to define the "ideal German man" from the time of the Greek statues which Winckelmann admired to the figures by Arno Breker which watched over the entrance to Hitler's new Reichs Chancellery. Beauty was expressed through a stereotype which would remain operative from the eighteenth century and eventually melt into the "Aryan type" the Nazis and their predecessors praised so highly. Many of the important racist writings, such as those of Hans F. K. Günther in the 1930's, simply repeated the ideas and descriptions we find in Winckelmann, claiming them as a monopoly of the Aryan race. Instruments were invented to measure the right proportions of the human face and classify the worth of men accordingly. This trend, which began at the end of the eighteenth century, was almost immediately applied to the classification of the human species.

Anthropologists were impressed by the "ideal type" represented by Greek art, though Winckelmann himself had been careful to disclaim any racial judgments. He posited the ugliness of the Jewish nose and the squashed noses of Negroes, but he immediately related this particular prejudice to an innate sensitivity peculiar to whites, while admitting, for example, that to Negroes a squashed nose might be beautiful.[20] But for most of those who applied the ancient idea of beauty, such caution was thrown to the winds. For example, the influential Dutch anatomist Pieter Camper (1722–1789) attempted to explore racial differences through a comparison of the facial and skull measurements of Negroes and monkeys. He presupposed aesthetic criteria which already defined and evaluated the progression of the human species. The ideal form was represented by Greek statuary, and the further a race departed from it, the lower it must rank on the scale of humanity.[21] Negroes became a species placed somewhere between man and animal. If the white race was to continue to symbolize beauty and nobility, it was important that it did not mix with other races and produce offspring that would lose the Greek ideal form. Thus the beginning of racial eugenics is closely associated with the crucial symbolism of Greek and noble beauty.

The ideal of beauty was transmitted not merely by anthropologists but also by important social and political groups. Gymnastics were supposed to train fighters for the liberation of Germany; but these freedom fighters, in order to be effective, had to represent an ideal of beauty which did not admit any distinction between aesthetics and individuality—the uniqueness of the individual and the cult of beauty which united all Germans. The compulsory gymnast's uniform was designed partly to obliterate any distinction between rich and poor gymnasts, and partly to make gymnastics easier. But it had another function as well. Its simplicity symbolized a strictness of form which, in turn, referred back to the ancient concept of beauty. Friedrich Ludwig Jahn, who in 1811 founded the gymnastic movement, condemned the departure from that noble simplicity of form which his gymnasts should symbolize: "the bigger the stomach, the more unsteady and turbulent man's looks, the emptier is his soul."[22] The student fraternity movement, from its beginning in 1810, worshipped a similar beauty, and this continued into the Youth Movement which began at the end of the nineteenth century. The constant reiteration that the true German must have a beautiful body repeats the worship of the Greek models.

The tradition was also continued in stone and mortar in the national monuments of the century. The nation depicted its quest for unity through Greek motifs and Greek temples. The *Walhalla* near Regensburg, built at the demand of King Ludwig I of Bavaria between 1830 and 1842 on the banks of the Danube in order to keep the spirit of German unity alive, was a Greek temple. The statues of famous Germans which filled it imitated the manner in which the Greeks had celebrated their own famous men. But the *Walhalla* was no isolated example. The so-called Hall of Liberation at Kelheim, the Hall of Fame and the Gate of Victory in Munich—each of these imitated Greece. The *Niederwalddenkmal* in the Rhineland, and later the *Völkerschlachtdenkmal*, built to commemorate the victory over Napoleon, repeat Greek motifs in their construction or in their friezes. At the same time, Frederick William IV of Prussia continued and elaborated classicism in the north. These monuments span the nineteenth century and, as the self-expression of the German nation, illustrate the "tyranny of Greece over Germany." The "good taste" about which Winckelmann wrote had found a home not only under the blue skies of Greece but also beneath the grey skies of Germany. Winckelmann had wished ardently that this taste might spread everywhere, but he did not foresee that it would in fact become a vital part of German national self-identification.

The development of artistic modes of expression was crucial, and the architects who were used to build these representations of the nation were trained in classical models. They journeyed to Rome and Greece to fill their sketchbooks with drawings of ancient monuments; and they were deeply influenced by the revival of classical architecture which had taken place in Prussia during the latter half of the eighteenth century. Men like Karl Friedrich Schinkel (1781–1841) and especially Friedrich Gilly exercised a continuing fascination on future generations. We have the testimony of Albert Speer, Hitler's favorite architect, of the importance of Gilly in developing his own artistic taste.[23] Friedrich Gilly (1772–1800) influenced future generations by his designs and his teaching, rather than by actual buildings. He received commissions only in the last years of his life, and none of them enabled him to build the monumental structures which were his special concern. But through the exhibitions of his designs for public monuments and new cities, and through his teaching at the architectural academy in Berlin, he guided future architects who did get the opportunity to put theory into practice. Schinkel, who rebuilt much of Berlin, and Leo von Klenze (1784–1864), who transformed Munich, were his pupils. But aside from such personal influence his designs, which survived his early death, exercised a compelling attraction.

These early classicists were reinforced above all by Leo von Klenze, the architect of the *Walhalla* who in the 1840's also rebuilt much of Munich to conform to the classical taste of King Ludwig I of Bavaria. Gottfried Semper and a host of other architects continued this tradition in the second half of the nineteenth century, and the example of such men provided the inspiration for Hitler's own taste. Through the Munich architect Ludwig Troost, Adolf Hitler came to admire Klenze's work.[24] Classicism survived all its enemies; not only did it make peace with romanticism—which in reality meant co-existence rather than fusion—but it also received added impetus as a reaction against the *art nouveau* (*Jugendstil*), the style so popular at the turn of the century. The architects we have mentioned were only the most celebrated examples of such continuity.

Yet, especially in the building of national monuments, Winckelmann's original definition of beauty underwent an important change. While he had praised simplicity and believed that a simple house could be more beautiful than a palace, the architects who tried to translate national feeling into stone and mortar no longer agreed. From the start of the nineteenth century, the classical tended to be confused with the monumental. They mixed the Roman tradition of the Colosseum with the Greek ideal of beauty. This urge toward the monumental, what Winckelmann would have called the exaggeration of form, was a logical consequence of the heightened national impetus: national grandeur had to be symbolized. Moreover, the eternal nature of the German spirit had to be taken into account. The monument must therefore be visible from a vast distance and dominate the natural environment which surrounded it.

This confusion of the monumental with grandeur and eternity has deep historical roots. It was influenced not only by Rome, but also by the massive forms of the Egyptian Pyramids (as we shall see later). Moreover, "monumentalism" was inherent in the combination of aesthetics and nationalism. The movement toward the monumental was further exemplified by public festivals which played a vital part in the national cult. For the urge to the monumental was an integral part of the growth of nationalism in the age of mass movements, when masses of the population were drawn into the agitation for national unity. Goethe had already perceived what was involved when he described the Amphitheatre in Verona during his Italian journey (1786). Within the theatre the masses are automatically formed into a unity, taking on one form and one spirit.[25] This effect is due both to the simplicity of the amphitheatre and to its monumentality. Throughout the nineteenth century political leaders as well as poets thought increasingly in terms of mass politics and mass democracy, and this development was reflected in the transformation of the original ideal of Greek beauty into monumental art.

Much later, Moeller van den Bruck's *Der Preussische Stil* (*The Prussian Style*, 1916) reaffirmed that the Prussian style was indeed the classical style which had predominated in Berlin at the end of the eighteenth and the beginning of the nineteenth century. He once more identified classicism and monumentality: through its monumentality, he says, architectural style receives an embodiment which allows it to portray domination and manliness. Moeller condemned romanticism as feminine, because it lacked the laws of classical form and substituted a weak and sweet feeling for a strong and true sense of beauty. The Romantic style could be admired, he maintained, but the Prussian style symbolized the sacred, which one could worship. Through its simplicity and monumentality it harked back to a time when man, hero, and artist were identical; therefore, it projected itself into eternity, despising everything which was momentary or accidental.[26]

Moeller retained the Greek ideal and repeated both Winckelmann's and Vischer's efforts to eliminate the merely accidental from aesthetics in favor of the eternally valid functions of beauty. Moeller's ideas were to pass into Nazi architecture. National Socialists complained bitterly that the monumental in art had decayed during the late eighteenth century as art became individualistic in a liberal age and was no longer able to speak to the community as a whole. The term "monumental," they claimed, derived from the word "momentum," sounded an appeal to activism. Moreover, a monumental style symbolized for the National Socialists moral greatness and the undiminished force of the human soul.[27]

But for all the ideological justifications of the monumental, it also served to solve a purely practical problem. Mass movements needed large spaces in order to accommodate the people who attended their festivals. During the second half of the nineteenth century this problem was already being widely discussed, mostly in connection with obtaining a "sacred space" in front of national monuments. But discussions concerned with the creation of the right environment for national worship were also concerned with the structure of festival halls able to hold some 75,000 or more people. The Hall of Congresses in Nuremberg where some of the Nazi party rallies were to take place was similar to the Roman Colosseum. The classical tradition was still relevant in 1933 and the architects even attempted to retain the Greek principles of a noble simplicity. But Hitler was only repeating a commonplace when he said that "We must always keep the people in mind and build stadiums which can contain 150,000 to 200,000 people."[28]

Nazi art and architecture was deeply influenced by the classical revival of the late eighteenth century, despite the criticisms it leveled against its individualism. The monumental was always superimposed upon the "noble simplicity" of Greek form and harmony. However, the classical ideal from the beginning had to face the Romantic movement and the revival of German symbols and myths within it. This confrontation led to a synthesis on several levels, one of which is exemplified by reference to the power of the Germanic soul which we quoted above, and which was used in order to justify the classical and monumental tradition.

At the beginning of the nineteenth century romanticism captured the imagination of many who were devoted to the ideal of German unity. Thus Ernst Moritz Arndt in 1814 suggested that a monument erected to celebrate the victory over Napoleon at Leipzig should be "large and wonderful like a colossus, the Pyramids or Cologne Cathedral." Arndt's proposal combines the monumental with Oriental and medieval inspiration, a typically romantic mixture of nostalgias. Friedrich Ludwig Jahn also advocated the building of national monuments (1800), coupling this desire with the romantic fascination with history. Monuments survive all times and the fury of all enemies, but they will be lifeless unless the history of the nation remains alive within the soul of the people. Arndt said nothing about the classics, but Jahn believed that ancient monuments could serve as a living example, for all peoples through all centuries made pilgrimages to Greek and Roman temples.[29] The classical tradition and romanticism did not merely confront each other within the rising spirit of national consciousness. They combined into a loose synthesis, or indeed co-existence, which was to determine the way Germans expressed their national spirit and its worship.

To be sure, Gothic elements, favored by much of romanticism, can be detected in some of the national monuments, such as the *Hermannsdenkmal* (see Plate 7). But the romantic and medieval impetus was rarely expressed through the construction of imitative national monuments. Those castles and other buildings which dated back to the earlier Gothic periods of history were used as scenery, as an already existing setting for the worship of the nation. The classical tradition was integrated into this medieval setting, with emphasis on the romantic and Germanic. The early student movement used the medieval Wartburg Castle, where the mastersingers had held their festivals and Luther translated the Bible, as the setting for an important demonstration of German unity. But when, later in the century, they built a monument on the Kyffhäuser Mountain, the romantic aspect was already present in its setting, the "Holy Mountain" on which it was built; the construction of the monument itself also has classical motifs. The romantic and the classical could exist side by side or, as we shall see, could form a closer union. But the romantic seldom replaced the classical.

Contemporaries were aware of this dominance of the classical, and many deplored it. Carl Bötticher, a famous architect, in 1846 praised a certain German style of building in which a roomy, large construction was made possible by means of high ceilings and arches. Such German architecture was preferable to the Greeks. A later commentator remarked in 1890 that with Bötticher's speech the Hellenistic tradition of Winckelmann had vanished from Germany.[30] Nothing could have been further from the truth. As late as 1886, Constantin Frantz, advocate of a medieval corporate state and a political writer of some importance, lamented that the revival of German national consciousness led to an aesthetic snobbery and had produced classical Germanias but no true German art. Writing in the *Bayreuther Blätter*, published by the disciples of Richard Wagner, he called for the revival of the true German Romanesque spirit. His accusation was correct, but his solution found no favor even though it seemed to correspond with romantic medievalism.[31]

The ancient idea of beauty and its function remained intact, continuing to delineate the "ideal type" of the German man and to determine the design of national monuments. But it surrounded itself with Germanic symbols. The wood and the oak were very important, and the people who gathered at public festivals and national monuments preferred such settings. This was especially true when national monuments became closely linked to public festivals during the second half of the century. Both became part of a cultic rite, and nearly as much thought was given to the gathering places which surrounded the monument as to the monument itself. Thus the actual monument on the Kyffhäuser was to be a part of a terrain on which the masses could gather, surrounded by a Germanic wood, to perform acts of national worship.[32]

At its maturity, the new secular religion of the Volk combined romantic and ancient elements in this way without marring the ancient concept of beauty, which thus retained its essential function. The worship of the Germanic landscape never replaced the dominance of Greece which is so obvious in most national monuments, as well as in the later representational buildings of National Socialism (the Nuremberg stadium, for example).

The romantic and the classical did not merely collaborate in providing the *mis-en-scène* for national festivals; they at times reached a closer synthesis. The Greek ideal of simplicity fused with a Germanic tradition which had exalted this ideal as part of the national heritage. German humanists of the sixteenth century (themselves influenced by the classics) had already endowed the German national character with an ethic which stressed simplicity and an upright character. Perhaps the rediscovery in that century of Tacitus' *Germania* played its part here, for Tacitus had contrasted these Germanic virtues with the decadence of Rome.

Moreover, the romantic shared, with the evolution of classicism toward the monumental, the move toward "heightening the effects of nature" and a love for the extraordinary. This desire to enlarge nature was realized through the use of open spaces, the arrangement of trees and stones. It could have assumed a playful form, as in the grottos which Claude-Nicolas Ledoux, the architect of Louis XV, constructed for the French king. But it did not remain so, and Ledoux himself linked the heightened effect which he sought to bestow upon nature with his attempt to produce the same effect through the extraordinary dimensions of his buildings.[33] Nature and buildings were both being remolded to impress man with the extraordinary, that which stood outside daily life and which symbolized the high point of human existence. The analogy between such concepts and the sacred was easily made, for cultic ritual needed also to be placed outside the ordinary, linked to extraordinary forces which sprang from the cosmos and from man's soul.

Classical style and Germanic romanticism also joined hands on another level, one which is exemplified by the most widespread of German national monuments: the Bismarck towers, built at the end of the nineteenth and beginning of the twentieth centuries, which dotted the nation in praise of the chancellor who had brought about German unity (Plates 1 and 2). Wilhelm Kreis, who built five hundred of these towers between 1900 and 1910, was worried by the dominance of classicism. Germans had to find their own style and cease to imitate foreign models. But he was unwilling to reject the classical tradition altogether, for he also felt that through its idea of beauty the noble soul peculiar to Germans could be symbolized. He found his ideal compromise in the tomb of the east Gothic king Theodoric at Ravenna (Plate 3).[34] Theodoric the Great (c. 454–526) had entered Germanic legend, first as a part of the Nibelungen saga and then through themes for fairy tales and adventure stories. He became the symbol of Christian knighthood.[35] But during the struggle for national unification the east Gothic monarch was transformed into a militant Germanic hero who opposed the culture and might of Rome. Felix Dahn's book, Ein Kampf um Rom (Fight for Rome, 1867), popularized the struggle of the Germanic Goths against the Romans in Italy, and Theodoric became the representative of a courageous and noble people. This tomb was, therefore, symbolic of Germanic ideals even while it retained a classical form in its construction.

Using this model to build his Bismarck towers, Kreis's archi-

tecture could fulfill the national purpose of those who sponsored them. According to its student sponsors, these towers
were built to imitate the way in which the ancient Saxons and
Normans had honored the graves of their heroes, by pillars of
stone without any decoration.[36] The tomb of Theodoric did
resemble a massive heaping of stones, but it also attempted to
retain classic form.

Kreis himself was influenced by the Prussian classical architecture of the end of the eighteenth century.[37] While the
tomb of Theodoric was the model for countless of his Bismarck towers, when it came to building more ambitious
monuments to the chancellor-hero, Kreis relapsed into classicism. Some of these were modeled on the Pantheon, which
seemed to fuse the beauty of ancient form with the monumental style peculiar to Rome.[38] Though Kreis constantly relapsed into classicism he sought at times to save himself from
it, not only by the model of Theodoric's tomb but also by
emphasizing the romantic German landscape as the most appropriate site for his monuments. As he put it: For the effectiveness of a national monument as a shrine of worship, the
landscape in which it is situated is of prime importance. But to
be effective within such a romantic and Germanic setting, the
building must have monumental and cubic forms. By stressing
cubic forms Kreis did not mean the abandonment of classical
harmony, symmetry, and proportions.[39] The meaning of classical beauty was to be united with the symbols of the Volk.
The monument erected by the German fraternity movement
at Eisenach to commemorate its fallen soldiers in the war for
unification, finished in 1903, illustrates the classical and romantic synthesis perfectly. The contemporary architectural journal *Bauzeitung* described it as a "Germanic temple" in the
form of a Doric rotunda. It symbolized a "monumental quiet"
and power restrained through form. Once again we receive
the force of Winckelmann's definition of beauty. But the
Greek example has now become Volkish: "the wonderful
Volkish harmony of Greek art," as the journal put it.[40] But

nature is also important here, for this art was combined with a mood induced by the native landscape in which it was set, and both together symbolize the unity of a common fatherland. Kreis was the architect of the Eisenach monument, or *Burschenschaftsdenkmal*, and its symbolism would hold true for the Bismarck towers as well. As always, and again in the Winckelmann tradition, Kreis used as little decoration as possible. Instead, the huge hall inside the monument was flooded with a "mystical sea of light" from the specially designed windows.[41] Not very original, Kreis was typical of many other architects of the time, and of an aesthetic which served to represent the nation.

Kreis was to live into the Nazi era and receive the lavish praises of Adolf Hitler.[42] Small wonder, for the synthesis he advocated was crucial to the liturgy of Nazi politics. He became an expert at constructing memorials to fallen soldiers during the Second World War and was chosen to design their cemeteries. Here too a romantic landscape surrounded what were essentially classical buildings.

The synthesis of the classical and German took one other peculiar form; Arndt's reference to the Pyramids was part of another important tradition. German architectural interest in Egypt dates back to the sixteenth century, and travelers to Rome could see obelisks strategically placed to give a heightened dimension to the papal *Roma Triumphans*. The eighteenth century witnessed an increasing interest in the use of Egyptian models. At the beginning of the century Fischer von Erlach, the most important Baroque architect of his time, enlivened his landscape designs by the use of obelisks and pyramids.[43] Other architects built pyramids such as that in the park of the Wilhelmshöhe in Kassel (1706), or even whole Egyptian temples (the Apis Altar of Johann Melchior Dinglinger in Dresden, 1731). Gilly took up this fashion and, typically, combined it with his love for classical forms. His sketchbook (1791) displays such a combination: a pyramid with a flattened top and a classical pillared entrance (Plate 4).[44]

Gilly's example, as usual, was significant. His student, Haller von Hallerstein, submitted designs for the *Walhalla* which combined the classical and the Egyptian, while at least one design for the monument to commemorate Frederick the Great of Prussia also followed Gilly's example.[45] Indeed, pyramids had come to symbolize the mysterious, reverential, and astounding. Moreover, they could be seen from a long distance away. Giambattista Piranesi's *Antichita Romane* (*Roman Antiquities*, 1756) popularized the pyramid as a symbol of eternity, and his book of copper plates became well known all over Europe. Here he attempted to show what ancient Roman cemeteries must have looked like; the eternity of time is represented by pyramids, obelisks, towers, and sarcophagi, all on top of each other or in close proximity. For Piranesi this was a monument to ancient Rome.[46] The pyramid was thus connected with eternity and also with Rome, whose architecture was so much admired as setting a standard for beauty and monumentality. Herder, too, praised the pyramid in 1774 for its simplicity and its synthesis of square and circle. For him Greece obtained its cultural inspiration from Asia and Egypt.[47]

The Romantic movement, with its love for the mysterious and unusual, was fascinated by both Indian and Egyptian cultures. As early as the seventeenth century, the Jesuit Kirschner had thought that India was an Egyptian colony.[48] Friedrich Schlegel attributed Egyptian art and architecture to impulses coming from the Indian subcontinent. He was filled with admiration for "the gigantic grandeur and durability of Egyptian and Indian architecture in contradistinction to the fragile littleness of modern buildings."[49]

Pyramids also had associations of grandeur and durability, and were therefore considered a sign of eternity. At the turn of the eighteenth and into the nineteenth century, they were particularly popular as tombs.[50] The symbolism of pyramids led the French architect Ledoux to believe that important buildings should climax in the pyramid style. Both Ledoux and

Gilly were attracted to this form because it facilitated the emphasis upon grandeur and massiveness. But Egyptian form never rose to typify the "concept of beauty": that was left to classicism. Friedrich Ludwig Jahn compared Greek and Roman temples with the Pyramids of Egypt. The pyramid had also outlasted time, but the national history which it symbolized was forgotten. The Greek and Roman temples still exemplified a glorious past. Clearly, the classical was a valid precedent for national monuments which "as symbols of national history embrace the fatherland with a garland of flowers, more firmly than iron and diamonds."[51]

Egyptian forms could be used within a classical framework in order to heighten the effect of the monumental. That was how Gilly used his pyramid, and it was how the Egyptian form entered the arena of national representation. It is no coincidence that Wilhelm Kreis's tomb of Theodoric also contains pyramidical elements or that Bruno Schmitz, one of the most prolific architects of national monuments, always returned to this form. Here, then, was an inspiration which could be used to extend the classical ideal of beauty toward the monumental and which would fill the beholder with even more reverence and astonishment.

National monuments illustrate most clearly the concept of beauty associated with the new politics and its development. But other symbols which were used in sacred national rites cannot be omitted. The sacred flame was of the greatest importance as a symbol of Germanism. Such a flame was intended to crown the Bismarck towers, but its symbolic use in nationalism goes back to the very beginning of the nineteenth century. When it came to celebrating the first anniversary in 1815 of the Battle of the Peoples, the German victory over Napoleon, most of the ceremonies throughout German towns and villages centered upon a "pillar of flame" which illuminated the hill or mountain on which it was built. At times, altars for these fires were constructed on public squares. This was the "altar symbolizing the salvation of Germany and at the same time an altar in praise of God. Let the holy flame of German unity cast its sacred light."[52]

The symbolism of fire and flame dates back to primitive times. Fire and torch were used to fight demons, and the power of the flame derived from the fact that it linked earth and heaven (often connected by lightning, which symbolized the cosmic or divine origins of the flame). No doubt some connection was made between sun cults and the sacred flame, though this does not seem to have been of importance in pagan Germany. The Christian use of the sacred flame was important as well: the Easter candle, the consecration of a flame. Some interpreters of the Bible saw in fire the symbol of God's love. But above all, the Holy Ghost was often given the properties of fire and flame in words and in pictures.[53] The eternal light over the altar further annexed the sacred flame to Christianity.

Christian and heathen symbolisms were mixed up together, but it was the sacred flame or the pillar of fire which dominated the ceremonies, though the people also went to church in order to give thanks to the Lord. The symbolism of the German oak was added, and men walked in procession wearing its leaves. Often such a tree was put in the midst of the flames, thus uniting the two symbols. Villages and towns thought of the oak as the "tree of liberty" made familiar through the festivals of the French Revolution.[54] The oak was one of the most sacred trees in primitive times, perhaps because of its imposing size, perhaps also because it had provided nourishment. "Holy oaks" could be found in all regions of Germany. Christianity also annexed this symbol; the worship of the oak was connected to the worship of the Virgin Mary. Her picture was found miraculously in the hollow of an oak, whereupon a chapel was built on that spot.[55] The symbol of the oak was, like the sacred flame, a part of popular piety and therefore easy to use in the cause of national self-representation.

In 1815 there was still a confusion of symbols, Germanic,

Christian, and even French, though the nationalistic festivities were meant to celebrate the victory over that nation. But the Germanic symbols, and especially the sacred flame, had already taken on a religious cast; they were a part of the cultic rites which produced a romantic mood of worship. The flame and the fire were to increase in importance as the center of the national rite, ultimately taking the place of the Christian altar in the making of a secular religion.

One further dimension should be added to the function of fire as conceived by the new German cults, and that is the idea of everlasting rebirth and, thus, of continual growth and development. The flame as it stood symbolized light over darkness, the sun as against the night. It reflected the mystical forces of the life-bringing sun which gave men strength and vitality. To the Nazis it meant "purification," symbolized brotherly community, and served to remind party members of the "eternal life process."[56] But this had always been the meaning of this symbol, connected as it was with the Goddess Freya, Giver of Light. Above and beyond this, the rising flames also stood for ascending life symbolizing "eternal rebirth."[57] Certainly here ancient Aryan legends played their part, for they had been rediscovered by the beginning of the nineteenth century. Indian antiquity was popularized as part of the Aryan heritage, which so often included the idea of "Karma": the constant rebirth of the soul. Toward the end of the century such a mystique became part of many German Volkish theories. The swastika itself played as yet no part in this symbolism—not even as a wheel of fire, as the Nazis often conceived of it.

The sacred flame thus symbolized a variety of meanings all based upon life, the cosmos, and the victory of light over darkness, the warm sun's victory over the cold of night. The summer solstice was an ancient folk festival now claimed by the newly awakened nation. The flag, too, had been one of the most ancient political symbols known to the armies of Romans, ancient Germans, Arabs, and to the Middle Ages in general. It played an important part in the formation of the secular cults of nineteenth- and twentieth-century Germany. The Church annexed the cult of the flag, giving it a religious as well as secular meaning. Indeed, during the Early Middle Ages, but even later, men saw a definite relationship between cross and flag.[58] In the Middle Ages the flag was a sign of victory in battle and, with its surrender, of defeat. But as a symbol it was also used by rulers in times of peace. The flag already had a long history behind it by the time of the wars of liberation against Napoleon. Earlier on, the possession of a flag itself was important, not its colors.[59] However, when the flag became a national symbol rather than a dynastic one, its colors and patterns became of prime importance. The Free Corps, which fought against Napoleon, as well as the student fraternity movement, invented the black-red-gold color combination which was to become symbolic of a unified Reich. These men believed that the flags of the "Holy Roman Empire of the German Nation" had possessed these colors, although in fact a set color scheme was unknown to earlier ages.[60]

Dress itself became symbolic among national groups. The students who gathered at the Wartburg Festival were asked to appear in imitation Germanic costume.[61] However, the uniform which Jahn designed for his gymnasts was not only Germanic, but was partly inspired by his admiration for the beautiful human body exemplified by Greek models.[62] Treatise on dress at the beginning of the nineteenth century shows that its symbolic value for the national cult was fully understood.

The classical theme reappeared continually throughout the nineteenth century and later. At times during the celebrations of the anniversary of the Battle of Leipzig in 1815, the placards carried by the crowds that pressed around the altar and the flame pictured Pallas Athena as "the wise goddess who has given this great victory to the world." The shield of Minerva was used to symbolize the horrible fate which awaited enemies of the German people.[63] The classics were always alive amidst Germanic symbolism—landscape and monuments and sacred flame—which recalled a long-lost national heritage.

This symbolism introduced an additional concept of beauty into the Germanic ideal type. The romantic writer Carl Gustav Carus accurately described the type in 1849. Determined by the force of the sun, he was light in pigmentation, endowed with blond hair and blue eyes. All of these characteristics reflected the life-giving strength which the sun symbolized.[64] Winckelmann had believed that under certain circumstances brown pigmentation of the skin could be beautiful.[65] This idea was now rejected. Once more the classical ideal of beauty and its function were retained. But it was now fused with blond looks; and clarity of skin, which Winckelmann had praised in Greek statues, now turned into an obsession with light pigmentation, with the kind of looks that became the Aryan ideal type. Manliness and virility were associated with such looks, the same manliness which Moeller van den Bruck detected in the monumental Prussian style of the late eighteenth century and Friedrich Ludwig Jahn claimed for his gymnasts. This "Germanic man" was celebrated in the sacred flame and in the festival of the summer solstice which became a festival of hope and confidence in the national future.

The examples of Germanic symbols which we have discussed—fired by the romantic impetus of the nineteenth century, and combined with the influence of classical models—became part of German national consciousness. These concepts formed the basis of the national cult, while the synthesis between the national monument and its setting produced the church of a new secular religion. This church was not a building of stone and mortar, but instead the whole setting in which the worship of the nation took place. It was the "sacred hill," with its equally sacred pillar of fire, the German wood echoing choirs which sang national songs, answering the oaths of brotherhood. The national monument was often an integral part of this *mis-en-scène*, the solid symbol which provided a basis for the setting. All of this formed the *"Kultraum"* or "cultic space" whose beauty would lift man above the routine of daily life and lend a higher purpose and unity to his struggle for existence.

These rites produced on a national scale the escapism and urge toward a fuller life which festive occasions also typified in private bourgeois society. For example, the festivities which Thomas Mann describes in his *Buddenbrooks* (1901) are filled with opulence. Here, too, beauty represented a life lived to the fullest. Thomas Mann was not alone in his concept of festivals; it was shared by the bourgeoisie and the working class alike. Thus Richard Wagner's wife Cosima wrote: "I love festivals and festive occasions, the comfortable intimate ones as well as those which display grandeur."[66] Indeed, she spoke for a much wider public than the Wagner circle when she added that all manifestations of religious enthusiasm must be viewed with deep sympathy. As soon as the festive occasion went beyond the family or circle of friends, when masses of men hitherto unrelated to each other became involved, these festivals took on a new dimension as cultic rites on behalf of an ideal which would draw men together in a common purpose.

This ideal was symbolized by an eternal concept of beauty. Whether it was nationalism or workers' movements, political manifestations became secular cults, and, as the rites of a secular religion, were suffused with myths and symbolism which expressed aesthetic ideals. The "people" were not considered merely as a gathering of individuals, but exemplified an idea of the beauty of soul which was projected upon the outward world. Vischer himself attempted to see the people in this light, and the mass movements of the century took this concept as the means of their own self-identification. The aesthetic concepts we have discussed became charged with political meaning. Indeed, they formed the essence and the framework of the new political style. This drama must now claim our more detailed attention, not just as a *mis-en-scène* but as the core of the new politics.

National monuments, for example, formed one of the most essential aspects of the self-representation of the nation. As national symbols they penetrated into the people's consciousness. We have mentioned them often in the preceding pages, but we must now examine their development in greater depth.

# CHAPTER THREE

# National Monuments

NATIONAL monuments—as a speaker at a festival commemorating the founding of the German Reich told his audiences —by revealing a universe of symbol and myth determine the secret music of our soul.[1] The historian Thomas Nipperdey has described national monuments as the self-representations of a democratically controlled nation, objectifying the ideals for which the nation is supposed to stand.[2] But it was not always so. Before the nineteenth century, such monuments had for the most part been erected in honor of kings or generals. Only at the beginning of that century did they start to encompass poets and writers, adding a cultural dimension to the political and military ones.[3]

The early monuments were statues whose symbolism lay in their facial expressions or dress. Plain at first, they speedily acquired symbols to surround them: for example, the horse on which a hero sat was led by classical representations of the goddesses of Peace or War, or he was crowned with laurels; or the pedestal on which a man stood was decorated by friezes illustrating his deeds and worth. Such monuments always had a symbolic meaning, but by the beginning of the nineteenth century this had become far more pronounced. National self-representation began to displace the less complicated and purely dynastic symbolism of an earlier age.

The "good taste" of classicism played an important role in the development of such national portrayal, for symbols taken from Greece or Rome brought additional meaning beyond the simple statue of the dynast. For example, Karl Friedrich Schinkel's design for the castle bridge in Berlin (1819–23) featured naked young warriors being crowned by Pallas Athena. And all the groups which decorated that bridge followed the same design.[4] Schinkel celebrated the victory of Prussia over Napoleon by imitating the Greeks' celebration of their warrior-heroes. Such classical ideas were leading toward a national representation that stressed abstract ideals rather than the specific personality. Schinkel also built the Berlin Museum, in the form of a Greek temple, and it is significant that a leading Nazi specialist on art believed that this museum was the only one of its kind during the nineteenth century to emphasize the "sacred": the reverence with which all art should be regarded.[5]

Schinkel's older contemporary Friedrich Gilly was to be of even greater importance in setting the tone for the future. His designs survived him to inspire future generations. The most important of these was his plan for a monument to King Frederick the Great of Prussia. At first, Gilly had planned to imitate the graves which line the Via Appia in Rome. However, his final choice of design was that of a Greek temple standing on an artificial mound, modeled on the Acropolis (Plate 5). The deeds of Frederick the Great were symbolized by a sacred building; the king himself was represented merely by a statue inside the monument. The design for this monument, which was never built, greatly influenced Albert Speer in his own work for the rebuilding of Berlin a century and a half later.

Unlike Schinkel, Gilly tended toward monumentalism. He was inspired both by Greek beauty and by the monumental Roman style, a fact which rendered him the eighteenth-century architect who had considerable influence on National Socialism. For later generations, the combination of Greek form and Roman massiveness came to represent the "sacred," as indeed it had done for Gilly himself. As one enthusiastic Nazi writer said, Gilly's designs could transform even a bath house into a "sacred building."[6]

The Prussian classical revival was not the sole source of inspiration for the future. In eighteenth-century France, architects also broke with the Baroque style. The French architect Ledoux adopted a classicism inspired partly by Egyptian forms and partly by Roman models. He believed that every building or monument must be a creation unto itself and clearly express its purpose. One of his pupils summarized this point of view: A church must induce reverence in the beholder and a prison fear. But Ledoux's basic ideal was similar to Winckelmann's concept of beauty—restfulness and lack of movement. Like many Germans, Winckelmann believed that these attitudes symbolized reverence and the sacred.[7]

Ledoux built the pavilions and columns which mark the "gates" of Paris, classical forms set on massive foundations. For the French classical school of which he was a leader also tended toward the monumental. It was an *"architecture parlante,"*[8] because it told the beholder of its purpose without the aid of unnecessary decorations. That purpose was expressed, more often than not, in monumental form. Boullée provides the other important example of this school of architecture in eighteenth-century France. He revered antiquity, but he combined its forms with cylindrical and cubic shapes, triangles and spheres.[9] The effect was a new massiveness and eccentricity. Yet, in the last resort, "symmetry, regularity and variety" provided the essence of Boullée's style—symmetry meaning economy of material and regularity simplicity of execution. Here the circle and the square symbolized the most valuable geometrical forms.[10] Boullée's architectural principles were very similar to Winckelmann's ideal of Greek beauty. The architectural school which arose in France during the last decades of the eighteenth century was not so different from the Prussian classical Renaissance across the Rhine. The monumental played its role here as well, and the most famous architectural handbook of the time, Jean Nicolas Louis

Durand's *Précis des Leçons d'Architecture, etc.* (*Summary of Architecture*, 1802), praised the Pantheon in Rome for its magnificence and its simplicity.[11]

In France, however, this style was not to last, while in Germany it could build on native foundations. Hitler later claimed to admire the circle and wanted to build a dome similar to Durand's or Boullée's designs for churches.[12] Moreover, Hitler's admiration for the Colosseum was reflected in Nazi buildings.[13] The Nazi ideal of beauty and splendor remained similar to the French school, though it is doubtful whether the Nazis had any real knowledge of the French movement. Albert Speer discovered Boullée only during the Nazi period; but once he had done so, he felt himself confirmed in his own architectural tastes.[14]

The "*architecture parlante*" symbolized the ideals of the beautiful and the sacred in a direct and unambiguous manner. Such utilitarianism was important to the growth of a national liturgy, for it could be easily understood by the people. This direct appeal, later to be called "propaganda" when it was used by twentieth-century mass movements, in reality expressed purposes going back to the classical revival of the eighteenth century. Architects in France and Germany were filled with a genuine intention to create forms of true beauty as they understood it, to imitate a noble simplicity which would liquidate the frivolity of the Baroque. Monumentalism, or "*grossissement*" as it was called in France,[15] played an important role from the very beginning. Public buildings must induce reverence and lift man out of the ordinary course of his life.

The word "sacred" has played an important role in our analysis. It symbolized the urge, even in the eighteenth century, to transform the political into the religious. German Pietism had already talked about the fatherland as a "magic space" (*Wunderraum*)—the "hidden fatherland."[16] Within the boundaries of Pietism, however, this space was still confined to man's soul and not yet translated into a concrete "sacred space" set aside solely for the self-representation of the nation. But this "magic space" did, in the designs of architects like Gilly, find outward expression in the creation of the immediate surroundings for the national monument.

Contemplation of a national monument should lead to cultic rites, to the worship of the secular religion of the nation. This meant that symbolism displaced mere visual representation of a personality, an idea which Gilly's design for the monument to Frederick the Great carried out. However, few architects as yet wanted to do away with a prominent statue of their hero.

A. F. Kraus, a contemporary of Gilly, submitted a design for a monument to Frederick the Great which further extended the cultic nature of such monuments. Kraus placed a bust of Frederick the Great upon an altar under which the king was supposed to be buried. Every year, the Prussian army was to gather around this altar in order to pay tribute to Frederick's memory. The tomb was surrounded by a wood in which monuments to patriotic Prussians were to be placed. A "pilgrims' road" (to use his own phrase) led from the City of Berlin to the altar. This design presented a conscious substitution of the worship of the Prussian nation for the traditional worship of Christianity. Kraus's design for the tomb was classical, and the statues of patriotic Prussians were thus to be cast in imitation of Greek models.[17] But the symbolism of the wood and the altar foreshadows by some twenty years the time when altars crowned by a sacred flame were used to celebrate the first anniversary of the Battle of Leipzig.

National monuments continued to follow classical models. To celebrate the granting of a Bavarian constitution by King Maximilian, a column was erected at Bleibach in 1818 which, through the more immediate influence of the so-called national column in the place Vendôme in Paris, continued a Roman tradition derived from Greece. But the column as a national monument also owed something to the Egyptian obelisks. These were at times conceived as the "concretization of a sun's ray," symbolizing the eternal flame of life. But though obelisks partook of the same aura of mystery and wonder which Egypt held for the eighteenth century, they were also a part of the classical tradition. The obelisks most easily accessible to the European imagination were those used in a striking fashion in the rebuilding of Rome by the popes of the sixteenth century. From such examples, Ludwig I of Bavaria built a bronze obelisk in Munich to commemorate the Bavarians fallen in the Russian campaign.[18]

The column, too, became an important symbol of strength and power, often likened to the strength and beauty of a tree. Yet the classical columns or obelisks failed to satisfy the urge for national self-representation. This dissatisfaction is well expressed by one participant in a patriotic meeting of 1832: "We erect columns to those who fought the battle of the peoples: but for a national monument which would reflect the majesty of the German People no room can be found upon the wide expanse of German land."[19]

This pessimism was mistaken. In fact, the free-standing column (*Ruhmessäule*) had a limited future before it, but the pillar itself became an important element of national monuments. The Renaissance had in fact made a detailed classification of pillars, based on an interpretation that went back to Vitruvius.[20] The Doric pillar was endowed with simple masculine qualities, while the Ionic, with its "tender" decorations, was considered to symbolize femininity. This tradition lasted into the nineteenth century, and the pillars of national monuments are apt to be Doric,[21] for the vigor and manliness of the nation had to be represented. Their strength and simplicity was supposed to symbolize national spirit. Germanic symbols, in turn, were objectified through the construction not of a pillar of stone but one simulated by fire, a column of light, and visible from afar. From such classical symbolism at the beginning of the century, we can trace a direct line to the construction of the Bismarck towers which themselves were crowned with a flame.

Not untypically, the national monument of the *Walhalla* was described as a "pillar-carrying" building, similar to the temples of the Acropolis.[22] For the early Greeks the pillar represented a statue and, as Winckelmann wrongly pointed out, the Greek words for "pillar" and "statue" remained identical even at a time when Greek sculpture had reached its artistic apotheosis.[23] The pillar was not merely considered a part of Greek architecture, but in itself came to symbolize Germanic manliness and the kind of beauty for which Greek art stood. Yet Egyptian examples also influenced the construction of symbolic columns, modeled not on the Pyramids but on the obelisks which the Romans had already used.

However, most national monuments built at this time were more elaborate. Leo von Klenze, a dedicated classicist, was influential in continuing this tradition as the chief architect of Ludwig I of Bavaria who ruled from 1825 to 1848. He had studied for a year under Gilly and then continued his studies in Paris, Berlin, and Rome. He met the Bavarian Crown Prince Ludwig in 1814—an association which was to last forty-eight years. The relationship of the Bavarian ruler and his architect was not without strain, and from 1839 to 1852 Klenze worked in Prussia and in Russia, where he built Leningrad's famous Hermitage.[24] But his true life's work was the virtual rebuilding of Munich as it still stands today, and the national monuments which he created for a king obsessed by the concept of German unity.

The most important of these monuments was the *Walhalla*, built outside Regensburg between 1830 and 1842 overlooking the Danube (Plate 6). Observers could mistake it for the final accomplishment of Gilly's famous design. King Ludwig had given explicit instructions: this sacred monument to German unity was to combine the style of the Propylaeum of Athens with the Pantheon in Rome.[25] But Klenze believed that the king's instructions were impossible to execute. He was wedded to Greek, not Roman, forms of architecture, and wrote of true architecture that it could not be invented any

more than could musical harmony or the rhythmic laws of
language. The "architecture of perfection" practiced by the
Greeks depended upon a divine order which combined divergent elements into one harmonious whole.[26] (It was Klenze
who, at the behest of Ludwig, journeyed to Greece and
through his influence upon Ludwig's son, the Greek monarch,
prevented the destruction of the Acropolis.)

Ludwig planned the *Walhalla* at the time of the Napoleonic
occupation, and gave it the name of the palace of the mythical
Odin (or Wotan) where those heroes gathered who had been
wounded or killed in battle. The saga of the *Edda* had described the *Walhalla* or hall "shining in gold" where Odin
daily chose his comrades in arms, a hall which symbolized the
field of battle.[27] The monument itself was in the form of a
Greek temple, 60 yards high and 136 yards long. The eaves
were decorated by figures which on the southern side represented the German states gathered around a victorious Germania, while on the northern side Hermann the Cheruskan (a
Germanic tribe) fought the Battle of the Teutoburger Forest
against the Roman Legions. Inside the monument itself were
two large halls, decorated on wall and ceiling with Germanic
gods and the symbols of their worship. Within the temple a
Teutonic note predominated in the form of a Greek model
combined with German symbols. The gods looked down on
the statues of famous and patriotic Germans—the heroes who
had entered *Walhalla*.[28]

Aided by the historian Johannes Müller, Ludwig spent
much time selecting those who should have a place in this
sanctuary. The basic principle of selection was based upon the
family of Germanic languages to which those honored had to
belong, corresponding to the important role which language
played in the development of nationalism. Thus not only
Germans, but Swiss and Dutch were included. Most of the
new heroes were rulers and generals; arts and sciences were
hardly represented.[29] Such omissions were corrected from
time to time. At first the Bavarian kings, subsequently the

German Bund, then the Bavarian government, and finally Hitler determined whose statues should be erected. (The latter suggested only the composer Anton Bruckner, and with a great deal of pomp and circumstance attended the unveiling of that bust.)[30] Today the Bavarian government again determines the price of entry into the hall of heroes.

The *Walhalla* was supposed to be a "sacred monument" for the worshipping of German unity. Ludwig, laying the foundations in 1830, stated his hope that Germans would be united just as the building united the separate stones out of which it was constructed.[31] *Walhalla* was to be a setting for national pilgrimages and, suitably enough, was opened in 1842 on the anniversary of the Battle of Leipzig. But the *Walhalla* was designed without planning a meeting place for the masses who would come to worship. Its crowded interior resembled a museum and there was no room in it for the celebration of national festivals. Much later, in the 1920's, a proposal was made to create a "sacred space" outside this monument, where patriotic plays and dances could be performed. At the same time, the problem was raised whether heroes who were not racially pure Germans had a place in the monument, something which had not bothered the Bavarian king.[32]

The *Walhalla* was by no means the only monument which Klenze built for his king. The Hall of Liberation at Kelheim, also created to celebrate once more Germany's liberation from Napoleon, took the form of a round temple. Inside there was again a sacred hall, filled this time not with statues of heroes past and present, but instead with representations of the battles fought against the French. In Munich itself Klenze built a "Hall of Fame" (also a Greek temple) in order to celebrate local Bavarian heroes. This hall surrounded the statue of "Bavaria," a colossus resembling Pallas Athena which to this day dominates the Hall of Fame and the large meadow around it.[33] Klenze and Ludwig could not have foreseen that the Bavarian revolution of 1918, which deposed the dynasty, would begin beneath their national monument. But unlike the

*Walhalla* or the monument at Kelheim, the "Bavaria," surrounded by a large open space, was built near a city and thus did become a convenient focal point for mass meetings.

Klenze worried about the largely imitative nature of his Greek models. Yet he fought bitterly against his rival for the king's graces, the painter Peter von Cornelius (1783–1867), who desired to create a more native, Germanic art. For Cornelius the Gothic had to be combined with native designs as in fifteenth- and sixteenth-century Italy. He was a romantic who had joined the school of Nazarene painters in Rome, men who attempted to revive Christian painting through the use of abstract symbolism. Cornelius did succeed in painting the frescos in the Munich museum of sculpture (the Glyptothek) which Klenze had built and which resembles Schinkel's Berlin museum. But Cornelius was not able to fulfill his ambition to graduate from painting to designing national monuments.[34]

Cornelius never really achieved a Germanic style, whatever this may have meant, and instead fought against classicism. Klenze, himself conscious of accusations leveled against his imitations of Greece, did not turn to some kind of Germanic past (as Wilhelm Kreis was to do later) but to another imitation instead. He copied the architecture of the high Renaissance for his Munich municipal buildings. To this day the central post office is a replica of the famed Florentine Orphanage, and the avenue which was meant for public and royal processions (Ludwigstrasse) is flanked by Renaissance palaces. Klenze and Ludwig I were not unique in their concept of national self-representation. Frederick William IV of Prussia (1840–61) was pursuing a similar course at the same time. The love of past history which such men shared did not necessarily imply a nostalgia for the ancient Germanic past. Rather, history for them was defined through the Roman or Greek tradition. Frederick William IV's building program for Berlin and Potsdam imitated the City of Rome and the villas of the Roman countryside. Moreover, when toward 1841 he himself designed a monument to Frederick the Great, it was

almost identical to Gilly's design.[35] The classical tradition became annexed to German historical awareness, and this was to
remain the case for many people during the nineteenth and
twentieth centuries. Adolf Hiter, as we shall see, followed this
image of Germany and despised the imitation of ancient Germanic art and architecture. He accepted a tradition which had
been in full force from the 1830's, linking such neo-classicism
not only to a concept of beauty but also to the virtues which
the nation symbolized.

The Italian Renaissance was also, at times, annexed to classical forms. The mixture of classicism and Renaissance proved
effective, and was transmitted to future generations by another influential architect, Gottfried Semper (1803–1879).
Semper believed that modern architecture must, above all,
continue and develop the traditions of the Roman Empire and
of the Renaissance. But he also believed that architectural
forms must grow out of the material used, and not be forced
into shape by the use of external decorations or Baroque-like
curves. Each building should have an autonomy of design that
reveals its own purpose.[36] The earlier French tradition of the
Ledoux school clearly influenced Semper.

Semper defined as beautiful that which combined crafts-
manship and symbolism.[37] He changed the classical ideal in
one important way: Winckelmann had believed that the colorful painting of buildings detracted from their classical
beauty ("color falsifies form"). Meanwhile, however, it had
been discovered that the ancients did in fact paint their buildings. Semper therefore did the same, and this led to a more
colorful Renaissance style, especially in private houses which
he built in some profusion.[38] Renaissance villas became the
favorite habitats of the German bourgeoisie toward the end of
the nineteenth century. An Italian who entered a villa which
Semper had built was led to exclaim, "E una villa di Toscana!"
But Semper always handled the Renaissance in the spirit of
antiquity,[39] a remark which by the way could equally well
apply to Klenze.

These imitations of antiquity and of the Renaissance were used to create a mystical Germanic spirit. Semper was a friend of Richard Wagner (both had fought side by side in the revolution of 1848) and he designed a theatre in Munich which was to provide the setting for Wagner's operas. Here Renaissance concepts of perspective and illusion were the inspiration for the startling use of lighting, and for the orchestra hidden from sight in order not to interfere with the dreams presented on stage. Dream and reality were to merge into a single experience.[40] In Semper's design for this theatre, the classical fused with the romantic as exemplified in Wagner's operas, and all these factors were combined in the service of Germanic worship. Wagner's festival hall at Bayreuth, when finally built, followed Semper's model.

Men like Gilly, Klenze, and Semper had set the tone for the national monuments, however many changes could be wrung on their themes. However, there exists one famous monument where the romantic predominated, symbolizing through its Gothic form a nostalgia for the medieval mystical and religious past. The monument to Hermann the Cheruskan (or Arminius) departs from the style we have discussed, while retaining the love of monumentality and the symbolism which attempted to represent a national spirit rather than an individual dynastic or military hero. Moreover, a discussion of this monument illustrates two principles which will be important for the future: the ceremonies or festivals which surrounded it at the inauguration and completion; and the way in which the monument was financed by universal subscription. For all its difference in form, it is also an integral part of the development of national monuments in the nineteenth century.

This monument was meant to celebrate an earlier war of liberation, the victory of Hermann or Arminius over the Roman Legions. It came about through the obsession of one man, Ernst von Bandel, and its construction spans most of the century (1841–75). It was begun when the memory of the wars of liberation against the French was still fresh in men's minds, and indeed Bandel was haunted by the French occupation of his native Rhineland.[41] But lack of money forced Bandel to abandon work when Germany became preoccupied with the coming revolution of 1848. He did not resume work on the monument until the example of Italian unity had given new heart to the German national spirit, and it was completed only during the euphoria which accompanied the actual achievement of German unity. The history of the *Hermannsdenkmal*, as it was called, mirrors the course of German nationalism in the nineteenth century.

Bandel had come under the influence of the classics and even produced some conventional classical sculpture. His imagination was captured by the monumental classical figures of the Danish sculptor Berthel Thorwaldsen. Yet he came to oppose Greek influence and turned to the Gothic instead, thus departing from the tradition of Gilly and Klenze. However, he shared with his predecessors the love of monumentality; for Bandel, too, monuments had to be simple, massive, and stretch toward the sky.[42]

The Monument of Hermann was to be a symbol of Germany's eternal youthful force (Plate 7).[43] Hermann still stands, raising his sword, ready to do battle at any moment. The massive pedestal which supports him was meant to symbolize the strength of the barbaric conqueror of the Roman Legions.[44] The statue of Hermann, huge and monumental, is that of a knight in armor; but the form of the figure itself is reminiscent of classical models (except that Bandel, a sculptor of mediocre ability, misjudged his proportions). Hermann's pedestal has some elements of the pyramid construction so popular with those who wanted to evoke massive force. But it consists mainly of Gothic elements, especially in the Hall of Fame which is contained within the pedestal. This hall was meant to house representations of famous Germans, but its form reminds one more of a Gothic cathedral than, as at *Walhalla*, the interior of the Acropolis. This part of the monument was never completed and the hall still stands empty today.

The surroundings of the monument are an integral part of the design. It dominates a hill in the Teutoburger Forest where ancient Germanic cults had left their trace. The "sacred space" which surrounded other monuments is missing. Instead, this monument is fused with the landscape in which it stands. Those who continued the tradition of Gilly and Klenze also believed that the landscape within which a monument was set would heighten its symbolism. But then more often than not the national monument retained its classical form alongside the romantic landscape.

There can be no doubt of the effectiveness of the *Hermannsdenkmal*. Even today, when many of the other monuments such as the *Walhalla* are almost forgotten, it is still a center of pilgrimage. The Nazis disliked and ignored it; perhaps because it was so eclectic and ill-proportioned, or more likely because Hitler thought that the Gothic, which forms an important part of this monument, was an archaic art form, unsuited to modern times.[45] However, one aspect of the construction of the *Hermannsdenkmal* was to impress Hitler: the way in which Bandel raised part of the money for its construction, for this led to a mass participation by German youth in the building of the national symbol. In 1863 Bandel wrote to the best pupil (*primus*) in every German high-school class in order to urge him to collect money for this "national deed."[46] This appeal proved to be a success, and part of the immediate popularity of Bandel's monument can be ascribed to the fact that a large element of German youth had participated in its construction. Hitler planned to adopt this device in order to raise money for his monumental Dome, a key feature of the planned rebuilding of Berlin.[47] Active public participation, so important in all of the new politics, determined Hitler's course of action in this instance. He did not in fact need to raise money in this particular fashion, which in any case would have paid for only a tiny fraction of his huge monument.

There is no evidence as to whether or not Bandel had the effectiveness of such participation in mind when he wrote to the high schools. More likely he simply wanted to overcome a financial crisis. Yet when, perhaps to his surprise, the schoolboys had collected a sizable sum, he proudly stated that the "*Hermannsdenkmal* was the first national monument erected by the entire German people."[48]

Eventually the king of Prussia, and then the German Diet, appropriated money for the completion of the monument, and Emperor William I gave Bandel a large pension. The foundations were laid in 1841, in ceremonies which have a wider significance, for they were to be repeated throughout the Second Empire whenever an important national monument came into being. The symbolism for which the national monument stood was acted out in front of it by various groups; high-school students attended dressed in ancient Germanic garb, and male choirs sang Arndt's famous song of the wars of liberation, "What Is the German Fatherland?" A cannon "liberated" at the Battle of Waterloo thundered the accompaniment. No one could mistake the purpose. The monument was unveiled, many years later, in the presence of the emperor. Male choirs, sharpshooting societies, and gymnasts each played a part in the ceremonies. A Protestant clergyman preached a patriotic sermon and a Protestant chorale was sung.[49] This mixture of the Germanic and the Protestant had not changed since the beginning of the century. In 1815, celebrating the victory over Napoleon, men had worshipped the sacred flame on its altar, only to go to church in order to give thanks to the Lord.[50]

The *Hermannsdenkmal*, then, illustrates a departure from the classical tradition. But it retained the ideal of monumentality and added the element of popular participation in its construction, and proved normative in the ceremonies which attended its beginning and completion. The so-called *Nieder-walddenkmal*, built between 1874 and 1885 on the banks of the Rhine by Johannes Schilling who had been trained in Rome, illustrates a further development in the history of national monuments (Plate 8). Its appearance was almost traditional. Built to celebrate German unity, it was once again modeled on classical forms in the huge statue of the Germania, and in the massive pedestal with its friezes representing peace and war as well as the German rivers Rhine and Mosel.[51] Through the way in which it was financed and sponsored, the *Niederwalddenkmal* marked a still closer bond between the national cult and the national monument.

For the sponsors attempted to imitate Bandel, to raise money by subscription from high-school students. But this time it did not work, the amount raised financing only one of the friezes.[52] The *Walhalla* and earlier monuments had been financed by German rulers who desired national unity. But once this unity had come about such financing was difficult to get, the nation was in existence and, though there were exceptions (like the *Hermannsdenkmal*), on the whole the Reich did not prove generous. As a result, national monuments came to be financed by special groups within the nation who wanted to give voice to their patriotism. The *Niederwalddenkmal* was financed by the Kriegervereine—associations of war veterans, originally formed after the wars of Frederick the Great in the eighteenth century, but increasing in number and significance as a conservative force in German politics during the nineteenth century. They were a loose federation of local organizations when the *Niederwalddenkmal* was conceived. Eventually, however, they formed a stronger union (Kyffhäuserbund) with a membership of over one million and felt a new need to focus their energies.[53]

That they sought to focus their energies by building a second monument on the Kyffhäuser Mountain (1896) shows to what extent such symbols in stone and mortar captured the patriotism of a large portion of the population.[54] But it also brought to the fore the limitations of national monuments sponsored by one particular group within the nation, and not by a ruler or by popular subscription. For the Kyffhäuser monument (Plate 9) entered into competition with the *Niederwalddenkmal* as to which would be a better setting for truly national festivals.[55] In this manner, it was thought, the monument would not merely represent the patriotism of one party or group, but would inspire the whole population.

Such an ambition meant providing a space in front of the monument for national festivals. Gilly had already provided such a sacred space for national worship and Arndt had advocated it. For them this space, as we have mentioned, had taken the form of a cemetery for famous Germans; but it had already evolved from a dead into a living space, one which was taken up not by graves but by living people acting out their national liturgy. Such a space now became of prime importance, for the use to which it was put would determine the difference between a living and a dead national monument. The *Niederwalddenkmal* had received such a space.[56] But the Kyffhäuser memorial could present a sacred space which was even more impressive. For this monument, in the shape of a fortress centered around the statue of Emperor William I, was built on one of Germany's holiest mountains, the Kyffhäuser, within which, it was said, the emperor Barbarossa slept until the restoration of the medieval Reich. A large platform in front of the massive monument could serve as the sacred space. In the competition between the two monuments in 1897–8, pragmatic considerations were not forgotten. The committee for "National Festivals on the Kyffhäuser" gave much thought to the transport and housing of large numbers of people who were expected to make the pilgrimage.[57] In the end, neither monument became the focus of truly national celebrations. But the competition itself remains significant. The idea of the "sacred space" had assumed a key importance which it was not to lose again, and national monuments tended to become inseparable from national festivals.

The solid monuments were to be surrounded by moving, singing, and dancing masses of people. But these were to be confined to the "sacred space," and did not touch the base of the monument itself. Yet toward the end of the nineteenth century there was an attempt to infuse the national monuments themselves with movement as expressed in their own construction. The sculptor Reinhold Begas wanted to make his monument to emperor William I, set in Berlin (1890), a "national hymn, a majestic choir."[58] He used classical forms but attempted to combine these with Baroque elements in order to give his design a feeling of movement that the other national monuments lacked. William I, for example, sits on a horse led by the Goddess of Victory. The "heroes of 1870" are walking by her side, perched upon a Greek quadriga. Lions guard the booty of war. Here, Begas preferred the curve to the straight line, though he used Doric columns to unite the monument's various elements. Still, all seems in movement; the dramatic predominates.[59]

Begas's emphasis on the dramatic proved unsuccessful. It departed too much from the simple, solid, and monumental style which had become the symbol of Germany's power and beauty. The dispute in 1912 over the design for the Bismarck memorial at Bingen is of interest here. The delicate, lively statue of a young Siegfried was submitted and fervently supported by Walther Rathenau, among others, as breaking with the tradition of monumental architecture. But the majority of the prize committee thought this young Siegfried too playful and sweet. For Bismarck should be remembered as a rock of iron. Rathenau and his friends regarded the monumental as a paean to brutality, but they lost out to a design by Wilhelm Kreis which continued the older, monumental tradition. Not without some truth it was said that a Greek faun could hardly touch the sentiments of the people.[60]

The drama of national self-awareness was not supposed to be expressed through Baroque movement or sweet playfulness. This is well illustrated by the most famous national monument to open the twentieth century, celebrating the one-hundredth anniversary of the Battle of Leipzig, the *Völker-schlachtdenkmal*, built between 1894 and 1913. This monument climaxes the construction of national monuments (Germany would not see their like again after the First World War). But it also summarizes, through its style, the history of national monuments we have attempted to describe. Designed by Bruno Schmitz, who also designed the Kyffhäuser monument, the *Völkerschlachtdenkmal* (Plates 10 and 11) combined classical forms with a pyramidal construction. Once again the monumental predominated; the personification of the fatherland or of individual heroes was avoided. Once more a massive structure visible from afar symbolized the fatherland and its victory: not a Greek temple like the *Walhalla*, but one in which the simple, solid mass created a monumental impression without the benefit of decorations or even pillars. Inside the massive foundations, we again have halls which symbolize the purpose of the monument. There is a crypt which honors those who fell in battle. Eight masks without eyes stare at the visitors. The "hall of fame" is on the second story of the building, filled with statues of those who led the war against the French.

The actual shape of the monument is close to Wilhelm Kreis's Bismarck towers in the attempted combination of the classical and the Germanic. There are echoes of the tomb of Theodoric in Ravenna as well as of the Pyramids. Yet the details are unified through the use of classical lines. The landscape surrounding the monument was to be planted with German oaks and the wood dedicated as a cemetery for famous Germans.[61] This recalls the "sacred space" of Gilly and Kraus. However, an open space was added, the "sacred space" on which a national festival should take place. German youth were to gather to stage gymnastic competitions in order to demonstrate the vigor and manliness of the nation.[62] Once more a national festival was thought necessary in order to make the monument come alive.

This monument was also financed by individual groups, when the attempt to raise money from schoolchildren had failed.[63] Now the gymnasts contributed,[64] and the German cities were supposed to make the monument their special project.[65] Here too one man, reminiscent of Bandel, was responsible for keeping the project alive—Clemens Thieme, a Leipzig architect. He founded a "League of Patriots" to finance the monument.[66] Eventually, however, groups like the male choir societies, sharpshooting societies, student fraternities, and a right-wing trade union of commercial employees also joined the effort. The first two of these groups and the gymnasts we shall meet again, for they were among the principle cultivators of the national cult.

The urge to imitate the function of the Pantheon existed in the *Völkerschlachtdenkmal* as in so many other monuments. Historical memories had to be appealed to as an integral part of the myths and symbols which informed the new style of politics. Friedrich Ludwig Jahn had already written at the beginning of the nineteenth century that such an appeal made the difference between "genuine" festivals and those which were artificially created.[67] Ancestor worship was essential for national theology, manifested by the statues within the monument and, in this case, by the tombs of contemporaries in the sacred wood. Past and present thus joined hands.

When the *Völkerschlachtdenkmal* was finally unveiled in 1913, those groups which had originally supported it formed the backbone of the festivities. The theme was taken from the earlier tradition of celebrations of the Battle of Leipzig: "Let us fight, bleed, and die for Germany's unity and power."[68]

The *Völkerschlachtdenkmal*, unveiled just before the First World War, never attained the popularity of the *Hermannsdenkmal*; no national gymnastic exercises were held in its shadow as planned. The war drove this monument out of men's minds, and after the war it attained no more than regional importance. Only in the new German Democratic Republic did it again become a symbol for patriotic sacrifice

—now in the name of the Socialist state. The fact that the Russians had participated side by side with Germans in the battle of liberation transformed the monument into a symbol of German-Russian friendship.

However successful or unsuccessful these monuments may have been, they did form a vital part of the national cult. Wilhelm Kreis, the architect of the Bismarck towers, summarized their purpose: through their appearance they lifted men above the routine of daily life and spoke to them in a new language by the harmony and firmness of their forms. The inside formed a "sacred temple inducing a reverential attitude."[69] This was the new church. The mystical and the elemental must be united. For the builders of national monuments this meant the use of monumental forms, of impressive masses, either in pedestals like that of the *Hermannsdenkmal* or in the structure of the monument itself as in the *Völkerschlachtdenkmal* or the Bismarck towers. For Kreis, monuments were "architectural mountains" equivalent to the sacred mountains that (like the Kyffhäuser) played their part in the national mystique.[70] The landscape which surrounded the monument was part of the total impression, and the "sacred space" this might provide fused living worship with reverential forms. Such architects made a sharp distinction between sacred buildings and buildings in which people lived and worked. Kreis, for example, also built skyscrapers and factories, but these in a simple manner related to a more modern architectural style.

The aims in building national monuments were clearly expressed. Toward the beginning of the twentieth century the architect Theodor Fischer wrote that "live church buildings" no longer exist. We must create buildings, he said, through which men can once more be formed into a higher, cosmic community. "Sacred halls" are needed in which man automatically "removes his hat and woman restrains her tongue."[71] Fischer himself built such a hall for gymnasts.

Throughout these developments the Greek ideal of beauty

remained intact, and indeed was further emphasized through the work of the individual sculptors who executed the figures and friezes. Almost all belonged to the classic tradition of monumental sculpture. Ludwig Schwanthaler, who executed most of the decorations for the *Walhalla*, put these in Germanic guise, for they were supposed to recall the deeds of German ancestors. But they were classical figures, whatever dress they wore. Franz Metzner, who created the statues for the *Völkerschlachtdenkmal*, was a self-educated classicist. Such examples could be repeated many times over. Fritz Klimsch, one of the most famous sculptors of the early twentieth century, was praised by Nazi Germany in 1940 on his seventieth birthday for having created "ideal types of classical beauty," adopting monumental forms. This was said to affirm the cultural politics of "our state." The importance of such classical sculpture as a symbol for National Socialism was aptly summarized by the playwright Hanns Johst, who remarked that the heroic world of antiquity overcomes the fatigue with life induced by Christianity. This heroic world calls forth the greatest deed of all: the creation of the Volk.[72]

Though nineteenth-century monuments had increasingly stressed the space needed for national festivals, this could not satisfy the appetite of mass movements after the First World War. The masses involved were growing in size, while mass meetings in the shape of national festivals became a widely used political technique. Restricted spaces had to give way to larger sites without losing the effectiveness of their sacred surroundings. There the Nazi criticism of older national monuments is of interest, and typifies the needs presented by an intensified use of the new politics.

Nazis were apt to contrast the memorial to the Battle of Tannenberg (where Hindenburg had defeated the Russians in the First World War) with monuments such as the *Niederwalddenkmal*.[73] Monuments, they believed, had to provide a framework for mass meetings. "The space which urges us to join the community of the Volk is of greater importance than the figure which is meant to represent the fatherland." Such a figure is isolated; it does not have the binding force which lifts us above individualism.[74]

The Tannenberg Memorial (1927) satisfied the Nazis' spatial ideals (Plate 12). The brothers Walter and Johannes Krüger had taken Stonehenge in England as their model, envisaging an ancient Nordic meeting place where festive rites were performed. The Krüger brothers thought of such formations in terms of a circle of leaders grouped around the chief, a circle in whose center "stands the strongest."[75] Stones defined the limits of this "sacred space." They first tried out such a design in the Soldiers' Memorial at Leer in East Frisia. There, pillars of stone were joined together at the top by a ring of stone, and a cross stood in the middle of the space which they formed.[76] Later, at Tannenberg, eight massive towers were united by walls. Within each tower the space was used differently: one was to contain a youth hostel, another the flags of battle, a third the tomb of Hindenburg and his wife, a fourth an archive, and the others a chapel and busts of participants in the battle; lastly, one tower was devoted to the memory of Bismarck.

Originally the Krügers planned to place a cross in the center of this ring of walls and towers, but that plan was abandoned. For the space was to be reserved for the gathering of crowds; 100,000 could thus take part in ceremonies within the monument.[77] There is no doubt that Tannenberg represented a new departure in national monuments. The Krügers may have used the theme of Stonehenge because of its ancient historical associations, but the result was a monument which surrounded a vast "sacred space," rather than being surrounded by it. No longer did this space have to lie outside the monument, as in Gilly's design, or indeed as in all later national monuments, such as that to the Battle of the Peoples by Bruno Schmitz.

The veterans' associations had taken the lead in preparing this monument, as they had sponsored the Kyffhäuser Monument earlier. The occupation of the province of Memel by Lithuania in 1923, a territory which was joined to East Prussia, spurred the preparations. Hindenburg, the victor of Tannenberg, gave his blessing to the design and attended the opening ceremonies in 1927, now as president of the German Republic.[78] The national ideal was clearly in the forefront; the invitation to the inaugural ceremony talked about the native hearth (*Heimat*) surrounded by waves of Slavdom, meaning the Poles. Significantly, a rabbi was prevented from taking part in the opening ceremonies, which were attended by some eighty thousand people. (The Social Democrats and the trade unions had refused to contribute to the erection of the monument in the first place.)[79]

The Nazis praised the design of Tannenberg,[80] but it played a singularly small role in their own ceremonial. Hitler and Hindenburg attended one meeting there in 1933,[81] and in 1934 it was the setting of Hindenburg's state funeral. But that was all. Perhaps Tannenberg was too closely connected with the field marshal and Hitler wanted none of his shadow. Still, the Tannenberg Monument must have attained some status, for unlike others (such as the monument to the Battle of the Peoples or the Kyffhäuser memorial), it was blown up during the retreat of the German armies at the end of the Second World War. The sacred memorial to victory over the Russians could not be allowed to fall into Russian hands.

However, the use of space, so prominent in the Tannenberg memorial, corresponds to the use of space at the Nazi Nuremberg party days. There, too, the space dominated the actual buildings which surrounded the masses, the buildings themselves almost fading into the background as a convenient framework for the participants. No direct influence of the Tannenberg memorial upon the *mis-en-scène* at Nuremberg can be traced, yet there was good reason for the Nazis to praise this new kind of national monument, for it certainly presented a stage in the evolution of such symbols which were to reach the point where the space for festivals displaced the monument itself.

The Tannenberg memorial was the only successful monument erected during the Weimar Republic. But it owed nothing whatever to the Republic, either politically or architecturally. When the Republic itself undertook experiments in the building of national monuments, they were unsuccessful; a shrine in honor of the tenth anniversary of the beginning of the First World War was planned (but never built) in the midst of a sacred wood and was conceived as a hall, bell tower, and home for veterans who would compose the honor guard.[82] Though all the veterans' associations backed this monument and its conception in 1924, it came to nothing. The Republic was paralyzed by rivalries among the various cities and regions offering sites. The monument itself was to have been traditional, setting in the foreground a sacred wood of the kind that Gilly and Arndt had thought particularly suitable as a memorial to heroic Germans.[83] The hall and tower idea we will find used again much later on a vaster scale in Hitler's Dome, as the centerpiece of the rebuilding of Berlin (Plates 18 and 19).

However, the Republic also sanctioned a more experimental approach to national monuments. Bruno Taut, for example, designed a huge crystal ball which was to dominate a city as a memorial to fallen soldiers. This design was never executed, but he did build a hall in the City of Magdeburg in order to honor the dead of the First World War. The inside of this memorial was given over to a library and reading room. This was an intellectual notion which broke with all past tradition and was therefore doomed to failure. Such modernistic designs were considered by some as a negation of patriotic and warlike themes.[84] National monuments continued to be viewed as sacred places, as secular, national shrines, frameworks for acts of national worship. Neither reading rooms nor crystal balls could fulfill this function. For example, the more

than seven hundred "shrines of honor" built for the dead of
the First World War during the first thirteen years of the
Republic were highly conventional: towers, columns, some
pyramids, and round temples foreshadowing Kreis's designs of
war memorials during the Second World War. Moreover,
such conventionality continued after 1945; those who wanted
to build monuments to the fallen of the Second World War
were once again advised to use the form of pyramids, obelisks,
and crosses.[85] Such symbols have a constancy in form and
appearance which defies any experimentation; traditionalism is
built into every popular faith.

Parliamentary republics were naturally unable to construct
effective representations of themselves, just as they failed to
create national festivals, a subject to which we shall later return. National Socialism went back to the previous tradition
of national monuments and sacred spaces as an integral part of
the new political style. Mass participation in rites of national
worship was stressed, and the nature of public festivals therefore determined the usefulness of a national monument. The
monument itself was, at times, given a stark simplicity so that
the space surrounding it could dominate. The Schlageter
Monument in Düsseldorf provides a good example of this. A
simple giant cross is part of a space surrounded by low
walls.[86] Other Nazi monuments were rarely this straightforward, but spatial considerations pushed most autonomous
monuments into the background.

National monuments were an effective part of the liturgy of
public festivals which the Nazis adopted and extended. The
development of the festivals themselves played a key role in
the self-representation and worship of the nation.

1. Bismarck Tower
at Heidelberg
(architect, Wilhelm Kreis)

2. Design for a Bismarck Tower (architect, Wilhelm Kreis)

3. The Tomb of Theodoric at Ravenna

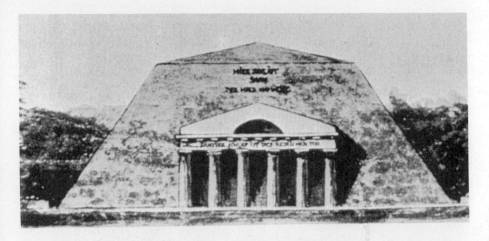

4. Design for a Pyramid (architect, Friedrich Gilly)

5. Design for the Tomb of Frederick the Great (architect, Friedrich Gilly)

6. The *Walhalla* near Regensburg (architect, Leo von Klenze)

7. *Hermannsdenkmal* in the Teutoburger Forest (architect, Ernst von Bandel)

8. The *Niederwalddenkmal* (architect, Johannes Schilling)

9. The Kyffhäuser Monument (architect, Bruno Schmitz)

10. Design for the *Völkerschlachtdenkmal* near Leipzig, with projected field for gymnastic festivals (architect, Bruno Schmitz)

11. The *Völkerschlachtdenkmal* at Leipzig (architect, Bruno Schmitz)

12. The Tannenberg Memorial (architects, Walter and Johannes Krüger)

13. *Thing* Theatre above Heidelberg

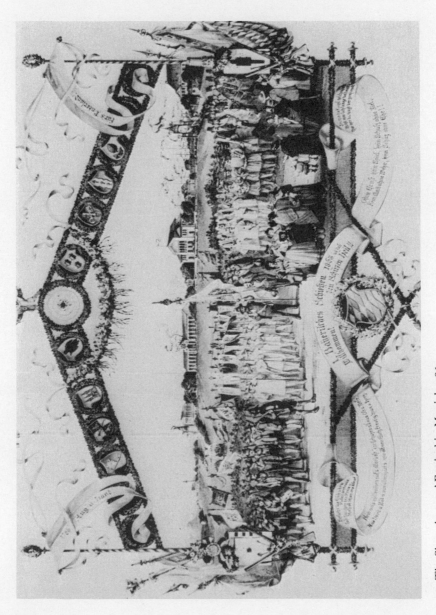

14. The Sharpshooters' Festival in Munich, 1863

15.  The Munich Workers' Gymnastic Society in 1905

16. Festival of May 1, 1933, on the Tempelhof Airfield, Berlin, staged by Albert Speer

17. Hitler Addressing a Party Day Rally at Nuremberg in 1935

18. Model of the interior of Hitler's Great Hall (architect, Albert Speer)

19. Model of the Great Hall, centerpiece of Hitler's projected rebuilding of Berlin (architect, Albert Speer)

# Public Festivals:
# Foundations and Development

THE NATIONAL monument and the "sacred space" which was often constructed around it were the setting for many public festivals. Such festivals became essential to the political style of National Socialism, and its leaders sometimes boasted that they had invented something new.[1] This was far from true. The management of public life under the Nazis had a history as long as the national monuments themselves; indeed, it was closely linked to the political aesthetics which the monuments represented.

Jean Jacques Rousseau had recommended to the Polish government the institution, every decade, of a patriotic festival to be held around a monument inscribed with the names of the great events of the past. In this way the Poles would obtain a higher opinion of their own capabilities and those of their fatherland. Public games and sports, festivals and ceremonies should be invented in order that the people might become imbued with the virtue of patriotism, and resist the distractions of theatres, operas, or comedies.[2] Rousseau's statements were prophetic, for games and gymnastic competitions were later planned around such national monuments as the *Kyffhäuser* and the *Völkerschlachtdenkmal*.

Rousseau's own model was ancient Greece. The Greeks had not transformed their theatres into "obscure prisons," but had held great and superb festivals under the open sky. Within this setting, men's hearts were elevated and ennobled.[3] By their very simplicity and lack of pomp and luxury, such spec-

tacles breathed a "charm peculiar to patriotism," which induced a martial spirit fit for free men.[4] Admiration for the
Greek sky we have already met in Winckelmann. Rousseau
linked this admiration, not with the beauty of art, but with
the effectiveness of public festivals. The setting was all-important for, as he wrote to D'Alembert, "spectacles are made for
the people and it is only by the effect which they have upon
the people that one can judge them." This effect must always
be an emotional one. Festivals should reflect human passions
whose roots are in everyone's heart.[5]

Rousseau's concept of the general will anticipated the theory upon which national festivals were to be based. The nation's own self-representation entailed a worship by the people
of their own passions. The French Revolution under the Jacobin dictatorship used public festivals as Rousseau had recommended, demonstrating how the "general will" could worship
itself, and in so doing created a new style of politics.

Such festivals were public cults whose purpose was not so
different from that of Christian rites, to make man more virtuous. But virtue here was defined in terms of antiquity, a love
of the fatherland which came alive through the symbols of
virtue supposedly inherent within the people themselves. Festivals were to be extraordinary occasions which lifted man
above the isolation of daily life, but they were also to recur
regularly and thus provide a sense of order paralleling the
"Christian year," with its regular cycles of holy days. Public
festivals were designed not merely to further the enthusiasms
of crowds, but also to form them through the use of an or-
derly liturgy. As far as festivals were concerned, Rousseau's
example related to and became involved in the already present
trend of eighteenth-century German Pietism. Such Pietism
was intensely patriotic. It tended to fuse the spirit of Christ
within man with the "inner fatherland," which should also
have space in every man's soul. The experience of community,
which Pietism stressed so much, consisted not only in an outpouring of Christian love, but also in love of the fatherland.

Both were matters of the soul, internalized, but within a liturgical framework. Volk festivals should be infused with a serious and reverential air, distinguished from Rousseau's festivals by their passion and enthusiasm.[6] Men were not only brothers in Christ, but also brothers through patriotism. A patriot must live in the state in the same way as one lives in one's loved one, the poet Novalis tells us,[7] and many Pietists held this opinion. Both Friedrich Ludwig Jahn and Ernst Moritz Arndt came from such a Pietist background.

Jahn, at the beginning of the nineteenth century, repeated what Rousseau had said earlier, but infused this with a consciousness of German history which could already be found among the Pietists. Jahn set the historical awakening of the Volk alongside the awakening of the Christian spirit in man: both are the beginnings of all creativity, as he once expressed it.[8] His models were not the festivals of the ancients, but the celebration of Germanic deeds. These deeds were those of the people themselves, not the actions of kings or bishops. He recommended as particularly suitable for civic rites the victory of the Germans over the Roman Legions (as celebrated later in the *Hermannsdenkmal*) or the revolt of the peasants against princes and bishops in the Early Middle Ages (as in the Battle of Merseburg).[9] He turned the cult of festivals away from ancient models or the symbols of the French Revolution toward the world of Germanic myth, thus giving national festivals a democratic direction. Yet Jahn, for whom the Greeks and the Germans both were "holy people," retained the Greek notion of beauty as an ideal type, even while surrounding it with Germanic symbols.

E. M. Arndt, Jahn's contemporary, was perhaps even more important in laying the foundations for a German political cult. He proposed the founding of a "German Association" (*Deutsche Gesellschaft*) in 1814 which would celebrate "holy festivals" in the name of all Germans. He suggested as especially suitable for such occasions the anniversaries of the Battle of the Teutoburger Forest, the Battle of Leipzig or, more generally, the memory of those great men who had sacrificed their lives for the fatherland. Arndt also added that the summer solstice was particularly suitable, for at that time every year traditional fires of celebration were lit on mountaintops. Arndt conceded that such festivals could include dances and feasts, but insisted that the historical connection be kept alive. Thus the deeds of Hermann must be retold at the festival of the Battle of the Teutoburger Forest, and the anniversary of the Battle of Leipzig must link that event to the earlier triumph which Hermann had won over the Romans.[10] Like Jahn, he believed that true national festivals must grow organically and be part of a revived historical consciousness. In contrast to Arndt's celebrations, the festivals of the French Revolution had not been able to draw upon the past, but instead had had to rely solely upon a correspondence with the Christian liturgical tradition.

From this point of view it is no surprise that Arndt came to the conclusion that a "festival commemorating the noble dead" might be the most effective. For here "History enters life and life itself becomes part of history."[11] Simultaneously with Arndt's proposal, the "festival of the dead" was introduced into Protestant liturgy. Friedrich Schleiermacher, a figure instrumental in setting the guidelines for Protestant liturgy in Germany, had first advocated this festival, and in 1816 the Prussian Church decreed the celebration of an annual religious service for those killed in the wars of liberation.[12] Celebrations of the glorious dead were to play an important part in later political liturgy and, indeed, to become central to National Socialism. Arndt's theory of festivals emphasized both a historic and an emotional dimension. They encompassed the human spirit and heart, while being designed by Germans in the German tradition. They were sacred rites, but not yet pagan ceremonies.

"It is obvious," Arndt wrote, "that Christians begin festivals with quiet prayer and a pious church service." Moreover, his suggested monument to the Battle of Leipzig was to be crowned with a cross and surrounded by a "sacred territory" to be planted with oaks. This would be used as a cemetery for great Germans. For Arndt, such a monument was at once "truly German and truly Christian."[13] Friedrich Gilly had also surrounded his monument for Frederick the Great with such a sacred space, but the Christian aspect was absent, swamped by classicism. However, throughout the nineteenth century national festivals existed in close proximity to the Christian tradition, not only borrowing from Christian liturgy but also employing the reality of prayer and church service.

Karl Hoffmann, at Arndt's suggestion, collected evidence of how the anniversary of the Battle of the Peoples was celebrated all over Germany in 1815. The Germanic symbols were always present in these ceremonies: men decorated with oak leaves, and the pillar of fire on the mountaintop or upon an altar in the square. More often than not, it was a Protestant minister or Catholic priest who preached at the "altar of Germany's salvation," even though he was apt to recite patriotic verse and mention God only in passing. Yet each festival ended with a regular church service.[14]

Similarly, when gymnasts and student fraternities, all disciples of Jahn, held their famous festival at Wartburg Castle in 1817, national and romantic elements predominated. Once again we have pillars of fire and torchlight parades up to the castle, so closely associated with Luther and the medieval festivals of song. The students burned supposedly "un-German" books, made speeches which reflected the cult of the Volk, but ended their celebrations with a service.[15] Indeed, such a service was regarded as a unifying element. Hoffmann's correspondents related with much pride how Protestants went to Catholic services and Catholics to Protestant services in order to celebrate German unity. The fact that Jews also joined in such Christian services was taken as heralding a new national unity (in one town they even joined in singing Christian chorales in the streets).[16] During the celebration of the anniversary of the Battle of Leipzig, the euphoria of national liberation silenced the voice of anti-Semitism which, however, was to make itself heard two years later at the Wartburg Festival. What were these church services like? The Protestant services consisted of common song, prayer, preaching, and the blessing. The confession of faith only gradually became a permanent component of religious service during the first two decades of the century. Similarly, the place of Scripture reading in the liturgy was, as yet, controversial, practiced in some churches but not in others. The Catholic Introitus psalm, Kyrie, and Gloria were often replaced by a sequence of three songs.[17] These songs were all-important, as they provided the opportunity for dialogue with the community. Friedrich Schleiermacher rejected the spoken responses common in Catholicism, and instead advocated a sung dialogue between the minister and the congregation.[18] Such a service was intended to stimulate the religious consciousness of the community. The minister was integrated with the community; unlike Catholicism, he was not to perform his own rite at the altar. Nor did Schleiermacher advocate the use of separate chants by the priest.

The church services had to be festive; this was the basic ideal of Schleiermacher's liturgy. Like festivals in secular life, they must emanate from the people themselves, and not be decreed by authority. During a festival poetry is read, songs are sung, and there are speeches. So it must be in a church service; the religious cult must take on a definite form. As a matter of fact, Schleiermacher believed in a certain freedom in the organizing of such a religious cult, although he also insisted that parts of the service remain fixed. Thus the text of traditional prayers was not to be altered, and even the sermon was supposed to follow a set form.[19] Schleiermacher was convinced, and rightly, that the congregation should not be disoriented by a rapid change in the liturgy. In the appeal to feeling, rather than intellect, such stability was necessary for creating and retaining the festive religious mood and for heightening religious consciousness.[20]

Catholicism was in agreement with the basic ideals of Schleiermacher's liturgy. But more than such Protestantism, it stressed the part played by art and architecture, the importance of symbols, and the role of the priest in creating the proper atmosphere, whereas the Protestants concentrated more upon song, sermon, and the primacy of the congregation, as well as upon common prayer.

The actual order of any given service may have differed from church to church and from state to state in Germany, but the liturgical rhythm and its purpose provided a constant example for the formation of secular festivals. If we take the descriptions of the fesival at Wartburg Castle we find that it opens and closes with a hymn: the Lutheran "Eine Feste Burg" ("A Mighty Fortress") at the start and the so-called Dutch Prayer of Thanksgiving at the end. This prayer was used at almost all national festivals as the concluding hymn; indeed, it became traditional patriotic fare.[21] At Wartburg the initial hymn, sung around the fire, was followed by a few words about justice and the German forest of oaks (the Introitus of the church service). More songs followed and then a speech, best described as a patriotic sermon, was made to mark the occasion. The "Credo" in this case was a living testimony of faith as all participants joined hands and took an oath never to forsake their Bund. Meanwhile, the church bells of the nearby town of Eisenach sounded their accompaniment.[22]

The liturgical rhythm in the church and the liturgical rhythm in front of the castle had clear affinities. The Wartburg Festival, like the celebration of the battle of liberation before it, forged one sacred national and Christian act of worship.

In any Christian liturgy, so a Nazi tract on political festivals tells us, one person speaks on behalf of all, and the congregation participates in the form of short appeals to God, through the Credo and, above all, through the hymn sung by the congregation. This order of service must be kept intact for secular festivals, the tract continues, because it expresses a fundamental psychological truth—it recognizes symbols as expressing, in a binding form, the spirit of the community. The theme of a Christian liturgical rite is therefore always the same: the confession of its sins by the congregation, the Credo, the explanation of Scripture, and, as the climax, common prayer and blessing. For the National Socialist this basic form could not be abandoned, but should simply be filled with a different content.[23]

The confession of sin, therefore, vanished from National Socialist ceremony, and instead the symbols of the words of the Führer—the Volk, blood, and race—took its place. Earlier, the same results had been accomplished with national symbols such as the flame, the oak, or monuments. The hymn had always been an integral part of such public festivals, as had been the Credo and the reading, again not of Scripture, but of patriotic poetry. The prayer and blessing were transformed by the Nazis into invocations of the national spirit or of racial ancestors. The ringing of church bells, which had accompanied the festival at Wartburg, was replaced by the sounding of trumpets. "As church bells alert the whole town to religious festivals, so fanfares or calls on trumpets should shortly before the beginning of the festival, remind those outside to participate."[24] Nevertheless, the Nazis quite consciously sought to separate their own festivities from those of the church. While in 1933 Goebbels spoke of cultic acts, by 1938 Hitler attempted to draw a clear distinction between religious "cults" and Volkish-political teaching.[25] This attempt to separate Christian and national cults was directed against the churches. But Nazi cults could not disguise their origins in the Christian tradition.

There was a tendency, in the second half of the nineteenth century, for public festivals to claim a monopoly of the "sacred." This logical development, however, did not become complete until the time of National Socialism. At every unveiling of a national monument up to the First World War a priest or minister still had an important function. He still preached a sermon even though surrounded by patriotic song and symbolism. This was more pronounced in Protestant than in Catholic regions. Though Catholic services also knew the hymn sung by the whole congregation, in the last resort the priest performed a different function (and even rite) at the altar from the congregation. The parallels here were present but not as clearly expressed as in the Protestant tradition of Schleiermacher.

Small wonder that it was Protestants and not Catholics who, during the Third Reich, attempted to fuse Christian liturgy and the national cult even further. But the Nazi festivals were autonomous; they adapted the liturgical rhythms to their own exclusive purpose. The Introitus, the hymn sung or spoken at the beginning of the church service, became the words of the Führer; the "Credo" a confession of faith pledging loyalty to Nazi ideology; while the sacrifice of the Mass was transformed into a memorial for the martyrs of the movement.[26] The Nazis stressed the so-called morning festival as helping to separate nationalist religion from Christianity. This took place on Sunday morning and was supposed to keep people from going to church. The "morning festival" not only made use of patriotic songs but also annexed the music of Bach, Händel, and Beethoven in order to create the proper atmosphere. Thus it made a "regular and binding appeal to the human soul and enabled members of the party to suffuse the national community with their faith."[27]

The parallels with Christian observance were obvious even when the festival finally stood upon its own feet and the traditional link between national and Christian worship had been broken. But from the beginning of the nineteenth century the national content of festivals had already developed through the use of their own symbolism. The symbols employed were appeals to the Germanic past and to historic memories sup-

posedly embedded in the Volkish soul. Festivals, Friedrich
Ludwig Jahn tells us, must embody transcendent ideals symbolized through the nation. They must link themselves with
traditions still alive among the people, and penetrate the unconscious.[28] The symbolism of the German oak, of a landscape replete with historical memories of the national past,
helped to fulfill these requirements. Jahn added to these the
dress of the ancient Germans, in order to induce an attitude
which would recapture Germanic virtues. Arndt agreed with
Jahn on all these points, as we have seen earlier, and also
advocated the return to Germanic dress which, together with
the German language, had suffered through the imitation of
foreign models. German dress was "natural and manly"; its
wearing would contribute to a regeneration of German
youth.[29] In addition to these attempts at historical continuity,
folk songs and folk customs which had survived the changes
of history were studied and resurrected as part of the national
ceremonial.

It was the awareness of historical continuity rather than
military example that led these men to propose that Germans
wear Germanic garb. To be sure, analogies to military practice were drawn. Thus the crowds gathering at the national
Hambach Festival in 1832 were likened to Napoleonic armies
on the march, and later Ferdinand Lasalle called his meetings
with workers a *"Heeresschau"* (military parade). Armies,
after all, were the largest formation of masses which existed.
But the immediate influence of the military tradition was
complex and indirect. It was certainly present in the *Aufmarsch* (the drawing up of groups before entering into a
hall), in the march rhythms which were often used, and in the
symbol of the flag. But the attempted uniformity of dress
during the first half of the nineteenth century, at least, was
rooted in a revival of supposedly Germanic traditions and
concepts of beauty which we have discussed already.

During the Second Empire, military ceremonial seemed to
defeat the dynamic of the national cult (as we shall see pres-

ently), but with the First World War it came to provide one model for the formation of masses, although always in concert with the already developed tradition of public festivals. The Third Reich tended to keep military pomp separate from its cult; at Nuremberg the army was given a ceremony of its own. Celebrations such as that of Heroes' Memorial Day did become military occasions, when units of all military forces marched carrying the tattered flags of the First World War. Where the military example played a role it was annexed to the national cult, rather than providing the most important model for Nazi ceremonial. The nationalist impetus did not feed notably on military models which, in the age of Arndt and Jahn, seemed devoted to its suppression.

The gymnastic organizations which Jahn founded in 1811 were supposed to bring an additional dimension to festivals. He believed that the ancient Germans had already competed in sport in order to show their manly nature and virility. His gymnastic festivals took place on a meadow outside Berlin (the Hasenheide), on days designated to recall the events of the wars of national liberation. The singing of patriotic or church songs, the patriotic sermon, torchlight parades, and the sacred flame all at times accompanied the gymnastic exercises.[30] The cult of manliness through physical competition became an integral part of such rites, and some national monuments specifically designed their sacred spaces in order to accommodate them.[31] For Jahn, such manly exercise got rid of the "sins of youth"; it turned young people away from the frivolities which Rousseau had castigated.[32]

The foundations of the national cult had been laid by 1832, when a national festival took place at Hambach on the Rhine. This was the first mass festival inspired by the aspiration for national unity. The celebrations of 1815 had been local, not centralized, while the Wartburg Festival of 1817 had encompassed only a relatively small number of student youth. At Hambach some thirty thousand Germans gathered, and it may well be true that this was indeed the first German mass meeting. Contemporaries felt reminded of Napoleonic armies on the march.[33] As one of the festival's initiators put it: "What youth had sworn to do at the Wartburg, the whole people should now swear to uphold."[34]

The festival was called together during the "German May," for at that time the ancient Germans had held their tribal meetings or *"Thing"*. But the revolutionary impetus behind the festival was emphasized when J. G. A. Wirth, a prominent figure at the celebration, added to the Germanic precedent the fact that Poland too had received its constitution in May. Poles were present and spoke at the festival, for the Polish struggle for national liberation—like the struggles of Hungary, Italy, and Spain also mentioned by Wirth—was seen as identical to the present German quest.[35]

An ancient ruined castle on a hilltop was, once again, the focal point of events at Hambach. The most imposing part of the festival was the procession to the ruin itself. This was well organized and contained deputations from all over Germany, women carrying the Polish flag, and a militia of citizens with a band. Dominating the processions were the black, red, and gold emblems worn by everyone, the ancient German dress and costumes worn by the students, and many flags. These often displayed the emblems of the Roman fasci on one side as a sign of strength and determination, and a wreath of oak leaves on the other. The procession was enveloped in patriotic song, of which Arndt's "What Is the German Fatherland?" was most popular.[36] At the castle the speeches started immediately; there were some nineteen of these lasting until late at night, interrupted only by songs and the noonday meal. Moreover, a speaker would often form a separate group within the crowd, for many people could not hear the main proceedings. It is possible that people felt themselves part of a *Thing*, but chaos certainly dominated this scene at the castle.[37] The masses were not really united except during the procession. Symbolism was confined to flags on the towers of the ruin, fires on the hills at night, and speeches. The kind of ritual that had dominated the Wartburg Festival apparently could not as yet be transferred to a mass meeting.

Nevertheless, the festival itself did become a symbol. Typically enough it was the procession, its most coherent element, which was reproduced in pictures, and on pipebowls, aprons, and snuffboxes. But Hambach hats, jackets, and even styles of beard also followed. Many localities found their own symbols to represent the meaning of Hambach. The "tree of freedom" was resurrected from the tradition of the French Revolution, symbolizing justice, but also now rechristened a "May tree" in many communities.[38] The symbols of Hambach were secular, though at the beginning of the procession to the castle the church bells had rung their accompaniment as they had at Wartburg. But in the speeches we find no trace of that union of Christianity and nationalism which Arndt had desired. Patriotic songs were not combined with hymns; rather, the melodies of the French Revolution predominated.

The Hambach Festival demonstrates how national liturgy, under the pressures of national frustration, tended to become increasingly independent of religious meanings and to find its model in revolutionary inspiration. However, as far as the organization of the masses was concerned, Hambach did not provide a viable precedent. There had always been processions in national festivals since they were easiest to organize. Much later on, these grew increasingly formalized as part of a liturgical whole, when they became known as *Aufmärsche*, taking on something of military discipline.

The further development of the national liturgy took place within a more restricted and settled framework than festivals like Hambach. A town or village provided its own organization for a festival held within its confines, and through its relatively fixed structure, could induce greater coherence among the inhabitants. The same held true for festivals sponsored by specific organizations for their members, even if they were nationwide, like the sharpshooting and singers' festivals. All these celebrations united even further an already closely knit crowd, not an incoherent, diverse mass like that which streamed to Hambach. Only much later, in the twentieth century, would a more fully worked out national liturgy provide a standard for highly diversified and random crowds.

The revolution of 1848 was directed toward the attainment of German unity, yet it did not lead to festivals which anticipated the formation of large and diverse crowds held together by a political liturgy. To be sure, traditional processions did take place, for example, before a representative of the Austrian emperor when he visited Frankfurt in 1848. Torchlight parades, processions by the trade guilds of the city, fireworks, and flags celebrated the occasion.[39] At times during the 1848 revolution the relevance of national ceremonial was denied, even by those who had practiced it earlier. For example, the students met, once again at Wartburg, in memory of the festival of 1817. But the difference was great, for there was no ceremonial in 1848, except a rained-out attempt at the close of the meeting. In fact, the motto was now: "No pretty speeches, no songs of freedom, no tears, no oaths, no celebration of the last supper."[40] This was an overt repudiation of the national festival which had taken place in 1817, and gives an indication of how a later generation, engaged in the serious business of revolution, viewed the past.

Instead of the old-style, pseudo-religious structure, the students organized a parliamentary debate. Their final resolution was free of mystic or patriotic tones, proclaiming concrete suggestions for the freedom to teach and learn and for the centralization of the German university system. They even rejected as Protestant and therefore one-sidedly clerical the singing of the Lutheran chorale "Eine Feste Burg" which had been so prominent in 1817.[41] Liberalism, for these students, stood in the way of the ceremonial of nationalism, and revolutionary change was viewed as a sober business. Not so the flood of national propaganda conveyed by newspapers, pamphlets, and songs which accompanied the 1848 revolution. By and large, however, the revolution tended to reject the cult of nationalism. Despite the short-lived revolutionary fervor, the national liturgy developed within a more restricted local and organizational framework, as is well illustrated by the next great mass celebration after Hambach, the "Schillerfeiern" of 1859. The search for national unity had been disrupted once again by the revolution of 1848. But in 1859 the time was thought ripe for another festival, for the hundredth anniversary of Schiller's birth seemed to provide a renewed link between nationalism and freedom. A cultural figure thus became the national symbol; the revolutionary tradition kept alive at Hambach through demonstrations of national liberation had given way to an internalization of national identity. An emphasis upon the "national spirit" (which seemed a natural consequence of the failure to produce concrete change in 1848) was increasingly bound to stress the need for national symbolism. Perhaps the urge to activism at Hambach had helped to stifle the full use of national symbols and liturgy.

The Schiller festivities were localized. Each town produced its own celebrations, not dissimilar to those in commemoration of the Battle of the Peoples which Karl Hoffmann had described so well. These festivals were often financed by popular subscription.[42] The male choir societies played a leading part, but the sharpshooting societies also participated. Moreover, almost everywhere all classes of the population joined in, workers as well as the bourgeoisie. Indeed, in Paris the Schillerfeier was the creation of German expatriate workers who belonged to musical societies, and one observer noted that he had never seen the "German proletariat" so united.[43] In Germany itself—for example, in Hamburg and Stuttgart—the workers created a large part of the processions with which the festival began. They joined with the bourgeoise, the gymnasts, singers, and small-trades people in celebrating the national festival. Only the nobility and the military were said to be hostile, which was understandable, as Schiller was a symbol of freedom and national consciousness.[44]

The fête was usually opened by processions, by now standard procedure. Sometimes such processions were enlivened by floats representing themes from Schiller's plays, and here the diverse groups carried symbols indicating their crafts. Flags were the rule of the day, and all members of the procession had to wear a common emblem. At Leipzig, members carried the rod of Mercury on which an owl perched representing art and trade.[45] Torchlight parades took place at night, and fires were lit on the surrounding hills. The parade usually ended at the market square where speeches were made and toasts proposed to Schiller and the German nation. Now and then cities made special use of their own effective settings. Munich, for example, used the Feldherrnhalle at the end of Klenze's processional street, the Ludwigstrasse. A torchlight parade of some five hundred students ended in front of the monument. Its loggia was decorated with a bust of Schiller, and the male choirs of the city around its base broke into song as the procession approached. The students then marched on to another square where they sang student songs and piled up their torches into a bonfire.[46] The use to which the Ludwigstrasse (designed for royal state processions) and the Feldherrnhalle were put on this occasion would occur again some seventy years later when the Nazis used the setting in the identical way to commemorate their dead of the Hitler putsch of 1923.

Apart from processions and speeches, the Schiller festivals abounded in symbolic representations (*Transparente*) and *tableaux vivantes*. Frankfurt was typical of many cities in constructing a huge mock-up of a Germania crowning Schiller with a laurel wreath, underneath which the different German tribes were represented. The municipal theatres presented *tableaux vivantes* from Schiller's plays, always ending with his apotheosis: the poet ascends to Heaven and is crowned by his predecessors from Livy to Shakespeare.[47] The national theme was crowded out in the theatre by the muses, but in the outdoor representations it was always present, Schiller and Germania proudly united.

Political parties did try to make use of this festival for their own ends. Berlin, especially, saw a small riot develop between the Democrats and the police. Elsewhere the Liberals tried to annex the festivities to their cause.[48] But such attempts ended in failure. The Catholic south joined the Protestant north in the celebration and, as at Hambach, the desire for national unity pushed the religious element virtually out of the picture.[49] The church bells tolled in many places at the beginning of the processions as they had done ever since 1814. But in Hamburg a veritable conflict arose between Church and festival. Schiller's anniversary fell on the important Protestant holiday of "Repentance and Prayer" (*Buss und Bettag*). Though the festival's sponsors pleaded that their city should join the rest of Germany in a common celebration, they lost out and had to postpone festivities to the next day.[50] Religious sentiment was a factor to reckon with, even though the festival itself no longer accorded the clergy a prominent position. Nevertheless, by 1859 at the latest, the national cult had become secularized, and not even the minister's restored function in Wilhelminian Germany could disguise this fact; the cleric would vanish finally after the First World War, never to be resurrected again.

The festivals which have concerned us were all infused with a feeling of historical continuity, a sense of being part of an organic whole, which we shall meet again in the choir, gymnastic, and sharpshooting festivals of the 1860's. To be sure, the national cult had not yet developed into a fully stabilized liturgy, and would not do so until after the First World War. The attainment of national unity in 1871 presented a grave problem to the continuity of the national cult, for festivals were now guided by the Establishment and could no longer draw their dynamic from unfulfilled longings. Before 1871 most German rulers—with the exception of a few, such as Ludwig I of Bavaria—had opposed national agitation, and this opposition infused the national liturgy with an *élan* stressing popular participation against the political Establishment. Jahn's opposition to "imposed" festivals reflected this dynamic. During the Second Empire, festivals were in danger of becoming artificial creations decreed by an official orthodoxy that threatened to rupture their link with the dramatic world of Germanic myth and symbol.

The annual festival to commemorate the German victory over France at Sedan of 1870 illustrates this. It was the first national festival which the Second German Empire created for its own glorification. The Protestant minster Friedrich von Bodelschwingh was the force behind the institution of the so-called Sedanfest. Bodelschwingh had founded schools and institutions for the poor, over which he maintained a strict regimen. His stern Protestantism emphasized discipline in daily life, as well as the discipline of war which God had sent in order to prevent decadence in time of peace.[51] He had been shocked by the festivals he had witnessed in the France of Napoleon III: "stuffing oneself with food and drink, dancing and jumping from morning to night."[52] Sin was on the loose (only to be expected in France) and the German Protestant minister believed that such sin would lead directly to another Paris Commune and the destruction of family values.[53]

Germany had to be rescued from such a fate. Bodelschwingh thought that the Germanic festivals which Tacitus had described might be useful here as a more productive way for people to spend their leisure. He turned to the celebration of the Battle of Sedan as a way of preventing national decadence, which for him equaled frivolity. The Franco-Prussian War, which had kept decadence in check and turned men's minds to patriotic sacrifice, was over, and other means to accomplish these ends had to be found. Inspired by Arndt, he looked to the past celebrations of the Battle of Leipzig as one other example of the synthesis between the religious and the patriotic.[54]

Emperor William II eagerly accepted Bodelschwingh's suggestion and the Sedanfest was instituted in 1871. The minister had put forward his own plan for its celebration. The Day of

Sedan was to begin with morning service in church and end with evening prayers.[55] But as the festival became established, and by 1873 obtained a certain amount of popular success, it did not remain as serious as Bodelschwingh would have wished, nor as simple. In 1883 in the provincial city of Oldenburg, for example, some 1,500 persons took part in a torchlight procession and singing, heard patriotic speeches until 1:30 A.M., and danced until 5:00 A.M. The usual patriotic organizations arranged these festivities, but in 1890, at any rate, the Socialist Workers' Cultural Association was also participating,[56] perhaps to prove its loyalty during enforcement of the anti-Socialist laws. The dancing would not have suited Bodelschwingh, who believed that after the speeches and evening prayer, people should go home to their families in order to relive the "beautiful day" once more, in their own circle.[57]

As time went on the Sedanstag was co-opted by various patriotic associations which gradually drenched it in bourgeois *Gemütlichkeit*. More important still, military parades moved to the foreground in the same way that they dominated the other Wilhelminian patriotic festival, the emperor's birthday. The people were excluded from active participation. In the memory of one of those who lived through such a Sedanstag in 1911, for example, this festival was a day of military display.[58] The festival was still further restricted as a national act by the opposition of the Catholics, who saw in it a celebration of those political parties supporting the anti-Catholic policies of Bismarck. For them it was sponsored by the Establishment, and biased toward one part of the Establishment at that.[59]

The Sedanstag was a failure,[60] in the end, because it had been organized from above in a conservative manner, had stressed discipline, and gradually excluded popular participation. It was therefore quite unlike the earlier celebrations of the Battle of Leipzig, which had emphasized Germanic myths and symbols, and had left room for universal participation. This breakdown was typical of the way in which things developed in the Second Reich. A democratic and dynamic element was lacking, not only in festivals, but in all political movements tied to the Establishment. The Social Christian Party of Bodelschwingh's friend Adolf Stoecker provides a good example. Stoecker wanted to create a mass movement, but his party was severely limited in its popular appeal by the restraints of Protestant orthodoxy and loyalty to the emperor. Even Stoecker's later emphasis on anti-Semitism, popular as it was, could not give the "Court Preacher's" movement new vitality. An Establishment frightened by the spectre of a political mass movement put an end to Stoecker's political activities.

Jahn had already stressed that no festival could succeed without popular participation and the appeal to historical myth and symbol.[61] Military parades and even church services could not take the place of such historical memories, and neither could the trend toward *Gemütlichkeit* within the closed circle of patriotic or trade associations. This lack of popular participation determined not only the unhappy fate of the Sedanstag, but also that of the celebration of the emperor's birthday. Here, too, military pomp and circumstance predominated, while the people watched from the sidelines.

The Nazis, in celebrating the Führer's birthday, also used military parades which sometimes lasted over four hours. But they also had recourse to cultic ritual. The central ceremonies were broadcast over the radio, and in every locality they were imitated by party organizations. The chief ceremony took place in Munich in the late evening hours. Flags, sacred flames, spoken choruses, and an oath sworn by all participants were framed in a darkness illuminated only by startling lighting effects[62]—a far cry from the Wilhelminian festivals, which one witness remembered mainly for the decorations on the helmets of the military.[63] The Wilhelminian festivities never broke through to become genuine rites with a liturgy that made room for popular participation. The dynamic that had assured the success of the festivals before German unification was missing, and Germany's glory was chiefly represented by marching soldiers.

The Sedansfest, like so many other festivals, failed in the Second Empire partly because it was enveloped in bourgeois *Gemütlichkeit* and partly because the powers that be were in fact afraid of mass movements. Festivals were now held to reinforce order and decency; they were to affirm the traditional way of life. Bodelschwingh's earlier emphasis upon the function of the family in the festival was especially typical, as the line dividing private from public festivals was easily lost. The fate of the male choirs, to which we shall return, provides a good example of this trend. From associations in which all could participate they tended increasingly after 1870 to become private groups performing at concerts, reducing the public to the status of spectators. These tendencies were inherent in the flowering of the bourgeois culture after 1870; the symbols of settled and comfortable middle-class life threatened to replace those of national revival. Jahn and his contemporaries had always held the fervent belief that a full stomach was opposed to patriotism and manliness.[64]

Just as some national monuments of the time adopted playful Baroque imitations, so the festivals, too, seemed to lack the seriousness of purpose their founders had intended. Bodelschwingh had failed in his attempt to defeat frivolity. Yet the social and psychological needs of national festivals were still clearly understood by many leading members of the Establishment. When a National Festival Society was founded in 1897, its support came from the "Central Commission for People's and Youth Sports" (*Volks und Jugendspiele*). This organization had been founded in 1889 in order to further sports in German schools, and was financed in large part by contributions from many German cities and towns (310 by 1899).[65] From its very inception, the commission attempted to introduce competitive sports into popular festivals in order to give them a stricter focus and seriousness. The founder, Freiherr von Schenckendorf, a physician and National Liberal deputy in the Prussian Diet, as well as the men on the commission, were not inspired merely by a love of sport; on the contrary, sport was meant to equip boys for the call to arms by the fatherland. The members of the commission were partly of the nobility, partly drawn from industry (such as von Siemens), and partly from finance (for example, the banker von Mendelssohn-Bartholdy). But academics were also included, as well as the president of the German Teachers Association and several directors of *Gymnasien* (high schools). Typically enough, the president of the Pan-German Association, Ernst Hasse, was also a member of the commission. These were men to the right of the political spectrum, conservative patriots with close ties to the army and the court. Small wonder that they believed popular festivals were to be "a union of all those who want to preserve the state." The commission wanted to see all sport transformed into competition, for this meant an effort of will to stay within the rules set by the sport, behavior conducive to "active obedience."[66]

Neither frivolity nor lack of discipline was desired at the Volksfeste. Not unlike Bodelschwingh, one of the members of the commission condemned the festivals of male choirs and sharpshooting societies, for they paraded through the streets to the people's applause, but afterwards celebrated at balls and dances. "Such frivolity does not silence class differences."[67] When the commission attempted to broaden local efforts by creating the National Festival Society, sociological considerations were of great importance. Class differences should be abolished at national festivals and everyone should compete, regardless of status.[68] Gymnastic competition, together with renewed devotion to the nation, would enable the existing class structure to remain intact while masking the awareness of class differences, and would also provide the emperor with serviceable recruits.[69] This German élite grasped full well the military utility of festivals, a factor which Rousseau had stressed but which is absent from the writings of Arndt and Jahn.

The initial Manifesto of the National Festival Society referred to Jahn, and took from his heritage the notion of the importance of a proper national setting for the reaffirmation of national consciousness through competitive sport.[70] The commission had already appealed to architects of national monuments to provide a place for sports, thus demanding in 1900 that every Bismarck tower should have a space on which *Volksspiele* could be held. They attempted unsuccessfully to buy a hill overlooking the old Leipzig battlefield as a site for competitive games, and offered to build a Bismarck tower there as well, so as to strengthen the "national spirit."[71]

The National Festival Society showed a special interest in the sites of the *Niederwalddenkmal* and the Kyffhäuser memorial as the scene of their proposed festivals. The competition between the two monuments, mentioned earlier, was directed toward becoming the site of these national festivals. The winning monument, so it was thought, could then claim a central part in the national liturgy. Though many German cities also competed and even submitted designs for sports arenas, the Niederwald was finally chosen because the monument was already a regional pilgrimage center. This despite the fact that the festival would have to take place quite far from the monument itself, since the surrounding landscape did not permit the construction of vast sports facilities.[72]

The Festival Society Committee members also tried to make use of the Sedan Festival for their own purpose, as they felt that the reason for its failure was that it did not fall on a Sunday.[73] In this they were sometimes successful. Thus in Dresden in 1900, after a meeting at the monument to the victory over France, everyone marched to the "Festplatz" where competitive games took place. While the judges deliberated, the male choirs sang. At Braunschweig, as in other parts of Germany that same year, the games took place a day before the actual celebration of the victory at Sedan, but they also began with a speech and a procession and ended with a "Hoch" to emperor and Reich.[74] But this success was only momentary. The National Festival Society failed to take into account the real reason for the failure of the Sedanstag. They could have learned from Jahn's own writings that festivals could not be artificially created as part of a conscious effort to unite the people behind the Establishment. Albert Soboul, writing about the French Revolution, distinguished between "imposed cults" and the spontaneous transference of the popular religious impulse.[75] The spontaneity itself was never a fact; all festivals are planned. But the carefully constructed illusion of spontaneity infused them with greater meaning.

Memories of distant times had to be part of this spontaneity, even if the festivals were actually honoring recent events. The wars of liberation had only just happened when they were recalled and celebrated in 1815; yet a conscious connection was forged between these wars and the struggles of the ancient Germans against the Romans. The National Festival Society members understood something of the theory of festivals; at least they were concerned with the site. But they had little feeling for the momentum behind such celebrations. In all fairness, it must be said that they faced an additional obstacle to the creation of popular enthusiasm, one which had for a long time plagued the Sedanstag and, for that matter, the celebration of the Fourteenth of July in France:[76] earlier national festivals had been directed against the Establishment, while these were supposed to celebrate the continuance of existing institutions.

Moreover, the parent Central Commission for People's and Youth Sports was plagued by the constant opposition of the powerful gymnasts with whom, in fact, they were competing. Admittedly, the commission attempted to take in all sports, from rowing to football, and even initiated training courses for sports teachers. But this ambitious program only managed to arouse the ire of the gymnasts still further.[77] After all, they were the true disciples of Jahn, and their festivals seemed to prove it. In any case, no specific national festival was ever held by the National Festival Society, though the work of the parent commission continued until the outbreak of the First World War.

The realization that national festivals were necessary in a modern nation arose on all sides during the Second German Empire, both from supporters of the Establishment and from its opposition. There is no clearer sign of this impetus than the place such festivals were given in the proposal for a new Jewish state which Theodor Herzl advocated during this period (in 1895). When he dreamed about the future Jewish state, he envisaged national festivals with gigantic spectacles and colorful processions. He was going to commission popular hymns, and believed that with the proper flag, "one can lead men wherever one wants to, even into the Promised Land."[78] He termed himself a dramatist and indeed his interest in the theatre was important. But he was equally fascinated with the problem of directing and leading crowds.[79] Herzl was a very unusual man, but his proposals for the drama of a Jewish state still reflected a general preoccupation with the masses and with the symbolism needed to harness them to a national mystique.

The very fact that during the Second Empire discussions about festivals and national monuments went on incessantly demonstrates that many people realized their importance as part of a new politics. But there was also a feeling that an older, dynamic tradition was in danger of suffocation. Popular religious impulse was no longer being transferred to national festivals. This problem was compounded by a new wave of national monuments which swept the country. People became bored with these symbols of national worship. As one architectural journal wrote in 1898: "A competition for another monument to the emperor William I will not help to focus public attention."[80] Consequently, there was a new concern with factors which could make a national pilgrimage site successful. Thus one design for a monument in memory of the Battle of the Peoples was favored because it featured a huge statue of a "powerful Germanic man," sword in hand. Such a statue had the potential for attaining the popularity of the *Hermannsdenkmal.*[81]

The preoccupation with a national pilgrimage site had always existed, but it now became the subject of extensive debate. The effectiveness of a national monument was said to depend upon its site, which must combine the autonomy of national monuments with a forum for national festivals.[82] It was widely held that a statue in isolation was not effective; the tradition which fused the national monument and the symbols that surrounded it was consciously assimilated.

In 1889, Bruno Schmitz submitted a design for a national monument planned to honor the emperor William I, which took the ineffectiveness of an isolated statue of the monarch fully into account. The monument was not to be built on a historic hilltop, like the Kyffhäuser memorial, but in the center of Berlin. William I mounted on his horse would be set in the midst of a square surrounded by colonnades, much like those Bernini had built at St. Peter's. A triumphal arch, reminiscent of the arch built by Gilly, would be placed behind the statue.[83] Though this design was never executed, Schmitz's demonstrated taste for the monumental and sense of space were to make him influential when he turned to other national monuments.

The very necessary "sacred space" around the statue represented a framework for mass meetings, and the masses themselves were only too ready to take advantage of it. For the appeal of the national mystique had not vanished in the Second Empire, even though it now faced new problems. We have noted the concern of the National Festival Society with political and class divisions among the population. Many workers continued to go their own way after the 1880's when Social Democracy became strong, though they also celebrated festivals to symbolize their particular aims. The Social Democrats founded male choirs and gymnastic societies, bending the traditions of nationalist associations to serve their purposes.[84] By the outbreak of the First World War the ritual elements of the workers' movement had also influenced the evolution of national festivals.

The Second Empire, then, raised the problem of the continued existence of a national cult during a time of political and religious conservatism. Its experience tended to reinforce the validity of ideas which founders of the national cult had put forward. Men's minds and hearts had to be renewed by new festivals as an expression of national regeneration. Within the Empire the nature of national festivals continued to be debated, not merely for the purposes of discipline or social structure, but also as a means of infusing national celebrations with a new dynamic spirit.

# CHAPTER FIVE

# Public Festivals:
# The Theatre and Mass Movements

THE TRIUMPH of middle-class values was complete in Germany even before national unification. The virtues of manliness, devotion to duty, discipline, and hard work were praised by men like Jahn, as well as by a whole body of literature which exalted the middle classes. National and middle-class ideals joined hands during the nineteenth century, and indeed it was the middle classes who flocked to patriotic associations and formed male choirs and sharpshooting societies. Not entirely, of course; workers, too, were drawn to and joined in the drive for national unity. But on the whole the Second Empire especially saw a general embourgeoisement of Germany in which the middle-class values of rootedness, order, and inwardness tended to become translated into *Gemütlichkeit* and love of opulence.

Yet if the national cult was to be rescued from official orthodoxy and suffocation, it was necessary to link it with dominant bourgeois ideals and utopias. The longing for myth and symbol had to be reawakened: the vision of a utopia was foreign to the stern mind of Bodelschwingh and only dimly understood by the aristocrats and big business men of the National Festival Society. Richard Wagner became the central figure in the revival of an emotional and religious nationalism which found its expression in myth, symbol, and festivals. Though in this sense he continued the work of Arndt, encompassing men's hearts and minds, the new nationalism was now much more closely linked to middle-class stability and utopian longings. The middle-class utopia of a healthy, happy, and ordered world was, in the last decades of the century, detached from reality. There was in fact little incentive to turn the dream into practice against the existing and comfortable order of things. The novels which these classes read by the million put forward the sentimental dream of a virtuous world, but in the same breath warned against upsetting the political and social order.[1] So the attempted renewal of a national mystique took place against this background. The sting was drawn from the anti-Establishment impetus of earlier nationalism, and the revolutionary ideals of Hambach were of course also liquidated.

Richard Wagner was not an isolated figure. He managed to create a cohesive circle of followers, dominated after his death by his second wife Cosima Wagner, and subsequently by his daughter-in-law Winifred. Moreover, his ideas had great appeal because they did not remain theoretical. The Bayreuth theatre was transformed into a pilgrimage center. Wagner's ideas and music evolved throughout his life; in this particular discussion we are concerned with his attempt to renew the national mystique during the Second Reich. It was this Wagnerian tradition which proved successful and was carried on until the end of the Second World War.

Once he had descended from the barricades of Dresden in 1848, Wagner became concerned with the maintenance of the national spirit which had, after all, inspired that revolution. The problem of man's fragmentation in modern society troubled him, and in order to solve it he arrived at ideas not dissimilar to those of Friedrich Theodor Vischer, who had also been a revolutionary in 1848. Art and its aesthetics could serve to reunite men, and to bring to light the true world filled with higher meaning. But for Wagner, unlike Vischer, this world was to be a primeval one, opposed to bourgeois art and culture as it had been evolving ever since the Renaissance. Wagner's world was based on the *Mythos*, or eternal Germanic truth, which provided inexhaustible material for the

German artist.[2] The *"Mythos"* implies that the world picture
has to be grasped through intuition. This intuition is defined
as an effort of the soul to rise beyond the present world to a
higher unity through ancestral memories. The *Mythos* is,
therefore, expressed through symbolism and art. The Romantic movement had sought to rediscover the memories of fore-
fathers through ballads, fairy tales, and legends.[3] Ideals of
beauty were an essential part of the *Mythos*, whether linked
with Greek or Germanic antiquity, or with a combination of
both.

We have seen how the principles of aesthetics became crucial for the new political style because they functioned as a
unifying element of the national cult. Wagner agreed with the
functional purposes of art but turned his *Mythos* into that of
the Germanic Volk. Hans Mayer has said quite correctly that
the *Ring of the Nibelungen* was meant to carry the *Mythos*
to the people. The Germans, Wagner believed, were characterized by an inner substance which had never changed; therefore, the ancient sagas were also an expression of the present.[4]

This was hardly an original idea, for the myth of the unchanging Volk dates back far into German history. It is, in
fact, a basic ingredient of German nationalism. As Hitler put
it: "Estates vanish, classes change, human fate evolves, something remains throughout and must remain: The Volk as a
substance of flesh and blood."[5] This reality was to be recalled
through the activation of historical memories.

Such a concept was basic to national symbolism long before
Wagner wrote that man conceived as a product of historical
change must be abolished and the people's memories awakened
to their original substance and strength.[6] As we have seen,
even festivals concerned with celebrating recent events, such
as those held in 1815 only a year after the Battle of the Peoples, had operated with symbols which harked back to an
ancient German heritage—the sacred flame, the oak, and the
so-called Germanic dress. And the Nazis continued this tradition. A survey of historical plays written during the Third

Reich shows that they always attempted to draw a parallel
with the present. Historical dramas tried to make history relevant by emphasizing the heroic.[7] The present was embodied
by the myth; audiences in the Third Reich were supposed to
see "no new material or characters, but the old and accus-
tomed through an everlasting regeneration of the human
soul."[8]

Wagner's idea of bringing the *Mythos* to the Volk was not
new when he discovered it. Freedom was a major theme of
this *Mythos*, as it had been during the struggle for national
liberation. Wagner's *Nibelungen*, from its conception in 1848
onwards, stressed the freedom of the people as against feudal
oppression.[9] We have seen that this theme was already present
in Jahn when he recommended the celebration of the Battle of
Merseburg where the peasants rose against princes and
bishops.[10] This form of democracy was basic to the development of national consciousness. It was the people as a whole
who counted and who worshipped themselves as the Volk.
Nationalism was not only supposed to free the nation, it was
also supposed to free each individual soul so that it could unite
with the Volk and become truly creative.

Wagner's connection with the tradition of the national liturgy seems obvious up to this point. When Hans Mayer calls
Lohengrin the black knight who rides between Death and
the Devil, we are again confronted with an image which had
played a large part in national literature ever since Albrecht
Dürer's famous woodcut. The knight became a symbol of
Germanic purity as against the temptations of the evil world;
the German will to survive history.[11] Art, we read in the
official *Bayreuther Blätter* (echoing Vischer once more), must
avoid the merely accidental fact of individualism; it must always stress the eternal and unchanging. Moreover, the concept of man as defined by the historical process does not begin
to exhaust the meaning of humanity. Man is, first and last, a
moral creature, and the world must be determined through
the eternal spirit of morality.[12]

This morality was linked to Germanic myths. But in the final period of Wagner's work, morality became a religious imperative as well. It is here that the Germanic is invaded by the bourgeois. When Wagner's mouthpiece and disciple Hans von Wolzogen tells us in 1884 that religion and art are the only two idealistic powers which can give true meaning to life, he is no longer speaking solely about ancient Germanic religion.[13] In Wagner's *Nibelungen* the free moral conscience of man is directed by the gods, but even here Christian elements of sin and repentance play their part. *Lohengrin* (1850) and *Parsifal* (1882) are based upon the myth of the Holy Grail, the vessel which contained drops of Christ's blood. The "holy blood" of Christ formed much of the Easter myth, and to realize its symbolic importance we have only to visualize the statues of Christ on the Cross, in which his spilled blood plays such a prominent role. But blood also played an important part in folklore and medicine. It was used for healing purposes, indeed endowed with magical qualities from ancient times to the nineteenth century. Hermann L. Strack has collected examples, from many regions of Germany, of men and women who used blood in order to cure illness or ward off evil up to 1892.[14] Christian and heathen elements mingled in the blood cult, just as for Wagner the Germanic knights were the guardians of Christ's blood. The Nazi poet Gerhard Schumann was staying within hallowed tradition when in one of his poems he called blood our "most holy property" and pleaded with God to keep it pure. This poem ended with a chorale from Luther's "Eine Feste Burg." Heathen mythology and Christianity were fused to define the eternal property of the German nation, its purity of blood.[15]

Wagner utilized the blood symbolism in this way but, in a more orthodox manner, connected it in *Lohengrin* and *Parsifal* with sin, repentance, and salvation. These, too, became signs of Germanic strength and morality. Here many Nazis, including Hitler, differed; for such Christianity was for them a slave morality. But for Wagner it both was sentimental and contained traditional Christian precepts, which were also those of middle-class morality. It might indeed be said that Wagner brought the *Mythos* not to the Volk but to the middle classes. There had always been an alliance between the ideals of the national cult and middle-class morality. They shared a common belief in honesty, manliness, and abstinence from frivolity; both condemned what Jahn had called the "sins of youth." Even in their use of Christian concepts and liturgical elements, *Lohengrin* and *Parsifal* did not stand outside the nationalist tradition, as we have seen earlier. But there is still an important difference between Wagner and the tradition of the national cult.

Wagner believed that Christianity had to replace the heathen traditions, that the Holy Grail must be of greater importance than the sacred flame. *Lohengrin* is set in the Middle Ages (the "age of faith") and is not, as in the *Nibelungen*, filled with ancient gods, sacred fires, and Germanic dress. Middle-class morality and Christianity were thus fused, directed together toward a national cult; the *Mythos* had become Christianized and robbed of all revolutionary sting. Bringing the *Mythos* to the people meant for Wagner combining the Christian and the German in a respectable and acceptable fashion; like the Jesuits in their Christianity, he wanted to make Germanic religion easy to join.

That is why he stressed the utopian and theatrical elements of his work. The most elevated works of art will be gratefully accepted, he wrote, if reality is first dissolved into a dream. Through this dream the people will be able to step into the seriousness of life. The unending dream of sacred Volkish revelations will return to them clearly, full of meaning. Leopold von Schröder, an expert on India who was closely associated with Bayreuth after Wagner's death, summarized this myth: "For the first time since the scattering of the Aryan peoples they can, once again, gather at a predetermined locality [i.e., Bayreuth] . . . in order to witness their primeval mysteries."[16] Wagner's *Mythos* could be enjoyed by the public as a kind of utopia, without actually having to fear any real change. But for Wagner, the *Mythos* and the dream world were only the means through which man would create a moral Volkish life.

Earlier, national self-awareness did not have to take such an approach to its symbols, myths, and festivals. No doubt the element of dream was present, but Wagner illustrates once more the self-conscious attempt to revive the national cult after the achievement of national unification, within a complacent bourgeois society. He was successful where organizations like the National Festival Society had failed. Wagner's work did stress the ancient myths, combined them with Christianity and middle-class morality; furthermore, he avoided abstraction by the construction of concrete works of art.

To see, really to see—that is the quality which most people lack. Do you have eyes? Do you have eyes?—this is what one would like to tell the world which is eternally talking and listening. . . . Whoever could really see, he knows where he stands [in the world].[17]

Wagner here meant true regeneration, not merely through the "inner eye," but by making the invisible visible. This was to be done quite concretely through works of art appealing to the senses, convincing men of truth through deeds and example.

These "deeds," his operas, were carefully staged. He paid just as much attention to the setting as had those who were reviving the national monuments and their sacred spaces. Wagner's own "sacred space" was total as well, an integration of both the staging and the hall in which the performance was to take place. He called the performances of his operas "festivals," and the opera house in Bayreuth was the "festival hall." Not only were his works to be played at certain months of the year, but they had a deeper meaning closely related to the tradition of national festivals. Performances of his works were to be removed from the cares of daily life and given an extraordinary, cultic setting in order to transform them into actual rites. Eventually Bayreuth became a national pilgrimage center.

Gottfried Semper designed the first festival hall, which was to have been built in Munich. When the actual hall was built in Bayreuth many of the original features were maintained. It was praised in the *Bayreuther Blätter* for being an "idealistic building" because it continued the classical and monumental tradition. The building, the paper said, symbolized a "noble restfulness," such as Winckelmann had praised over a century earlier.[18] The orchestra was hidden from view in order to heighten the romantic and dreamlike quality of the staging; for Wagner's scenes were filled with rustling woods, the sacred fire which surrounds Brünhilde and the mysterious light which suffuses the Holy Grail. The combination of classical and monumental forms with romantic settings and symbols should be familiar by now—it had been in use for over a century before Wagner built his Festival Hall in Bayreuth.

Though this latest national revival was set within a traditional framework, it brought some changes in the nature of both the myth and the festival. For here the people did not participate directly; the dream was presented to them by others. The audience was to assimilate it through the inner eye, while actual participation was confined to the prevailing "festive and sacred mood," as one of Wagner's disciples put it.[19] Through such a mood Wagner wanted to draw audience and actors together into one worshipful whole. The activism of the students at Wartburg, of the gymnasts, and even of the male choirs, was missing. His was in fact a Catholic rite rather than the transference to national worship of the Protestant liturgy. Such festivals presented a spectacle and induced a euphoric mood; but they did not create an activism which might help to induce political change. Change was lifted onto a purely moral plane. That concrete impetus for action which had informed national festivals before unification was now missing.

Wagner made the earlier tradition acceptable to those who wanted to maintain the status quo but who still longed for a national religion. Through his understanding of the nature of national festivals and his artistic skill, he succeeded in creating a pilgrimage center which helped to transmit the national cult into a new, more conservative age.

Cosima Wagner, the composer's wife, worked some twenty-five years after his death to extend the cultic elements of Bayreuth. For her the Germans were superior even to the Greeks, for they put their contemplation of the beautiful into the service of life itself. Small wonder that every manifestation of religious enthusiasm, including Buddhism, filled her with sympathy.[20] For Cosima Wagner, the religious was a predominant element in her love for right-wing patriotic causes. Both Wagner and his wife felt that the Germanic and the Christian were exclusively German properties. Their racism and anti-Semitism is well enough known. The emphasis on salvation meant a need for a devil, easily enough found in the Jews. Cosima's racism existed long before Houston Stewart Chamberlain became Wagner's son-in-law. Then Cosima enthusiastically embraced his ideas of an inevitable race war.

The "Wagner cult," which began upon Wagner's death, was founded by the master himself. The idea of the need for a racial nobility to preserve the Volk was adopted under Chamberlain's influence,[21] and it was the Wagner family which, much later, persuaded Hitler to exempt from military service descendants of Aryans who had made major contributions to German culture. The contention of Francis Galton (1822–1911), that superior fathers also produce superior children, was accepted and endorsed; the idea fitted in so well with the unchanging qualities which the race was supposed to possess.

Wagner had also worshipped the heroes of his operas. Men like Siegfried, Parsifal, or Lohengrin for him symbolized virtue. What was presented on stage became fact in the Bayreuth circle: a leadership cult developed, first of the master himself, then of Cosima, and finally of Winifred Wagner, the wife of Wagner's son. The correspondence was between Houston Stewart Chamberlain and Cosima Wagner illustrates this well, for the son-in-law always addressed Cosima in terms of exaggerated reverence. Here the virile and manly played little part; rather, the hero symbolized a moral posture. Wagner's earlier activism had become a sentimental religiosity which was deepened by Cosima herself. It is typical that one of her criticisms of Chamberlain's *Foundations of the Nineteenth Century* concerned his slighting of the power of Christian prayer.[22]

The influence of Bayreuth and of Wagner's operas on Hitler's mental development does not need additional proof. He was awed by the Wagner circle, which to so many on the right represented the living of a truly German life.[23] But he was also taken with Wagner's construction of his festivals, with the way in which he represented the "Aryan soul" on the stage and through his music. Though Hitler was to value this dramatic form less than festivals in which the people could actively participate, the Wagnerian tradition was kept alive.

Wagner typified the urge toward a new kind of theatre which would break the bonds of the old stage and involve the people in a mystic festival. His influence was not confined to Germany. Inspired by Wagner, the Italian poet Gabriele D'Annunzio dreamed of a new theatre where he envisaged immense, unanimous crowds assembled under the stars. In this setting, the poet's art would bring to "those rough unconscious souls," through the mysterious power of rhythm, an emotion as deep as that felt by the prisoner about to be freed from his chains. This vision is similar to that which Goethe had felt while contemplating the ancient theatre at Verona, but now D'Annunzio transformed it into a mysterious communication of the artist with the people.[24] D'Annunzio's vision of the new theatre was intimately linked to the politico-liturgical forms which he later put into practice during his sixteen months' rule of the City of Fiume in 1919–21. Mussolini, in turn, derived many of his ideas of political rites and festivals from D'Annunzio's rule over that city. Such ideals about a new type of theatre did flow into political liturgy, in Germany as well as in Italy. They were not confined to the inspiration derived from Bayreuth.

New theatrical forms, important for the development of national liturgy, arose simultaneously with the cult of Bayreuth and yet independently of it. The possibility of a "Theatre of the Future," as it was called, had already occupied the minds of some who regarded traditional theatrical forms as outdated and confining. Thus the Swiss writer Gottfried Keller had been inspired by an open-air performance of *Wilhelm Tell* during the "Schiller Year" of 1859 to propose a community theatre, set in nature, which was to combine male choirs with Volk plays. Keller believed that such a theatre could have a meaningful part in the Volkish mythology; he called his proposal the "Stone of Myth" (*"Am Mythenstein"*). At the same time, Eduard Devrient, the actor, held that the Passion Play performed every ten years at the village of Oberammergau provided an excellent example for a national theatre.[25] This was not a play directed or created from above, but a true people's play, which had ties with ancient local traditions. From 1850 onwards, and especially in the 1860's, many people suggested open-air theatres in the simple setting of nature as fitting for a revival of the stage. The plays could involve masses of people in Germanic and heroic performances, with lay players taking over some of the roles.

During the Second German Empire, this "Theatre of the Future" was a subject of general discussion. It would certainly come closer to fulfilling the cultic needs of true patriotism than official festivals had. Ernst Wachler, a pioneer of such new forms, referred in 1903 specifically to the more profound nationalism of the German Youth Movement, which should be captured by this Theatre of the Future. Such men wanted to abolish the conventional stage and transform the audience from spectators into participants. Wachler also mentioned

Gilly, Schinkel, and Semper as having tried to reduce the distance between actors and audience by pushing the stage forward into the auditorium.[26] The cultic interests of these neo-classicists was again prominent. The classical theatre at Orange in Provence served Wachler as another example of what could be done with staging. The orchestra was lower than the stage, thus heightening the visual effect of the performance. Moreover, the colossal dimensions were impressive; the theatre at Orange could hold ten thousand people.[27]

Equally important was the fact that such a theatre did without decoration; the inside of the stage allowed only for simple scenery. Simplicity was of the greatest importance here, as we know it was in the construction of national monuments. The Elizabethan theatre also exercised its influence over these architectural reformers. During the romantic period, Schlegel had already praised such simplicity as being especially attractive to the people. It allowed for rapid changes in scene without having to move heavy scenery; indeed, most of the scenery was permanent, a part of the construction itself.[28] Considerations of this nature were important when large numbers of people were on stage and when plays often took on the appearance of *tableaux vivants*.

Wachler himself rejected lay acting, because a trained speaking voice was essential in such a vast auditorium. The plays performed in his "mountain theatre" in the Harz— opened in 1907 and the first theatre of its kind—were a mixture of Germanic dramas and the classics, including Shakespeare.[29] While Wachler's theatre was built under the open skies, he acknowledged the importance of settings which, as we have seen, were widely debated at the time. He believed that the Kyffhäuser or Niederwald monuments, as well as Wartburg Castle, would be excellent sites for a cultic open-air theatre.[30] This was at precisely the same time that the National Festival Society was choosing the "sacred space" around the *Niederwalddenkmal* as a *mis-en-scène* for its abortive attempt to create a national rite.

Many open-air theatres came into existence at the beginning of the twentieth century, but the "opera in the woods" (*Waldoper*) at Zoppot in East Prussia deserves special mention here because it impressed the Nazis and may directly have encouraged them in their own attempt at a cultic theatre. Founded in 1909, this opera began to specialize in Wagner shortly after the war, terming itself the "Bayreuth of the North." Mass action on the stage was emphasized, and the operas were given before crowds which seem to have averaged nearly ten thousand at a given performance. At first no scenery was used, but eventually the stage became more conventional within the natural setting. For Alfred Rosenberg, the Zoppot "opera in the woods" had transformed the open-air theatre into a cultic rite. And the famous singer Lotte Lehmann exclaimed that, "Within the cathedral of the German forest music is transformed into a divine service."[31] Art, nature, and Volk were the main ingredients in most open-air theatres, but here they were combined with the Wagnerian mystique through the skill of the opera's long-time director, Hermann Merz, who was also one of the earliest National Socialists.

Open-air theatres were not always set within the Germanic landscape, but certainly at times used the backdrop of medieval town squares and a movable stage. On such occasions a part of the local population itself would join in producing the play.[32]

The principles of these theatres were also transferred indoors. The *"Reformbühne"* (reform stage) in Munich (1889) worked within a plain setting, without movable scenery, and with a stage pushed into the audience.[33] The "people's theatre" (*Volksbühne*) in Worms (1890) was very similar; simplicity was not confined to the stage, but heightened the interior effect of the whole building.[34] The thrust of these reforms is clear: the stage must guide men into the reality of dream and illusion; and the dreams should be filled with national content. Furthermore, actors and audiences must form a unity. The action on the stage was meant to be conducive to national worship, at times closely related to the concept Wagner wanted to realize at Bayreuth.[35]

Lay participation was furthered through the development of the "lay play," the word "lay" here being used in the primeval sense of belonging to the Volk, to the community.[36] The roots for this stemmed from the Oberammergau Passion Play, for example, whose actors were members of the village. Such theatrical form was extended by the German Youth Movement, much of it introduced for sheer fun but also because a lay play could deepen the sense of community among youth groups. With the second purpose in mind, they made use of choir plays (or choruses of movement) and speaking choruses (*Sprechchöre*).[37] Both of these had a long history behind them to which we shall return. Their use transformed simple lay plays into cultic dramas no longer performed for sheer pleasure but with a national purpose.

The plays of the Youth Movement before the First World War were moralistic rather than crudely national. They took their themes from the Middle Ages and preferred to act out the analogies and symbolism of traditional morality plays. Their favorite before and even after the First World War was the *Dance of Death*, in which Death dances with king, peasant, knight, and judge. Praise and blame were given to individual figures who left the common dance for a separate dance with Death and then joined in once more. Here hypocrisy, frivolity, vanity, and usury were condemned in a reaffirmation of "honesty and truth" (as opposed to the hypocritical world of the older generation).[38] Such a lay play minimized the gulf between actor and audience while also combining words and movement.

After the First World War, the Youth Movement continued this tradition, and soon a number of associations were formed to further the lay play, for example, the Bühnenvolksbund of 1923–32. But at the same time medieval themes tended to be replaced by those of modern authors. Rudolf Mirbt, prominent in the lay play movement, recommended dramas like Hanns Johst's *Prophets*, which contrasted the Roman and the German man, and whose central figure was Martin Luther. At the same time he wanted to retain the simplicity of setting of the lay plays. There must be no curtain and the lighting should be natural, candles indoors, torches outdoors. Artificial light not only denies the illusion which must be part of the play, he said, but also tends to exaggerate it beyond true emotionality.[39] Clearly, the lay play was becoming increasingly nationalistic and formalized.

Such a theatre of amateurs, in which the actors were said to form a true community, influenced political rites which drew upon their forms and experience. As Wagner had renewed the national impetus in his way, so the Youth Movement also represented an effort at national renewal both before and after the First World War. Wagner and the Youth Movement infused their national consciousness with a religious spirit. The urge toward symbolism and myth was obvious in the Youth Movement's preference for medieval plays like the *Dance of Death*.

The plays which groped for new theatrical forms were conceived as *"völkische Weihespiele"* (Volkish cult plays). But few of these plays actually existed. Much praise was heaped on Hans Herrig, who in the 1880's constructed such plays on the Greek model, using lay actors as, for example, in the Luther Festival at Worms (1884). The action on stage was commented on by actors in front while choirs (sometimes hidden) pointed out the moral. His example proved successful, and one dramatist who composed seven such plays (but without much success) wrote in 1922: "The invisible choirs . . . serve to awaken and call to voices within one's own breast: the listener becomes a participant."[40]

For Herrig, cultic plays and popular theatre were identical. The "people's theatre" had to confront the people with a festival, and like all festivals, must contain both religious and monumental tendencies.[41] Here the cultic play and the public festival comprised one unity of form, a trend inherent in all

"Theatre of the Future." Hanns Johst, who was to become a leading Nazi playwright, summarized in 1928 the aim of the theatrical development we have been discussing: the function of the theatre was to create a community of faith.[42] Wagner had expressed the same ideal. Moreover, the beautiful was never considered a thing in itself, but had its roots in an atmosphere which produced reverence in the service of the national cult. For Johst the cultic theatre performed the same service as mass meetings: it lifted man out of his isolation and integrated him with his Volk.[43] Finally, the ideal of the theatre as a cultic rite was taken over by Rainer Schlösser, for a time in charge of theatres in Goebbels' Ministry of Propaganda and Enlightenment during the Third Reich. "Cultic theatre," he stated, "must be an act of religious worship."[44] Schlösser believed that the lay plays came close to meeting this criterion, though for him they were too aesthetic, performed by an élite rather than directed toward the masses. Yet the Hitler youth had used such lay plays as propaganda weapons during the Nazi struggle for power.[45] Schlösser himself recognized the cultic nature of lay plays, but wanted to broaden their content in order to emphasize German historical events and their relationship to the cosmos. Thus a different kind of drama would be needed, as well as a new kind of auditorium which could hold vast masses of spectators. Schlösser thought that he had found such a theatre in the earlier model of the so-called *Thing*, which the Nazis furthered during the first years of their rule.[46]

The *"Thing"* plays (whose name was taken from the old Germanic meeting places) were performed in an outdoor setting, and the audience was supposed to become involved. They often joined in saying the "Credo," in responses, and the choral singing. The demand made on dramas was high. The use of too much oral expression, even choirs, was said to alienate the audience. Moreover, music by itself was not thought good enough to hold the action together. Plays for the *Thing* must be dramatic, and the artistic laws governing traditional drama had to be observed. But, above all, the *Thing* was a cultic theatre, national self-representation on stage. Schlösser disqualified all earlier related art forms as merely "predecessors" of the *Thing*, whether *tableaux vivantes*, lay plays, processions or festivals, the dance, oratorio, or pantomimes.[47] Yet choric movement plays, which developed out of the male choirs (as we shall see in the next chapter), were also considered essential to the *Thing*. Wilhelm von Schramm, a passionate advocate of this form of theatre, thought that it reached the height of effectiveness when choirs, as cohesive groups, acted out the drama. For in this case the purposes of the *Thing* were fulfilled—men dominated not as individuals but as types, and the emphasis was placed upon the common joys and tribulations of the Volk. The inner conflicts of the individual which had informed the conventional stage became symbolic of the race soul.[48] The new art form would need a new type of artist, one who was not easily forthcoming. It was hoped that every town which possessed a church would also possess a *Thing*, and the first "Thingplatz" was opened near the City of Halle in June 1934 before an audience of between five and six thousand people. Alfred Rosenberg asserted that the *Thing* theatre should be regarded with the same reverence as a church.[49] The cultic nature of such rites is seen in stark relief through this parallel of drama and church.

When Goebbels inaugurated the Heidelberg *Thing*, he proclaimed that "from out of these stones will spring the renewal of Germany."[50] It did not happen. For one thing, the right plays were lacking, in spite of Nazi efforts to encourage their production. Conventional plays had to take their place within the *Thing* setting, in many instances ruining the effect of the new theatre. Finally, after 1937, Goebbels gave up and the *Thing* movement died a rapid death.

Hitler had presumably never supported it. His theatrical tastes were old-fashioned, dominated by his Vienna experiences in the opera house. Certainly his many sketches for new theatrical buildings show no innovation whatsoever; a conventional auditorium is usually joined to an equally traditional stage. Hitler himself made fun of the imitation of ancient Germanic forms and customs. Bayreuth was about the limit of what he could stand in the way of theatrical innovation.[51]

Yet within the conventional theatre the ideas which we have discussed were not totally abandoned. The Wagnerian theories remained alive. Benno von Arendt maintained this tradition during the Third Reich, as official stage designer for the Reich (*Reichsdramaturg*). Stage setting and scenery, he tells us, are not meant for experimentation (a sentiment Hitler must have liked), nor are they self-contained. The task of staging, rather, is to produce the highest possible sense of illusion for the audience, and thus to fulfill their dreams.[52] The magic of theatre must compensate for the reality of life. This was also Wagner's dogma, without his principle of Christian regeneration. The stress upon illusion, upon *not* disturbing the mood of the audience with experimentation, was common to all Nazi cultural endeavor.

The Nazis concentrated on the drama of national festivals rather than upon more formal dramatic representation. *Thing* auditoriums such as that shown in Plate 13 were used to celebrate the summer solstice (the chief such *Thingstätte* still remaining, on a hill above Heidelberg, is now occasionally used for rock concerts). Yet the "Theatre of the Future" did add another dimension to the liturgy of national worship. The earlier Volk dances which were performed at national festivals, the choirs which sang there, and the *tableaux vivants*, were all systematized into a cultic rite through the choreographical influence of the new theatre. If indeed the actual drama of the new theatre proved unsuccessful during the Third Reich, the concept and form for which it stood were assimilated into Nazi liturgical rites.

The masses were supposed to be inspired by such performances, but they could not effectively participate in the drama and tended to become passive spectators. However many people could be accommodated in a *Thing* auditorium, this still could not provide the movement and excitement needed to hold the attention of large masses of people. To create a worshipful mood was one thing, to keep a large mass meeting on the move quite another.

Hitler could not simply adopt the *Thing* or indeed the "Theatre of the Future" as the framework for the formation of masses. Both tended to exclude universal participation, but the right kind of plays were lacking as well. Moreover, Hitler despised the revival of old Germanic customs.

The forms of such theatre could be used, but a different kind of inspiration had to be added, one which sprang out of the development of political mass movements themselves—not all modern mass movements, but those to which Hitler himself along with the Nazi leadership had paid close attention.

## II

In *Mein Kampf*, Hitler pays tribute to Dr. Karl Lueger, lord mayor of Vienna from 1897 to 1910: "If he had lived in Germany, he would have ranked among the great minds of our people."[53] Lueger's Christian Social Party recognized the value of large-scale propaganda; he himself was a virtuoso in influencing the psychological instincts of the broad masses of his adherents,[54] and he lived by constant agitation, among Viennese workers, artists, and bourgeoisie, making his presence felt at every popular festival. The Christian Social Party adopted the symbols of the white carnation and a red cloth with a white cross woven into its fabric. These were displayed whenever the lord mayor appeared. A "Lueger March" was especially composed for the occasion. He saw himself as the general of a popular army. Indeed, a Lueger cult came into existence, spawning medals of the leader, photographs of him, and busts; at meetings he was presented with laurel crowns and silver vessels. He organized his followers not so much through bureaucratic means as by continual rounds of meetings which took on the appearance of popular festivals.[55]

Here were symbols both living and dead, the living symbol provided by Lueger himself.

To be sure, this was largely a leadership cult such as France had known at the time of General Boulanger, or Ferdinand Lasalle had practiced during the inspection of his "popular workers' armies" many years earlier. But Hitler experienced the Lueger cult directly, and undoubtedly learned from it. His criticism in *Mein Kampf* concentrates upon the lack of a single clear goal on the part of the Lueger movement, which he saw as the absence of racism. Lueger's anti-Semitism, Hitler felt, though on the right track, was too ambivalent to exert a decisive influence upon the masses.[56] Moreover, the Christian Socialists could not be truly national, given the conditions of the Austrian Empire. Hitler sensed Lueger's cynicism, but was aware that as a mass movement the Christian Social Party had not yet broken through to the new politics as it might have done. For Hitler this new politics meant providing a clear goal ("The people don't understand handshakes") and, eventually, creating the liturgical form through which this goal must be expressed. Though Lueger obtained the living participation in his movement of a vast cross section of the population, and was surrounded by the symbols of his party, he himself was not yet, as leader, an integral symbol of a national cult. He remained above the crowd. He was not the kind of effective leader of crowds Le Bon had described, one who was an integral part of the masses and a living symbol of the myth shared by leader and led. Le Bon saw such a leader exemplified in General Boulanger, nearly a decade before Lueger came to power in Vienna. However, neither Lasalle, Boulanger, nor Lueger worked from within a well-developed national cult, as Hitler was finally to do so successfully later. Lueger's festivals lacked much of the "sacred" nature of the tradition of national festivals. His party was a committed Catholic movement and his attendance at Mass played a major part in his political strategy. Catholicism stood side by side with the festivals which he attended and created, but this, rather than profane symbolism, played the more prominent role as the "sacred" rite of his Christian Social Party. This was a dominance which German national festivals had never accepted and which Hitler was to reject.

Mass movements such as Lueger's depended upon the actual charisma of the leader; the rites of national worship as the mediating element between leader and people played only a minor role. These movements were apt to vanish when the leader stumbled or died, as their base was too personal and lacked the proper theological foundations. Hitler, observing the rapid collapse of Lueger's movement after his death, seemed to have learned this lesson. During the Third Reich he was careful to designate certain political rites as final. A fully fledged national liturgy was very important since, as Hitler said, this would make it possible for any successor to appear to be a great leader, even if he were a mediocre person.[57] Hitler obviously believed that no one of his own quality could succeed him, and therefore the national liturgy had to help guarantee the continuity of the Third Reich after his death.

For all this, Lueger had pointed to the future. The Christian Social Party possessed a dynamic. It was popular, and had won its victory over the Establishment of the Empire when the emperor was forced by public pressure into naming Lueger as lord mayor of Vienna. The other Austrian mass movement in which Hitler showed an interest was hardly successful. Georg von Schönerer and his Pan-Germans did arouse mass interest through constant agitation, but they remained a splinter group. Hitler liked their nationalism and anti-Semitism, but this movement could not really serve as a cultic example, for Schönerer was much too vain and unstable to allow anything to detract from his person or to succeed in developing a national ritual. Yet Hitler blamed Schönerer's failure on the actions of his followers in Parliament. They were right to enter Parliament, but once inside, Schönerer's followers started to behave like any other political party, thus depriving themselves of effectiveness. The lesson Hitler drew here was more important than that which he had learned from Lueger: "Mass meetings prove the only path to an effective, because immediate, personal swaying of the masses."[58] Hitler took this lesson to heart when it came to organizing his own movement.

Some Nazi leaders looked to mass movements within Germany itself, especially to the peasant movement in Hesse led by Otto Boeckel.[59] Boeckel, between 1885 and 1894, did forge a movement which used a dynamic approach toward its followers. Endless rounds of mass meetings were the order of the day; speakers were sent to the most remote villages; and followers were organized for such actions as establishing the cattle markets from which Jews were excluded. Moreover, the founding of consumers' and producers' cooperatives, which dominated all economic activity, was important. The peasants had a hand in running such cooperatives and thus took part in producing the goods they needed, as well as in selling what they themselves had grown.

Anti-Semitism was central to Boeckel's movement in a region where Jews were the middlemen as cattle dealers and moneylenders. But the "League of Peasants" also put forth a social program directed against finance capitalism and all middlemen. The abolition of interest charges was important to Boeckel in order to circulate more money among the people. Indeed, he wanted to end all speculation with the "fruits of the soil," to nationalize foreign trade, and restrict useless industry. Anti-Semitism was only one aspect of the program; Boeckel also anticipated the ideology of National Socialism. But in an ideological turnabout, he combined such opposition against the Establishment with loyalty to emperor, Reich, and the Protestant faith.[60]

When Boeckel was accused of financial irresponsibility, especially in regard to the cooperatives, he fled Hesse at once. With his absence the movement changed direction. It became, in fact, an agricultural pressure group, and some of his successors eventually became members of the Nazi Party.[61] Boeckel himself died in obscurity, though the Third Reich built a museum in his honor at Marburg, an electoral district he had easily captured at the height of his power, receiving one-quarter of a million votes in 1893.[62] Boeckel's was a mass movement, but he had worked mainly with written propaganda and through speeches. The newspaper he founded was effective; many peasants came in touch with such reading matter for the first time.[63] His meetings and speeches attracted many young people to his banner, and he ran a regular speakers' bureau for "itinerant preachers" who were sent throughout the countryside.[64] Yet all this was not enough to keep a movement going.

The "League of Peasants," like Boulangism or Lueger's Christian Social Party, was tied to one man, and when he defaulted the movement collapsed or changed direction. There was much to be said for Hitler's own idea, that a fully formed liturgy would carry a movement along no matter who the successor to the original leader turned out to be. Otto Hirschl, Boeckel's successor, was interested principally in economic matters, and in 1904 made peace between his Hessian League and the conservative union of farmers (*Bund der Landwirte*).[65] The conservative element in Boeckel's ideology had triumphed over its opposition to the Establishment.

Nevertheless, the Nazis had reason to look back to such examples. Like the Youth Movement, these were movements which at some time had opposed the Establishment and thus provided, it seemed, a more dynamic expression of the people's wishes and longings. Such rightist mass movements were not the only precedents which impressed National Socialists. Indeed, the organization of the masses of the left produced, if anything, an even greater immediate impression. Shortly after his arrival in Vienna Hitler had already watched "breathlessly" a huge mass demonstration by the Austrian Socialists.[66] After the First World War, Communist demonstrations and their techniques of organizing mass meetings were not only discussed but also, to a certain extent, imitated by the Nazi Party.[67] Nazi liturgy was not merely a mirror of Socialist mass organization, it worked largely from within the nationalist tradition; but the contribution of the workers' movement to mass meetings and mass organization was of major importance.

Within parliamentary régimes the creation of a truly national cult proved difficult. Here even the pomp and circumstance and the heroic postures of a leader were absent. Republics depended upon a consensus formed through the clash of interests played out in the parliamentary forum. Not only did this present a dreary spectacle, which often lacked clear direction, but it also prevented the strong leadership that could have supplied this sense of purpose. Moreover, the free play of diverse interest groups prevented the kind of national unity which might enable the state to sponsor cultic ceremonies necessary for the new politics. Committed Republicans believed in reasonable debate which would lead to stability, and thus had little sympathy for the new politics in the first place. Still, from time to time even Republicans saw the need for public rites in order to lend a new dynamic to their own state.

During the Third French Republic, one theologian called for the creation of civic festivals to compensate for weak executive leadership. Like the National Festival Committee in Germany, he wanted to institute gymnastic competitions and to center these on a national symbol.[68] He suggested Joan of Arc for this purpose, which demonstrates that, though a Republican, he was forced to turn to a royalist symbol, evoking memories of France's past, something which Republican symbolism alone was unable to do. After all, the two previous French Republics (Jacobin and 1848) had divided the nation.[69] Moreover, the one national monument built in the Third Republic, Jules Dalou's "Triomphe de la République," with its symbols of peace and plenty, remained stillborn.[70] The German Empire admitted to similar problems, as we have seen, but her national cults and monuments helped to overcome them.

The parliamentary German Republic after 1918 was in a similar position to the Third French Republic. In France the festival most closely connected with the founding of the Third Republic, that on the Fourteenth of July, had not caught on as part of a national cult. Except at its inception, July 14 remained a day of amusement (frivolities, Rousseau would have called them). With some desperation it was suggested that the fête be linked with a celebration of the Battle of Formigny which had helped free France from British domination in 1450[71] (Father Jahn would have approved such a suggestion). The difficulties encountered by the Fourteenth of July celebrations are not so different from those experienced by the Sedanstag in the German Empire.[72]

The Weimar Republic, too, attempted to institute a festival to celebrate its founding as a way of uniting Germany's divisive elements. "Constitution Day" (August 11) was supposed to induce loyalty to the new Republic. But even the official publication, published as a directive for the celebrations, displays an astounding ambivalence. Joy over the constitution is mixed with bitterness for the suffering of the German people. Nothing in the world is perfect, states the pamphlet, all is in flux, even constitutions; and the Weimar constitution leaves room for organic development.[73] It is almost unnecessary to list the self-defeating factors in this government publication of the Weimar Republic. A symbol must be eternal and here it was made relative; a national festival must include an outpouring of feeling, which cannot be mixed with pessimism. A collection of speeches made on Constitution Day further proves the point; they are dry and academic, lacking any *élan* or even emotional Republican appeal. They are lectures, not confessions of faith.

Theodor Heuss recalled that the legal and technical work of constitution making could not have captured the popular imagination. Since Constitution Day fell in August, the schools were on holiday and so was the bureaucracy. Neither schoolboys nor bureaucracy could be forced to participate, therefore the army in garrison towns had to be relied on for support.[74] Certainly this provides additional testimony to the impoverishment of what was originally designed to be the chief Republican festival. We have already mentioned that of the few national monuments built in Republican times only the Tannenberg Memorial, because of its association with victory in an otherwise lost war, captured the imagination of the people.

Parliamentary government certainly did not lend itself to the new political style. Some effort was made to imitate it through the mass organization founded to protect the Republic, the Reichsbanner. This had its flag and its mass meetings, but the lack of a charismatic leadership was sadly felt. No doubt, at times, the *Aufmärsche* of the Reichsbanner with their massed flags were effective, but the speeches, sometimes given by ministers of the Republic, tended to be lengthy and boring. Moreover, at times the mass meetings in which workmen's sports organizations participated ended up in tents where beer was provided and popular music played. The mixture of serious intent and beer-drenched socializing recalls the nineteenth-century festivals of the male choirs or sharpshooting societies, but it was totally unsuitable to twentieth-century mass action. However, when the Reichsbanner was transformed into the Iron Front (*Eiserne Front*) in 1930, a more concerted effort at mass propaganda was undertaken. Short speeches became the rule and the dialogue between speaker and masses was encouraged. Yet, the Social Democratic Party opposed such methods and was suspicious of the new dynamic. As a result, the Iron Front remained a splinter group supported by the workers' sports organization, the trade unions, and the former Reichsbanner.[75] It was a poor cousin compared to what Communists and Nazis could accomplish with their organizations. A government based on discussion and compromise had no real interest in grasping the traditions of a national cult which seemed opposed to rational control of the state.

The importance of rationality in the affairs of government could not easily be shared by those who had participated in earlier national festivals. Moreover, at the precise time when the Weimar Republic was halfheartedly and unsuccessfully attempting to institute a festival of its own, national liturgies were actively being revived and extended by its political enemies. The political right opposed the new politics to the parliamentary government of the Republic.

The Republic failed to come to terms with the dynamic of nationalism and mass politics. After 1918, however, the national liturgy recaptured the *élan* which had informed it before unification. Long before the dynamic was endangered by the Second Empire, important groups within the population had extended and preserved this liturgy. We have already mentioned gymnasts, male choir societies, and sharpshooting associations. Though they held their own festivals as well, they often performed at the sites of national monuments, or as an integral part of public festivals. In this manner they, too, were among those who gradually but steadily molded the ultimate shape of the national liturgy as it would appear in the Third Reich.

# CHAPTER SIX

# Organizations Take a Hand

NATIONAL monuments and public festivals together provided the myths and symbols that comprised a national liturgy appropriate for national self-representation. However, they did not exist in isolation. During the nineteenth and into the twentieth century, certain organizations were crucial in preserving and adding to the new secular religion. At a time when particularism dominated the politics of Germany, men felt the need to join together in order to keep the love of fatherland alive.

A network of private, specialized associations began to spread throughout Germany during the last third of the eighteenth century. These associations were intended to fulfill two functions: first, the "ideal purposes" of public service and reform which arose out of the new self-awareness of the Enlightenment; and, second, the meeting of social, cultural, and professional demands. Such associations tended to be democratic in their cross-class appeal, and patriotic as well. Typical, for example, was the "Association of German Scientists and Doctors" of 1810 which, despite its title, was meant to encourage the "inner cohesion of the scattered sons of the great fatherland."[1] Many purely patriotic associations also came into existence; we mentioned Arndt's "German Association" earlier. But most important were the gymnastic, choir, and sharpshooting associations. These were undoubtedly the largest of all such groups, and maintained their mass impact even after Germany had attained unity.

We have already discussed the influence of Friedrich Ludwig Jahn and the gymnasts as they, in a sense, pioneered the ideals of German national self-representation. "Love of fatherland through gymnastics," as Jahn described his movement, was based on the presupposition that "teaching and life as a whole form one unity."² The unity of body and spirit was a vital precept, expressed through the ideal type which pervaded all of Jahn's political aesthetics. The Greek ideal of beauty was prominent here as well; it idealized a hardened, lithe male body, whose contours were made particularly visible by the uniform Jahn invented for his gymnasts. The character, too, of this ideal gymnast was a combination of individuality and the Volkish spirit of his group.

The gymnasts saw themselves as the catalyst of national regeneration. Jahn connected such ideas immediately with public festivals, which for both him and Arndt were crucial to the functioning of the patriotic spirit. "Almost all Volk festivals have vanished because gymnastics have been neglected or have degenerated," he said. "That which is memorable in history is renewed through the spectacle of masculine power; the honorable deeds of the ancestors are renewed through gymnastic competition." Why was this so? "The chaotic movements of a Volk do not produce a festival, the formless crowd merely creates the atmosphere of a fair."³ Deeds and symbols were essential for the maintenance of continuity in crowds, otherwise festivals would be mere orgies. The creation of gymnastics was part of Jahn's concern for meaningful national rites; for he realized that such rites meant the channeling of a chaotic crowd into a mass disciplined in part through the performance of "sacred acts."

That is why even the earliest places where gymnastic exercises were performed were more than mere meadows; what Jahn termed "sacred work and spirit" needed the proper surroundings. He called the Hasenheide, where the first gymnastic displays took place, a "Tie," a name given to ancient Germanic meeting places.⁴ This included space for both meetings and rest. Song, the martial note of trumpets, short speeches, holy flames, all had their place as part of the gymnastic festivals.[5] But there was no place for frivolity. When Berliners went out to the Hasenheide to watch the somersaults, they were in fact making a pilgrimage to a national festival.

Jahn applied such national purposefulness to an organization which intrinsically could have done without it. The male choirs and sharpshooting societies applied the same principles to their activities and thereby drew them into the realm of national actions when they, too, would have survived on their own.

Jahn linked his gymnasts with the fraternity movement, also founded as another expression of national purpose, another way to draw youth into patriotism and preserve it from "enervating waste of time, lazy dreaming, lusts and animalistic excesses."[6] The Wartburg Castle Festival was in reality a joint enterprise of gymnasts and fraternities whose membership overlapped to some extent. Indeed, a gymnastic festival, well incorporated into the liturgical rhythm of Wartburg, ended the ceremonies. And that was how Jahn wanted it to be.[7]

The gymnastic movement was a success from the start. Around 1818 in Prussia there existed some hundred organizations with about six thousand gymnasts. All of Germany may have contained twelve thousand gymnasts by that date.[8] Increasingly, though in small numbers, workers and artisans joined the movement, which lost its purely student character, both middle- and upper-class, though it was never to do so entirely.[9] In 1820, gymnastic associations were proscribed as hostile to the Prussian régime. But this attack served only to increase their membership. Despite some setbacks, membership rose rapidly after 1848; by 1862, there were 134,507 gymnasts; by 1880, 170,315.[10] For the year 1863 we have a breakdown by social classes, from which it becomes apparent that most members were artisans and merchants. Manual and industrial workers formed 6.68 per cent of the membership, while artists, scholars, and students provided no more than 2 per cent.[11] Student domination had definitely given way to a cross section of the population which, however, was still not as balanced as that of the choral societies. This statistical breakdown may underestimate the participation of the workers, for we know how popular gymnastics was among them by the 1880's and 1890's. However that may be, it is clear that gymnastic enthusiasm had become a mass movement.

Its ideology remained Jahn's. Until the revolution of 1848 he had stressed national awareness as well as individual freedom and voluntarism. The gymnasts were a cohesive group from the beginning: not only did they perform gymnastics together, but they wore the same uniform and used the German "Du" and the greeting "Heil" among themselves. They were a regenerative élite within German society, in which young men joined of their own free will. Anti-authoritarianism was an important principle as long as the struggle had to be waged against the kings and princes of the German reaction. As we have mentioned earlier, most German rulers were opposed to nationalist agitation, and they were backed up by the loose German federation dominated by Austria. But even then the link between individual freedom, cohesiveness, and nationalism among the gymnasts was tenuous. The liturgy of the festivals in general stressed national symbolism to strengthen these tenuous links; yet, at Wartburg, for example, anti-Semitism as well as a trend toward a more authoritarian world view had been present during the burning of books.[12] Nevertheless, for the first generation of gymnasts, the move toward nationalism not only entailed transcending regionalism (as gymnastic festivals from 1841 onwards did), but also a variety of political viewpoints within the organization.

Leading Republicans such as Ludwig Bamberger were members, since Jews were not excluded from participation.[13] Just as in the celebrations of the Battle of Leipzig throughout Germany in 1815, religious diversity was welcomed if it meant transcending confessional differences for the sake of national unity.

The revolution of 1848, however, changed this combination of nationalism, freedom, and a modicum of tolerance. The gymnasts at this point followed the trend of the times and took part in the reaction against the revolution. In 1848, Jahn repudiated tolerance, for the Jews were said to favor a democracy not rooted in the Volk.[14] The idea of the Volk now moved to the fore. The "German Gymnastic League" (*Deutscher Turnerbund*), founded in 1848, proclaimed the "unity and cohesiveness of the Volk."[15] Freedom was no longer perceived as a value on its own, but was produced only through such unity. Members who had been revolutionaries were repudiated.

Gymnasts now thought of themselves as standing above all political parties. But this attitude did not necessarily support the status quo, for it was closely related to the progress of nationalism. Through 1870 nationalism was kept alive in a multitude of mostly local festivals. But even when the Second Reich was founded, many gymnasts thought that true unity had not yet been attained. At times they refused to join the adulation of chancellor and emperor. Moreover, it seems that individual freedom was still a goal as we learn that in the Wilhelminian Reich, unity and freedom had not kept pace with each other.[16] Unification in the Second Reich seemed to them sterile, as did its festivals imposed from above.

The festivals of the gymnasts continued to integrate physical exercise with national symbolism and ritual. The gymnastics meadow (Turnwiese) still existed, but the "Tie" now also contained a festival hall. Such halls, built for the occasion, were replete with a stage on which mass choirs performed, and galleries which held the flags of the individual groups. This was a cult hall, not yet fully developed in its idea, but already providing specific space for national gymnastic celebrations. Such halls also became commonplace at the national festivals of male choirs and sharpshooting societies. They were often built by leading architects and dominated the *mis-en-scène*. For example, the hall built for the seventh national gymnastic festival in Munich (1889) was surrounded by four fortress-like towers crowned by obelisks.[17] The classical forms were united with Egyptian splendor and monumentality, a tradition which, as we have seen, was also exemplified in many monuments throughout the century.

For variation, a flag tower could at times dominate the exercises. Paul Bonatz built such a tower for the national gymnastic festival of 1933; it contained eleven stories covered with a hundred flags from every German province.[18] But this was rare compared to the more versatile hall in which choirs could sing and patriotic plays be performed.

The development of gymnastic societies, from the first exercises which had taken place on a meadow outside Berlin, involved no new inventions; it merely extended what had already existed. Nevertheless, these festivals were central for Jahn and his successors. That gymnastic competition furthered the development of the ideal German type but, more important, had become a part of national liturgy, was clearly understood by the end of the nineteenth century.

At that time national monuments rivaled each other in winning a space on which gymnastic festivals could be held.[19] Gymnasts themselves saw the shade of the monument as a particularly apt setting for their rites. It is no coincidence that Albert Speer has compared the "sacred space" underneath the *Niederwalddenkmal* to the "Zeppelinwiese," that stadium where many Nazi Nuremberg rallies took place.[20] Both provided a suitable setting for the acting out of a national liturgy through movement and rhythm. Certainly for gymnasts the sport itself determined the nature of the act; but for many patriots in the Second Reich, gymnastics not only led to hardened bodies and therefore good soldiers, but was always conceived as a national festival.

This brand of nationalism considered itself separate from

the official military pomp and circumstance of Wilhelminian festivals. Gymnasts deepened their patriotism by rambling through the German countryside. Later they made contact with the German Youth Movement, founded in 1901, for which rambling constituted a major activity. This movement, in turn, made Jahn one of its heroes.[21] Gymnasts shared with members of the Youth Movement the ideal of the nation as an expression of inward spirit rather than of mere outward power, of the embodiment of the "beautiful" in nature and the human body. Rambling was one rite shared by the two movements, linking the eternal German landscape to the eternal spirit of the nation. The Youth Movement rites centered on songs, dances, and plays. The dance, rather than gymnastics, was important to the youth, for sheer power, they felt, should be sublimated into rhythmic, aesthetic, "poetic" expression.[22] Here the spiritual predominated whereas for Jahn, true significance lay in the power of the body, particularly since he did have actual military prowess in mind. The European reaction which grew out of the Congress of Vienna had to be fought actively, not solely by deepening patriotic spirit.

The gymnasts, like the Youth Movement, stressed the importance of small groups and, in light of this, opposed all mass sports. When, after 1883, large sports associations such as rowing, swimming, or football clubs were founded, the gymnasts stood apart.[23] Some of the symbols, too, were common to both, such as flags, holy fires, and folk dancing. Both also saw in common song the symbolic expression of national emotion. But then, both movements were indeed made up of youth and therefore shared a common vision of themselves.

One leader of the gymnasts, Edmund Neuendorf, was also the national leader of a large Youth Movement organization (*Wandervogel*), and there may have been many other personal links. But these were never as close as the gymnasts' earlier links with the fraternity movement, for the gymnasts were always careful to maintain the integrity of their own organization. Moreover, among the gymnasts adults played a leading role, quite different from the Youth Movement slogan of "Youth among itself."[24] Neuendorf, typically enough, was openly Volkish, while at the same time stating that nationalism as an overt plank in a party platform was highly suspicious. Nationalism, he held, was an integral part of the German spirit, and its open advocacy in the Second Reich could lead only to shallowness of feeling. While he wrote that "He who cannot hate can never love truly," he prevented the exclusion of Jews from his Youth Movement association.[25] He combined a mystical cult of the soil with Jahn's ideals of beauty and virtue. Neuendorf's outlook is worth stating, for it is typical of the cross currents within the gymnastic movement.

While the German gymnastic organization fought the Austrian gymnasts for excluding Jews, all "internationalism" was nonetheless condemned.[26] As a result, from 1892 onward separate workers' gymnastic organizations sprang up in opposition to the traditional gymnasts. But, as we shall see, these still shared with the parent organization the impetus toward cult and ritual which seemed to be built into German gymnastics, whether directed toward national regeneration or social justice. After 1918, the original gymnasts of the Deutsche Turnerbund accentuated the militarism in their tradition by their anti-Republican activities, by collecting signatures against the peace of Versailles, and by supporting the German Navy League and the Association of Germans Abroad.[27]

Naturally enough, this hostility to the Republic led to an increased emphasis on cult. They opposed their own festivals to those of the Weimar Republic such as Constitution Day. Hermann the German was celebrated in the Teutoburger Forest and a bust of Jahn was placed in the *Walhalla* accompanied by much ceremonial.[28] The gymnastic festivals were now equipped with a special hour of worship. This had always been a part of the festivals, of course, but now it was extended to special evening meetings, "spiritual gymnastics," as they were called. Here everyone participated, reciting old German sagas or fairy tales and retelling events from the German past.

At the same time, folk music and folk dancing were practiced with increased intensity.[29] Such evenings were supposed to form a contrast with the beer-infused gatherings that had often accompanied the meeting of gymnasts in the past. They were to win back a "truly honest Germanic humanity."[30] In 1927 Neuendorf proclaimed: "According to Jahn, gymnastics was part of a world view, and it must become this once more."[31] Politically, Jahn's world view was now tied to the conservative German National Party and not to the National Socialists. This was also true for the sharpshooters. But it was the Volkish right wing of the German National Party which attracted the gymnasts. Yet the Nazis managed to make some inroads into the organization; certainly by 1930 many of the local leaders had joined that party. Neuendorf himself joined in 1932.[32]

Hitler fully realized the importance of the gymnasts as a force in German life. He attended the gymnastic festival at Stuttgart on July 30, 1933, together with von Papen and Goebbels, and flattered gymnasts by calling them the best example of the life forces of the Volk. Though in 1933 Neuendorf, by now a Nazi, was the "leader" of gymnasts, all was not going well for them. Like so many other organizations, they wanted to maintain their own identity even in the Third Reich. But this naturally proved impossible, and when in 1933 H. von Tschammer und Osten became the Reichssport leader he soon seized power among the gymnasts as well.[33] The Deutsche Turnerbund was first subjected to Nazi control and, after a respectable interval of time, dissolved altogether in 1938. Such was the fate of all these organizations, whether gymnasts, male choirs, or sharpshooters, who had done so much to form the national liturgy and to preserve it for more than a century.

Gymnastics had been one of the crucibles for the formation of German national consciousness. At the borders of the Reich, in Austria and the Sudetenland, the gymnastic spirit was aggressively nationalist. Austrian gymnasts introduced an

Aryan paragraph into their membership rules by 1880 and the Austrian Gymnastic League was close to the Pan-Germanism of Georg von Schönerer. After the war, Konrad Henlein made the German Gymnastic League in the Sudetenland the gathering place for the Volkish movement. He restructured this organization according to the leadership principle and sought to advocate "manliness and a heroic attitude toward life."[34] But gymnastics also traveled beyond Germany and the Germans. The Czech equivalent to Henlein's Sudeten gymnasts, the Sokol movement, adapted the theory and practices of the German gymnasts to its own national ends, including their festivals and symbols. Jews, too, had formed their own societies by the turn of the century, which became forums for the discussion of Zionism, itself a nationalism seeking spiritual origins. Jewish gymnasts in fact cited Arndt's words that "The spirit rises from the flame," and repeated that Jews long "for freedom and fatherland."[35] But that fatherland was the Jewish Volk. Nevertheless, old heroes—Geibel, Uhland, Scheffel, the literary representatives of German consciousness —were revived, together with Yiddish songs.[36]

Thus, gymnastics performed an equally important function all over Central Europe; they preserved and extended the awareness that national consciousness is best expressed through liturgy and symbols, in festivals and their surroundings. But the gymnastics organizations were not the only ones important for the development of the new politics. Other organizations, too, included a cross section of the population, performed certain rituals, and displayed certain symbols as expression of their patriotism; of these the male choirs and the sharpshooting societies were the most significant.

## II

Male choirs came to play an important role within national ceremonies. From the second half of the nineteenth century, no inauguration of a national monument or festival could do without them. They were an integral part of the national liturgy and made their own contribution to its development. The revival of the folk song in the early eighteenth century had laid the foundations for this development, but its immediate origins were the bourgeois quest for culture in the age of the Enlightenment, and the decline of church music at the beginning of the eighteenth century. Though bourgeois church choirs went out of fashion at this time, smaller Pietistic communities still emphasized the song as central to their religious worship. The "brotherhood community" (*Brüdergemeinde*) cultivated simple song; their example would, at the beginning of the nineteenth century, serve to re-emphasize singing in the Protestant service.[37] Nevertheless, specifically church songs and church music were pushed back into the purely religious sphere, though they continued to influence the activities of the secular choirs and were sung at many national festivals during the first part of the nineteenth century.

By the time the new century began, the cultured person ideally not only acquired an appreciation of the ancients, but also musical tastes. To cultivate one's own voice and to sing together within the circle of one's friends had become fashionable. Domestic festivities now included the performance of music, and girls sang as they sat around the tea table in the afternoon.[38]

Musical academies were called for which would teach and refine the art of singing. The most famous of these, the Singakademie, was founded in Berlin in 1790; its influence radiated throughout Germany to reach Russia and France as well.[39] In 1809, Karl Friedrich Zelter founded his Berlin singing circle (*Liedertafel*) where men met outside the home in order to sing together. This was the first German choir organization not related to any church. The time of its founding was also the age of Napoleonic conquest, and from the beginning the singing circle struck a strong patriotic note. But the circle itself was exclusive: to belong to it gave social prestige as well. Indeed, until 1909 it never exceeded a mere 190 members.[40] This was because Zelter wanted to found a settled bourgeois and national society in which singing was an extension of bourgeois domesticity. "The formalities and conditions of bourgeois life provide our support," as the Mannheim singing circle around 1810 put it.[41]

These narrow horizons were broadened by Hans Georg Nägli (1773–1836) who, quite independently of Zelter, founded singing circles in Switzerland in the 1800's. He wanted to create a large bourgeois musical movement and therefore drew a sharper line between private and public singing. Music, he said, must leave its domestic confines to become a general instrument of culture and education. Nägli fought against the splintering of musical life into small and exclusive circles because it prevented the "rise of a private into a public activity." His own wider circle attempted to aid in the creation of a "decent, refreshing, patriotic publicity."[42] The future function reserved for such choirs stood out more clearly in Nägli's formulations than in Zelter's more exclusive patriotic aims.

The bourgeois exclusiveness for which these forerunners of the male choir movement originally stood was to haunt their future development. Throughout their history they faced the problem of breaking out of their narrow confines and becoming truly national organizations. They were to feel the pressure to drop their exclusiveness and to draw all the people within their orbit, to use their art in order to play a meaningful part in the national liturgy. Through song, musical life was to fuse with social life, and the patriotic impulse was present from the very beginning. Those who sang together, in a sense, also lived together, and this under the impetus of the struggle for national liberation.

The most popular songs of the period were certainly not exclusive to singing circles. Songs of national liberation and freedom were taken up by everybody, not just by one social sector of the population. They were meant to be sung within the Germanic landscape: in the woods, or even in the cafés of Berlin's parks. Such songs were appeals to national unity and demanded that their message be spread to all who could help attain it.

A striking example of the patriotic power of song is provided by "The Watch on the Rhine" (*Die Wacht am Rhein*). This song, based on a poem by an obscure government official, was written in 1840 when it seemed as if France was about to extend its frontier to the Rhine. Instantaneously, "The Watch on the Rhine" became one of the most popular songs in the disunited nation, not only in the Rhineland but throughout Germany, sung—contemporaries tell us—in living rooms and in the streets. The song became a symbol through which the masses could share their enthusiasm for the fatherland.[43] The male choir societies could not remain deaf to such a phenomenon, the more so as the songs from the wars of liberation (many composed by Arndt) had already attained lasting popularity.

Though their members were for the most part bourgeois, they comprised from the outset a variety of social classes. Some male choirs were founded during the first half of the nineteenth century. The first of these was probably the "Singgesellschaft" in Meigen in 1801 which, at first, stuck close to the Protestant hymn book. By the 1840's they were singing at neighborhood fairs.[44] But such beginnings were sporadic at best. The revolution of 1848 meant an interruption of male choir activities, so that it was during the 1850's and 1860's that they finally reappeared as strong and lasting associations.[45] National unity had been frustrated; now the same dynamic that had inspired the common struggle against Napoleon was translated into an urge to bring divided Germans closer together. What was better suited for this purpose than folk songs or songs of national freedom? Choirs participated in national festivals, but even in the absence of such rites their weekly or monthly meetings reinforced the patriotic spirit.

Certain local societies began to develop a ritual. At first they had given public concerts or simply provided social evenings for their members, but soon they acquired a flag, which

was consecrated amidst the participation of the whole population. Even in small towns like Ettenheim (with a population
of about 19,000) they celebrated festivals and singing competitions which also attracted neighboring communities. At
Ettenheim, for example, such a festival in 1896 started with
the church service and included a procession, concerts, singing competitions, and dancing. At times the gymnasts and
veterans' associations joined in; at Ettenheim the male choirs
were closely associated with and strengthened by the fire
brigade.[46] Choirs seem to have taken every opportunity to
perform, at fairs, sharpshooting festivals, carnivals, and in
taverns.[47] The patriotic and national impetus, especially
strong in those choirs founded after 1848, was always to the
fore.[48]

It was only a matter of time until the many individual choir
societies formed themselves into one organization, leaving the
exclusive singing circles out in the cold. The appeal for the
founding of the "German Choral Association" (*Deutsche
Sängerbund*) in 1862 stressed the necessity of unity among the
"German tribes" and collaboration in supporting German
strength and power.[49] The association sponsored yearly festivals and choral competitions which soon took on the nature of
national festivals. Choirs marched through the towns with
flags and emblems (the German oak was present as well),
listened to patriotic speeches and poems in the festival hall,
and sang their songs. Often the sharpshooting societies and
gymnasts joined in the celebration of these "Sängerfeste," and
they quickly took on the appearance of mass demonstrations.

But when German unity had become a reality in 1871, the
choir societies faced the same problems as the festivals and
national monuments. The bourgeois traditions of exclusiveness
threatened to reassert themselves. This did not mean that after
1871 the public was ignored; it was simply lowered to the
status of audience. Male choirs had always given concerts for
the public, but this form of entertainment moved again to the
forefront. Choral societies began to admit members who no

longer participated in their musical activities. As a result, the purely social aspect of their meetings assumed ever greater importance. At the same time, those who performed no longer sang with one voice but practiced ever more complicated musical harmonies.[50] These would impress an audience at concerts, but would mean that the people could not participate. The official Journal of the Sängerbund tried unsuccessfully to stem this tide. Private concert performances, which did not carry the song to the Volk, were condemned.[51] The function of the choir as part of the national cult was seriously endangered.

Moreover, the social divisions of the Second German Empire came to play an important role. Even in the 1850's, Jews had founded their own choral societies, for the time when they had been urged to join in the singing of songs to celebrate the Battle of Leipzig was long past.[52] But most choral societies did contain a cross section of the population despite the social fissures which were making their inroads upon the Second Reich. Nevertheless, we read constant complaints that each profession was forming its own separate choir, with teachers and bakers in the vanguard.[53] And the upper classes were no longer active in choral societies. Craftsmen, small merchants, and workers supplied most of the members.[54] This combination remained intact even after Social Democratic workers began to form their own separate choirs and founded the "Workers' Choral Association" in 1894. But even so, many workers remained loyal to the original Deutsche Sängerbund. Though its social base narrowed, it never became an exclusive petit bourgeois organization. Membership statistics are hard to come by, but we do know that in 1895 some 82,000 singers were a part of the organization.[55]

At the same time that choral societies faced these problems, the emphasis upon nationalism was increasing. Devotion to the nation was what bound the diverse choral societies together through the memory of the roles they had played in the struggle for unification. Now, during the Second Empire, this patriotism was too often confined to songs sung at "comfortable" evenings supplemented by beer, dance, and light entertainment. But the societies in fact never quite withdrew into their own inner circle; they constantly took part in national events of all kinds, the celebration of Bismarck's sixtieth birthday in 1875, for example, and in the inauguration of most national monuments. At times they joined with the gymnasts and sharpshooting societies in order to plan a festival, as for example on the occasion of the conquest of Metz (1870) or the Sedanstag (1877).[56] Hermann the Cheruskan (Arminius) was a favorite figure with the choirs. A choral work celebrating the anniversary of the Battle of the Teutoburger Forest enjoyed great popularity.[57]

The Deutsche Sängerbund, through its newspaper, tried to further new and old patriotic songs; its pages were filled with advertisements for such compositions. Emperor William II was conscious of their continued and "respectable" patriotism and himself attempted works for the male choir. Unsuccessfully, however, for even the *Sängerzeitung* criticized his products as "not always very fortunate," though it took some pride in the fact that the emperor was also a singer.[58] Songs of freedom were rare now, being replaced by songs of praise acceptable to the Establishment. But the "Sängerfeste" did continue the national rite as it had been practiced before unification.

The Austrian choral societies were also a part of the Deutsche Sängerbund; by 1912, out of a total membership of 160,000, some 30,000 singers were Austrian.[59] These men had not attained national unity by joining the Reich: for them the struggle for national liberation was still a reality. Austrian choral societies attempted to introduce a new *élan* into the Bund. Here the song was still considered a revolutionary weapon; they wrote to their German brothers about the "wave of aggressiveness by the Slavs," and exhorted them to show more love for the Volk.[60] Anti-Semitism played a definite role in Austrian choirs, which excluded Jews, while in

Germany this question was studiously avoided. The Austrians, who made themselves heard often enough, reminded German choirs not to forget their mission to embrace all the Volk regardless of national boundaries.[61]

National concerns continued to inform the German choir societies later, during the divided Weimar Republic. Then they attempted to further the unity of all Germans in conformity with their old tradition. Thus the societies not only kept the Austrian choirs within their organization, but included all Germans living abroad. Indeed, choirs visited German communities outside the boundaries in order to strengthen their sense of Volk.[62] The Sängerbund now exalted the fact that it stood above the political parties and desired a Germany as free from divisiveness as it was itself. The choirs, they said, served the entire fatherland.[63]

The troubled Weimar Republic seems to have given a new impetus to the choirs and their festivals. Forty thousand men and women appeared at one of these festivals in 1924 and the Sängerbund itself counted 500,000 members by 1925.[64] But pride in standing above political parties did not necessarily mean disloyalty to the Republic. Choirs took part in "Constitution Day" as they had taken part in similar celebrations under the Empire.[65] Perhaps the tradition of support for the Establishment was strong enough to overcome any overt anti-Republicanism. In fact, the Republic granted subventions to the Sängerbund.[66] It should also be noted that, unlike sharp-shooters and gymnasts, the male choirs had always participated in all kinds of local, political, and nonpolitical festivals—their love of singing pushed political loyalties into the background. This fact must also be taken into consideration when examining their attitude toward the Republic, in which their ability to adjust to the new régime differed so markedly from that of the other groups.

However, the choral societies continued to celebrate such patriotic festivals as the anniversary of the inauguration of the *Hermannsdenkmal* and praised Bandel as a worthy successor to Hermann himself. Germans, so the Deutsche Sängerbund tells us, love to look up to a heroic figure.[67] National monuments must remind us of the consciousness of national unity, especially in times when there is no national leader. These sentiments hardly constituted positive support for the Republic, even when it was passing through its most quiet and settled years. The Sängerbund continued its Wilhelminian traditions into the Weimar Republic without, however, taking an openly hostile position toward the new régime and even, at times, collaborating with it. The gymnasts and the sharpshooting societies, so closely related to the choirs through common festivals and common patriotism, did not compromise with the German Republic in this manner.

Directly after the First World War, choral music broadened out into a new art form. Erich Streubel founded the "choral movement play" (*chorisches Bewegungsspiel*) in which, through a combination of music and movement, choruses could be used to present a dramatic effect. The structured movement of an entire choir would lend a whole new dimension to its participation in the national cult. "Rhythmic choirs" could be used to "fuse music and visual representation."[68] However, within this genre music tended to be pushed into the background. Streubel himself was influenced by the so-called rhythmic plays (*Bewegungsspiele*) which, starting in 1919, emphasized group movement to symbolize the plot. The modern dance played its role here, for it stressed rhythmic movement and a consequent group unity. These choirs sang and moved, but they also engaged in dialogue with a single speaker—a kind of interchange between priest and congregation. Streubel described one play as the following sequence: choirs in rhythmic movement take up chants and pass them on; heralds speak verses; and loudspeakers announce songs in which the audience is asked to join. Over a decade later the Nazi *Thing* theatre was to take up the "choral movement play" as singularly effective in symbolizing the community of race and Volk.[69]

Choir performances had now become plays, or rather full-fledged liturgical rites. Music at times tended to vanish completely and the so-called speaking choirs took over. The words of the liturgy stood out more clearly, and pithy phrases by the choir could be substituted for longer songs. The workers' movement pioneered here, as we shall see later. Their mass festivals after the First World War provided a living example of such a liturgy. The Nazis at first used the speaking choruses lavishly and not without giving credit to the Communists for having developed this form.[70] But the style soon proved too artificial, and plays which could be used for this purpose proved hard to get. Moreover, Hitler himself with his passion for opera seems to have preferred music drama to such "word dramas."[71] Nevertheless, the spoken part of the chorus remained part of the doxology of Nazi mass meetings, while the choral play as such receded into the background.

Choirs continued to function in a more traditional way, even when they engaged in a dialogue with either a speaker or the masses themselves. They were as essential to the rite of national worship as they had always been. The combination of music and liturgical text had throughout been a basic element of sacred ceremonies. The Nazis even used organs to underline the worshipful mood, and Hitler himself commanded the installation of a giant organ in the Nuremberg Hall of Congresses.[72] Quite apart from the common singing at most Nazi meetings, the choir's role in national festivals reached its climax during the Third Reich.

When the Nazis came to power, the Sängerbund hoped that it would be able to continue its usual function of taking a part in national festivals as an independent organization. It did, at first, participate in newly revived festivals like Harvest Day or the Festival of Work.[73] The Sängerbund attempted to adjust to the new régime by emphasizing folk songs and sponsoring *Volkslieder* competitions. But the tradition of concerts and exclusiveness was still strong, despite the efforts of the leadership to combat such practices. The Nazis had criticized the

fashionable four-part harmony as preventing popular participation in choir song. The call went out for "open singing," in
which everybody could join.[74] The Sängerfest of 1933 was
called a "sacred hour for all Germans," standing above party,
but the Nazis were suspicious of this claim despite its rhe-
toric.[75] Overtly they courted this important organization;
Wilhelm Frick as Minister of the Interior, and Rudolf Hess as
well, assured the Sängerbund that Nazi choral organizations
would not compete with it. Hitler received the leaders of the
Bund in 1933. The hated rival, the workers' choral society was
liquidated.[76]

In spite of such gestures, however, some choir leaders
looked back regretfully to the Weimar Republic, where they
had gained the support of the state which was now being
slowly withdrawn. Nazi choir organizations did continue to
exist and to dominate Nazi liturgy. Indeed, the more Nazi
choruses were used, the more surely the Deutsche Sängerbund
became integrated with Nazi organizations. Alfred Rosenberg
took over the organization in 1934 when Hitler put him in
charge of the ideological supervision of the Nazi Party.[77]
Rosenberg took a special interest in the form and content of
public festivals and published a journal devoted to that subject. In his hands the Sängerbund was permitted to die a slow
death. At the very hour when the traditional function of the
male choir was heightened in a veritable orgy of song, the
organization dissolved into a part of the Nazi liturgy.

The Nazis saw to it that the male choirs shed their "bourgeois" past. They had to give up concerts, as well as their own
festivals (though this did not happen until 1939); they had to
serve the community in cultic rites; and finally, they were
forced to abolish choral competitions and the awarding of
prizes.[78] This was an attempt to guide the male choir back to
its historical origins before it had fused social togetherness and
national purpose. Small wonder that the Nazis stressed the
participation of choirs in rites like the "morning festival"
which took the place of Christian observance. But they also

envisaged choirs as supporting the discipline necessary for the "fighting actions" of the Volk community.

The choirs had to abandon much of their classical repertoire: the *Volkslied* took the place of Germany's great composers.[79] The Nazis themselves were troubled by certain traditional choral music. For example, the "Dutch Prayer of Thanksgiving" had to be changed, though this chorale had been traditional ever since the choirs were founded, sung at almost every national ceremony. They objected to the phrase "God the just," and to its ending, "God give us freedom." The Nazis discovered that this version of the prayer had been adapted by a Jew from earlier sixteenth-century editions, and to them it followed that the emphasis on justice was typically Jewish; that it divided the Volk into good and bad according to preconceived notions. "God give us freedom" was derided as patriotic cant, even though it had been considered especially relevant in national rites before unification.[80] Now men stood in prayer before "God the Father" and ended by asking for God's support against all enemies.[81] But nothing is as difficult to change as liturgical form once it has established itself. "God the just" lived on even in an official Nazi book of folk songs, while the appeal to freedom was universally dropped.[82] The Nazis, who usually grasped the meaning of festivals and liturgy, failed this once, even at their own celebrations.

But such failure was a rarity, as the success of Nazi festivals and their mass organization can testify. The male choir was effectively used in its old and new forms. Other traditional organizations with a national purpose were equally successfully integrated into their celebrations. The relationship between gymnasts and the Sängerbund was very close. Toward the end of 1920, the official newspaper of the choir organization was managed by the *Turnerzeitung* (*Gymnastic Journal*).[83] The connections with sharpshooting societies were equally intimate.[84] All three organizations liked to recall Bismarck's statement that sharpshooting societies, gymnasts, and male choirs had made an essential contribution to German unity. And they took great pride in the verse: *"Turner, Sänger and Schützen sind des Staats beste Stützen"* (Gymnasts, Singers and Sharpshooters provide the best support for the State).[85]

## III

The sharpshooting societies (*Schützengesellschaften*) were founded after 1800. Those in regions like the Rhineland were encouraged by the French occupation, which wanted to create a citizens' militia.[86] Elsewhere they practiced their shooting on behalf of German liberation from the French and eventually the Rhineland societies joined the national effort. Such societies were formed by small local groups; often, many different sharpshooting associations existed within a single town or village. Munich, for example, possessed one such society in 1812, 16 in 1870, and 206 by 1914. After the First World War their number declined again and Munich had some sixty-five sharpshooting societies after the Nazis seized power.[87] Like the male choirs, the sharpshooting societies spread all over Germany and perhaps became even more popular in the villages and countryside.

They did more than practice their shooting and sponsor competitions. Social considerations were important, and not just the drinking of beer or wine and a comfortable get-together. Some societies also created pension funds for their members. They were "settled" organizations from the beginning and usually established a link with some princely dynasty, whereby the prince would become their honorary president.[88]

Those shooting societies which existed in Catholic regions were prone to stress the religious element, perhaps in memory of the medieval guilds with which they sometimes identified themselves. Their festivals were often combined with religious processions, and indeed among some of them church membership was compulsory.[89] The combination of religious feeling and national consciousness confronts us here once again, but this time it was linked more closely than mere clerical participation, or the adaptation of Christian liturgy to political purposes. The statutes of the Bonn guild of sharpshooters can serve as an example. In 1840 it enjoined participation in the festivals of the fatherland, and at the same time called upon shooters to contribute to the glorification of religion and especially of church festivals. The statutes then called upon the members to practice shooting in order to further social communion and to amuse the Volk. Finally, they emphasized the upholding of the bourgeois order.[90]

This mixture of patriotism, middle-class pride, social togetherness, and gaiety is reflected in the statutes of other societies as well. Within Protestant regions, however, the religious element was often dropped. Were these then overtly bourgeois organizations? They contained a large proportion of rural members who were not middle class but who may have aped middle-class manners and morals. But from the 1850's on, a certain number of workers joined the sharpshooting societies.[91] The societies were bourgeois in their emphasis upon the hierarchical political order, socializing, and gaiety which they advocated, but not necessarily in their social composition. Yet their literature links the bourgeois with the Volk. In 1865, for example, one of their publications called for the awakening of the "Bürger" (middle-class citizens) from their slumber, so that they might carry arms for the defense of the fatherland—but added in the same breath that an army must spring from all of the Volk.[92] The Schützen seem to have equated the Volk and the middle classes.

Sharpshooting societies also formed a national organization of their own in 1862, almost simultaneously with the call for the founding of a German Sängerbund. While national sharpshooting festivals were to take place every two years, regional festivals continued to exist and flourish in great numbers as well (see Frontispiece and Plate 14). Friedrich Theodor Vischer, who attended the festival for the founding of the national organization at Frankfurt, has left us a graphic description: it fell into two parts—the shooting competitions and the festival proper. A festival hall stood next to the building where there was noisy shooting. Within the hall a banquet took place which was always a part of all these celebrations (choral societies included). Patriotic speeches were made, but a festival play entitled *Germania* was also presented. Finally, the whole assembly joined in singing led by Tyrolean sharpshooters.[93]

The religious element was missing from this and subsequent festivals. No doubt church attendance continued to be important in Catholic regions, but where Protestants and Catholics mixed, the proceedings became secular.

Were such festivals cultic rites? Vischer maintained that they were indeed political acts, not merely political meetings.[94] The mood of the people and their active participation in events overshadowed the speechmaking. Vischer's description of the festival clearly shows that a speaker's effectiveness was produced by his presence rather than by what he had to say. In fact, he could barely be heard above the noise in the festival hall, and the patriotic content of his speech must have been so familiar anyway that there was no need for anyone to actually listen.

The speaker, like the festival play or the common singing, was a symbol. The speakers of antiquity and of the earlier days of agitation for German unity had impressed the audience by the content of their speeches. But now a speech had to be effective even before it was given; its situation within the whole *mis-en-scène* was what guaranteed its success and the success of the whole festival.[95] This also held true for the individual singing and gymnastic festivals. By the 1860's at the very latest, speaking at these occasions had largely lost its traditional communicative function and became part of the liturgical rhythm of the occasion.

The "Schützenfeste," like those of the singers and gymnasts, were also in the tradition of true national festivals. Their liturgy, however, was not yet clearly worked out. The sharp-shooters themselves called their festivals "national." A German Volksfest, so we are told, should not merely mean enjoyment, but must have an ideological center. That center, at the second sharpshooting festival in Bremen in 1865, was a huge Germania. At an earlier festival, this symbol had been set on top of the temple in which the prizes were kept.[96] Now the statue was placed directly opposite the entrance gate, close to the hall which contained the flags. Thus the symbol of national unity would be surrounded by flags from all the diverse German lands representing the local sharpshooting associations.

The setting for these festivals became ever more formalized. The whole territory on which the festival took place was made into a single unit of space, sometimes through the construction of a main portal in the form of a medieval castle gate. The festival hall, the *Gabentempel* (where the prizes were kept), the hall of flags—all of these were specially designed by famous architects.[97]

Yet for all this, the festival still did not represent total unity; the frivolity and enjoyment, officially deprecated, were nevertheless present. Shooting competitions interrupted the ceremonies, and personal amusement was still an important reason for attendance. Beer flowed freely and the site was often surrounded by stalls offering food, drink, and games. Such festivals were both national rites and fairs. Nor were banquets the most promising setting for the development of a national liturgy (Jahn had already condemned full stomachs as unpatriotic), though they had often provided the framework for patriotic meetings not only in Germany but also in France.

The sharpshooting societies continued their activities under the Second German Empire without much change, supporting and being supported by the Establishment. Their attitude to the Weimar Republic differed from that of the Sängerbund; it was hostile from the start. In 1922, for example, their official newspaper praised the camaraderie among the sharpshooters which demonstrated that the new spirit of the times had made no inroads into their ranks. Indeed, the sharpshooters now instituted "patriotic evenings," similar to those which the gymnasts created at the same time. But unlike the gymnasts, these evenings provided outside entertainment: male choirs, an orchestra, and dancing. Middle-class *Gemütlichkeit* was combined with patriotism, but then their official newspaper in Bavaria admitted that "sharpshooters, for the most part, come from the middle classes."[98] Military discipline also provided a constant theme. Sharpshooters praised Albert Leo Schlageter, the Nazi hero who had fallen in the fight against the French occupation of the Ruhr Valley. Standing in front of the statue of Bavaria in Munich in 1923, one of their leaders declared that before such heroism flags must be lowered, while a band played the song of the "Good Comrade."[99]

Naturally, shooting societies stressed the need for military preparedness in a defeated Germany. But under the shadow of National Socialism they went beyond mere assertion and in 1933 held a shooting festival in Bavaria to honor the right-wing Free Corps at which both its leaders, von Epp and Escherich, were present.[100] These buccaneers found favor among the sharpshooters; they had attempted to fight the Poles at Germany's eastern border and, in addition, had put down the left-wing revolution in Munich. Sharpshooting societies also believed that they stood above all political parties, supporting the "Germanic man" who found joy in the use of arms and was filled with Teutonic spirit, camaraderie, and love of fatherland.[101] As the crisis of the Republic deepened in 1932, the societies bemoaned the "Umsturz," the German revolution of 1918, and wished that it could be wiped away by a miracle.[102]

Their attitude was reactionary rather than National Socialist. The ties which they had forged with dynasties and princes since the beginning of their existence, and which extended through the Second Empire, asserted their influence. Most sharpshooters remained monarchists at heart. Unlike the singers, they seem to have retained only few of their working-class members, and after the war became what they had always essentially been, a predominantly middle-class and rural organization. Youth apparently stayed away from the sharpshooting societies even before the First World War. Moreover, shooting was expensive, requiring the ownership of rifles and other equipment. This undoubtedly further restricted the membership.[103] Their festivals, in many of which male choirs took part, were not, as far as one can tell, in any way connected with Republican celebrations.

When the Nazis came to power the leadership of the sharpshooters' association asserted that it did not have to prove its national attitude by issuing a proclamation.[104] The sharpshooters participated in the ceremony during which Hitler laid the foundation stone of the "House of Art" in Munich in 1933. They marched on the Nazi Day of Work with flags and uniforms.[105] Above all, they attempted to gain favor by emphasizing the importance of "the people armed," to which the societies had certainly made a contribution.[106] The Nazis, however, dealt them the same criticism as that of the male choral societies: they were too exclusive, too much of a "Verein" (association). This even though the societies had always made an effort to emphasize the shooting of man-made birds or simple targets ("open shooting"), which required less skill and meant that more people could participate.[107] They attempted what the choral societies had attempted with the abolition of the four-part song. But since there were special skills involved in both choral singing and shooting, these attempts tended to result in failure, especially with ever more elaborate competitions for prizes. Thus the general public was still excluded from participation.

Attempts at popularization, then, were to no avail. In 1934 the Nazis forced a change of organization on the sharpshooting societies, strengthening the control exercised by the Deutsche Schützenbund. They then took over this central organization themselves. Like the male choirs, the sharpshooters too were now integrated into the Nazi state; and the three thousand larger local organizations were put at the disposal of the army.[108] The tasks they performed at national rites became less important in themselves than in their service to military training. This subservience to military ends was planned by the Nazis only for the duration of rearmament and the war. Martin Bormann, the Führer's secretary and a powerful man in the Reich, planned eventually to integrate sharpshooters with village festivals celebrating local customs and traditions.[109] Nevertheless, sharpshooters played a secondary role in the liturgy of the Third Reich. They marched and took part but did not help set the tone as the male choirs were able to do.

As a large patriotic association, however, they did provide an example for the organization of masses. Together with the gymnasts and the singers, they formed one large patriotic group which supported and participated in national rites for over a century before the Nazis came to power. Their festivals were not the usual political meetings, as Vischer had remarked, but acts which certainly helped to form and preserve the national cult.

## IV

The element of movement, of process, which accompanied and unified disparate parts, was essential for the successful functioning of national festivals. What could be more fitting here than the introduction of dance? Folk dances had always been used to fill the "sacred space." The German Youth Movement had stressed dancing as liberating the body and putting it in touch with the rhythm of the cosmos.[110] But the appearance of the modern dance movement after the First World War began to have a separate and important impact on the national cult in the 1920's. Though by no means a real national movement in the sense of involving a cross section of the population, its prime characteristics of song, rhythm, and physical movement linked the modern dance to both choral and gymnastic societies; these characteristics also lent themselves so easily to cultic ceremonies that its impact was sizable despite a relatively small number of devotees.

During the sharpshooting festivals, the crowd was still chaotic as indeed it had been at the Hambach Festival earlier. Space and movement had to be fused in order to form a liturgical unity with mass participation. The modern dance showed a concern for such unity, and it is not surprising that Albert Speer, who organized so many of the Nazi festivals, felt drawn to Mary Wigman, one of the founders of the modern dance.[111]

Mary Wigman, in common with all the founders of the modern dance, stressed both bodily movement and the space into which the body was projected. The dancer, so Wigman held, forms the space around him; not an existing space, but one which is irrational, created by the expansion of dance rhythms which dissolve all that is merely corporeal.[112] Wigman did believe in the effectiveness of solo dancing, especially when transposed against a large group of dancers. Yet groups, the "dancing choirs which make a statement," were the most effective in forming space and creating an atmosphere. Such dancing choirs became symbols, a group of human beings who fused into one moving body with a single goal.[113] The formation of space through such a group in rhythmic movement was basic to the modern dance as practiced in the 1920's. A preoccupation with lighting was added to the attempt to create meaningful space. Wigman asserted that light must have equal weight with dance, music, and words.[114]

Of equal importance for the development of concepts of space and movement were the rhythmic gymnastics which Emil Jacques-Dalcroze practiced in his school for rhythm, music, and physical culture in the garden city of Hellerau before the First World War. Dalcroze (1865–1950) had started out as a musician and music teacher in Geneva, but from 1911 onwards he made his home in the experimental garden city (the first in Germany) where the architect Heinrich Tessenow built a hall for his school. Dalcroze was influenced by Isadora Duncan, but her emphasis on the release of the body from conventions did not satisfy him. Instead, he sought through music and rhythms to discipline a new dance form. "To bring order into the movements (of the body) means educating the spirit to rhythm."[115]

Dalcroze also believed that light was a key factor in forming space. The open-air theatre had pioneered in this area, but its light was natural and not subject to the discipline of artistic creativity. Light must not only help form the space but also highlight the beauty of the human body, which should not be done by singling out the individual (as in the theatre), for that would destroy the communal effect.[116] Dalcroze's dance was group dancing, and he praised Hellerau for possessing a spirit of community. An artistic link must also be forged among the dancers themselves and with their audience, Dalcroze maintained.[117] Gluck's *Orpheus and Eurydice* was popular with the students in Hellerau as it was with Wigman. Here light and darkness could be used in symbolic fashion; the Furies dance in the mystical light of the Underworld while Orpheus and Eurydice strive toward the light of day.[118]

Dalcroze eventually failed in Hellerau, though his theories were taken up in Gustav Wynecken's boarding school at Wickersdorf, as well as in the United States.[119] Nevertheless, his ideas and Wigman's were similar. Their preoccupation with space, movement, and light obviously had liturgical qualities. Indeed, Wigman and Dalcroze both regarded their dances as rites, generating a mood wholly dissimilar from that produced by the technical finesse of traditional ballet. Mary Wigman talked about the "fairy tale of the dance," and regarded her version of the "Dance of Death" as the highlight of her creations.[120] Together with space and light, movement fraught with symbolism pervaded this dance form. Audience and actors had to share the identical mood.

It was Rudolf von Laban, after the First World War, who

lifted the modern dance out of the halls or theatres where it was usually performed into the realm of festivals. He had been impressed by the "festive restraint" of military parades, but as a close associate of Wigman's he wanted to fuse this impression with the existing theory of the modern dance. What was needed was an art form which stressed "communal movement and leaping, festive walking, and virile running."[121] Dances must be "choirs of movement," a concept which Wigman and Dalcroze shared; they must give to performers a "common experience of joy in movement," as Laban put it.[122] For Laban the essence of the dance lay in its festive nature,[123] and indeed the others had called their performances "dance festivals." Like them, Laban felt that a festive mood would enhance the experience of community between performers and spectators, and thus provide a contrast with the idleness and gluttony of daily life.[124]

The traditional meaning given to festivals could hardly have found a more concise expression. Laban practiced what he preached. He traveled around the country organizing festivals for various groups. His special interest was workers' festivals, for the devotees of the modern dance were progressive in their politics. However, Laban would offer his services to many other groups as well. Through Laban the ideals of space, light, and symbol were made available to a wider audience, always combined with the discipline of rhythm and "choruses of movement." Whenever Laban received a commission to organize festivals he would first train a choir of movement for it, and sometimes rehearse speaking choruses as well. These groups would be schooled in common movements, especially festive walking. His basic idea was to create joy in the common experience of movement and thus to "conquer the space."[125]

Laban, like Wigman and Dalcroze, founded his own dance theatre and became ballet master of the Prussian state theatres. Interestingly enough, he had also worked at Bayreuth, and the few dances Wagner wrote had a deep influence upon him. But in 1936 he had to leave Germany for exile in England, and it was there that his work continued through the Ballet Joos. Mary Wigman did appear during the Youth Olympiad in Berlin in 1936, where she produced some choric dances; then she fell silent as well, appearing only for a farewell performance in 1942.[126] Yet despite the political differences of these artists from National Socialism, the Nazis continued to encourage this dance form. In 1934, the Reichschamber of Culture sponsored a "German Dance Festival" which practiced the modern dance. Alfred Rosenberg's cultural organization proclaimed the "dance of movement" as an important element in the creation of all festivals.[127]

National Socialism also used a related tradition in concert with the modern dance, the "aesthetic gymnastic" of François Delsarte (1811–1871), which had already found disciples toward the end of the nineteenth century. This school tried to produce "noble movements" that would contrast with modern nervousness and restlessness. Each bodily movement had to be based upon a clearly defined thought; moral energy must inform physical movement. Sudden movements were condemned, for the theory was meant to produce an inner harmony and discipline as well as restraint.[128] Delsarte himself was an odd person who had passed from Saint Simonism to Christianity. His system attained great popularity in the United States, but it also furthered the "festive movements" of which Laban had written. Because of its discipline and idealism, the Commission for People's and Youth Sports had recommended it at the beginning of the century.[129]

Mass movements like National Socialism were vitally concerned with the principles of space and movement; this led eventually to a call for greater gymnastic training for dancers (which the modern dance had already included in its curriculum). Gymnastics too were now said to uphold a "higher principle of beauty," not by themselves, but in conjunction with the theory of the dance.[130] Already in 1902 such a combination was held to produce joy in a beautiful body, a joy which was essential for appreciating the concept of beauty that derived from the Greeks.[131] Father Jahn himself had put forward similar ideals. Beauty was, once again, linked to the national cult and the combination of gymnastics and dance was supposed to lead to its objectification through man. This past tradition certainly gave modern dance a greater national respectability than it could have obtained through its founders.

The importance of the modern dance as a liturgical rite needs no further demonstration. To be sure, military examples played a large part in the way masses were organized by the National Socialists. But there is a good reason why Albert Speer and others during the Third Reich were drawn to this art form. In order to inform Nazi festivals, the preoccupation with space, with community, with discipline of movement and, not least, with rhythm, was necessary. Significantly, too, some of those concerned with Nazi festivals were also attracted to Paul Whiteman's jazz[132] and the *Rhapsody in Blue*. Whiteman, who practiced "symphonic jazz" with massive bands, was known as the "king of the bandleaders." Here too rhythm and new uses of light were integrated with group action. Similarly, the modern dance joined space, movement of choruses, and light in a novel manner. Some Nazi experiments with lighting were of course purely pragmatic. Albert Speer arrived at his dome of light for the mass meeting of party functionaries on the Tempelhof Airfield in 1935 as a result of the demands of the terrain he had to work with and from watching anti-aircraft lights in the sky.[133] But those ideas on light which we have discussed in this chapter nevertheless exerted a clear influence on the presentation of many Nazi ceremonies.

The building blocks of a new political style were being constructed. Each association which we have discussed played its part, drawing more and more people into the practice of festivals and liturgical rites. The modern dance added further, cohesive elements, chiefly in the 1920's. But the foundations for the fully fledged liturgy which the Nazis made use of were not yet completed. The final development was stimulated by the workers' movement as well. Though we have already referred to this from time to time, its contribution to the development of the new politics warrants a closer look. But first we must retrace our steps, beginning with the development of liturgical form among the workers in the second half of the nineteenth century.

# CHAPTER SEVEN

# The Workers' Contribution

THE LABOR movement made its own contribution to the new politics, developing a political liturgy which was to impress even its enemies. A disciplined mass movement had existed ever since Ferdinand Lasalle founded his General German Workers Association (*Allgemeiner Deustcher Arbeiter Verein*), the first real workers' movement in Germany, in 1863. Lasalle was a master of agitation designed to build a mass following. He used flyers, newspapers, and a constant round of mass meetings to accomplish his purpose. Typically, he considered his followers an "army" and his speaking tours were known as "army inspections" (*Heeresschau*). Lasalle, like Lueger later, had a well-developed instinct for the political style which would attract the masses in the coming age.

Mass agitation was an integral part of his leadership of the workers' association. "What is above all important for the political struggle is the winning of those who are indifferent and to involve the greatest possible numbers [in the movement]."[1] His meetings developed a definite form of their own, even if they did not achieve a definitive political liturgy. The arrival of the leader in a town and his entry at the meeting began to assume prime importance; Lasalle was met at the railway station by a deputation, choral societies gave him a concert under his hotel window, and then a procession formed from the hotel to the meeting hall, which consisted of carriages decked with flowers; sometimes choral societies accompanied the procession, and at other times triumphal gates were erected over the street. Within the meeting hall the *"Bundeslied"* was sung, for Lasalle fully recognized the power of communal song and had a special anthem composed for his movement. The halls were covered in flowers, sometimes gathered and put together by the children of workers. The focal point of every meeting was Lasalle's speech, which could run for over two hours. Here the speaker and the content of his message were crucial, as the liturgy of Lasalle's meetings did not transform the speaker into a symbol.[2]

Yet contemporaries have told us how Lasalle's meetings took on the character of the founding of a new faith. Lasalle himself wrote: "I had the constant impression this is how it must have been at the founding of new religions."[3] Lasalle was the "prophet" and the atmosphere surrounding him was "sacred," worshipping the unity of the working classes and not of the nation, though national themes did creep into his speeches. Lasalle, it must be remembered, was the heir of the democratic agitation of 1848, a believer in the national democracy which had suffered shipwreck in that revolution.

The burning faith which suffused his meetings was supplemented by political tactics which encouraged activism and served as an additional stimulus to unity. At Lasalle's meetings his enemies were kept in their place; but when his opponents held meetings, his own followers appeared en masse to take them over.[4] This kind of warfare would continue for many years.

But Lasalle's strong leadership in fact hindered the development of a fully worked out liturgy; a personality cult grew around the figure of Lasalle. Certainly, leadership was to be seen as equally charismatic and important for later mass movements, but later, too, leader and followers were united by strong common myths; they had no need to confront each other starkly because the political liturgy acted as a mediating institution. Friedrich Ludwig Jahn undoubtedly had charisma, but the movements he founded remained self-sufficient because of their rites of national worship. His presence was clearly felt at the Wartburg Festival, for example, though he was not there in person. The cult of the leader had to be integrated and balanced with the liturgy of politics. The leader existed and was worshipped, but only as part of the totality of the religious impulse. Neither Lasalle nor Lueger was a leader of this sort; their political style was intensely personal.

Yet the cult which sprang up around them and which they directed did find a stable form of its own. The arrival and entry of the leader played a cardinal part, as we have tried to show. This was part of an old tradition: the "joyous entry" of kings into their capitals had always been the occasion for pomp and ceremony. But in the nineteenth century masses of people took an active part; such an entry no longer centered on the ruler whose activity alone dominated the proceedings. From now on, arrivals and entries became impressive documentations of the unity of a movement. The labor movement played an important part in this development. Eventually it was no longer solely a leader like Lasalle who entered, but rather a crowd in serried ranks, carrying flags as their symbol. Among later Socialists, the "cult of the flag" replaced the cult of the leader, much to the distress of those who wanted to see more fully ritualized festivals. For the impressive entry remained often the only festive part of Socialist meetings, the rest being filled with speeches and debates. The Nazis and other rightist groups were to combine the *Aufmarsch* with liturgical practices. Unlike the right, there were no charismatic leaders in later Socialism, and when they did exist, the cult of personality was frowned upon.

However, the labor movement continued to develop institutions upon which a more complete liturgy could be built. They involved themselves in the choral societies, and from 1875 onwards many class-conscious workers withdrew from the German Sängerbund to form their own organizations. These new groups coincided with the formation of Social Democratic electoral associations.[5] In 1894, workers' choral societies formed a united organization (*Arbeiter Sängerbund*) with a membership of 19,322. The movement spread rapidly, until by 1911 it contained some 148,000 singers.[6] The workers' choral society was now as large as the older German choral association. Yet many workers remained in the Deutsche Sängerbund. It was estimated that in 1907 in the Saxon town of Chemnitz, for example, about 60 per cent of the members of this "bourgeois" organization were, in fact, workers.[7] The growth of the workers' choral association was accomplished against strong opposition. Lasalle had realized the importance of community singing, but the Social Democratic leadership was not so easily convinced. Perhaps this was because some of the members of workers' choral societies were not at the same time members of trade unions.[8] But a more fundamental problem was involved, one which would haunt the Social Democratic Party into the future. Its leadership was suspicious of the new political style: their interest was directed toward the education of workers in Marxist theory and the perfection of the Social Democratic Party organization. They were reluctant to involve the masses in Socialism through the use of myths and symbols.

Nevertheless, the workers' choirs made their way into Socialist festivals. May Day, first celebrated in 1890, provided a strong impetus for the formation of workers' choirs. The bourgeois Sängerbunde had refused to meet the strongly felt need to enhance this festival through song, for they drew the line at supporting such radicalism. Therefore, workers' choirs took their place. Nevertheless, as late as 1929 we hear complaints that the Social Democratic Party did not make enough use of them.[9] This, though these choirs attempted to stress workers' songs, songs of freedom, and massed choruses. In reality, such songs were in scarce supply and the repertoire of workers' choirs included many of the same kinds of songs which the bourgeois choirs used. The workers' choir association lamented the absence of proper Socialist songs as late as 1925.[10] Perhaps it is typical of the spirit which prevailed that we rarely find mention of Marx and Engels in the history of these societies (no locals seem to have taken their names from these founders), but that a great deal was made of the Lasallian tradition (societies with his name abounded).

Certainly it is telling that when Erich Mühsam, the famous anarchist, presented his collection of "revolutionary, fighting, marching, and satirical songs" in 1925 he claimed that the Marxist "international" was almost unknown to Socialist youth. Satirical songs directed against the Establishment which had flourished in 1848 were now completely forgotten. Instead, the youthful "red fighters" sang a song taken from a patriotic hymn of 1914.[11] The workers' chóirs were to blame for the lack of revolutionary vigor, for like their bourgeois counterpart they tended to provide settings for social evenings and the performance of concerts, rather than concentrating on political agitation.

Erich Mühsam advised Socialists that the nationalists had always recognized the importance of song to help maintain a fighting spirit and firmness of will, and that the Socialists should do likewise.[12] The workers' choir associations did take part in Socialist festivals and, still more important, held their own national "Sängerfeste," which tended to become ever more elaborate. The festival procession predominated (as it had for Lasalle), for in this way organized singers could influence the uncommitted masses which lined the streets. If we select as our example the Bavarian workers' "Sängerfest" of 1914, the parallels with bourgeois organizations again spring readily to mind: the procession contained gymnasts and cyclists (a popular working men's sport); order was maintained by members of the workers' gymnastic association; flags were carried and songs were sung.[13]

Once again we are confronted by the mixture of social gathering and festival. The opening ceremony in the festival hall was typical. It began with a march from Wagner's *Tannhäuser*, to whose theme the choirs entered the hall. There followed the overture to Mozart's *Marriage of Figaro*. Then

Kurt Eisner (four years later to lead the Bavarian Revolution) spoke, no doubt a fiery evocation of a better world, and after this a "song of freedom" was sung by everyone present. The opening ceremony ended with music from Bizet's *Carmen*, Bavarian folk tunes, and skits by a Bavarian humorist.[14] The sacred mood induced by the first half of the ceremony gave way to a Volksfest in the second. The end of the session featured lighter entertainment than most bourgeois Sänger-feste provided. In those at least, the patriotic theme was kept intact throughout, but here the class struggle dissolved into Bizet's *Carmen*. There is no record of the singing of the "International."

The processions through the town became more elaborate as time went on, and indeed the Socialist movement empha-sized marches and processions through the streets (which we will find repeated in May Day ceremonies). In the "Bayrische Arbeiter-Sängerfest" of 1925 we are no longer faced with the rather simple march of 1914. Now the procession was opened by heralds riding horses, carrying the standard of the move-ment and blowing their fanfares; there followed floats with *tableaux vivants*, the first representing the ancient Germans marching to the festival of the summer solstice. Germanic songs were sung, Germanic dress worn. A youthful "blond" Germania with a lyre was flanked by two oaks. Two hundred singers took part in this marching representation of Ger-manism, surely an odd feature in a procession of Socialists.[15] This *tableau* might have warmed the heart of any patriotic organization, and it is thus difficult to reconstruct why it was used on this occasion. It certainly highlights the patriotism of German Social Democracy—perhaps the Republic which they supported should find its way back to the traditional national liturgy? Perhaps, also, the workers' choirs had not, after all, been able to separate themselves from the very traditional forms of the bourgeois choral societies. We might add that they were not to find a specific Socialist tradition which could have been used for their myth and symbol, though here

Thomas Müntzer or the peasant revolts of the sixteenth century might have been of use. (The Social Democrats during Weimar were the Establishment, and it was in fact the Nazis who firmly annexed the peasant rebellions for their festivities.)

The next *tableaux vivants* of the procession is easier to understand. The procession took place in Nuremberg, and medieval Nuremberg was here symbolized through its patricians and singers. A pastoral idyll followed, as well as a pageant presenting the "power of song." The procession covered all history from ancient Germans to modern freedom. At the final pageant the Goddess of Freedom appeared breaking her chains, and the cart on which she rode was decorated with the colors of the German Republic.[16] Germania at the beginning of the procession and the climax of freedom and Republicanism at the end, led the spectator to view the Republic as anchored in Germanic myths. We shall never know if this was consciously intended, but it seems a reasonable hypothesis. If this is so, then the Social Democrats in this instance used a nationalist tradition which was implied in some of their literature, but which was in fact appealed to more by the Communist Party.

Workers' choral societies took part in and even led some Socialist demonstrations, like those for the extension of the franchise in 1910.[17] But the largest workers' demonstration, May Day, was to be silent: "No call, no song."[18] Indeed, it became fashionable to stress such silence because it was calculated to impress by its sheer massiveness. "We have the numbers, we are the masses, we have the power," was demonstrated by silent marches which, as the official party newspaper put it, bore witness to the maturity of Social Democratic workers.[19] The choirs lost out here.

The Paris Congress of the Second International in 1889 proclaimed May Day (May 1) as a world festival. Their idea was to demonstrate the solidarity of the working class and to call for world peace and unity. May Day was supposed to be a demonstration, not a festival.[20] Therefore, the march of workers through the town was crucial; a provocation to the bourgeoisie which took its Sunday walk, a demonstration that streets, parks, and gardens belonged to the working classes; on May Day they "conquered the streets."[21] Such marches were influenced by military models but were also filled with chiliasm, the longing for a better world. The Lasallian "founding of a new religion" continued to play its part in Germany. At one such procession the workers carried a banner with a slogan taken from Lasalle's earlier organization: "The workers are the rock upon which the Church of the future will be built."[22] The religious was once more linked with the secular to form the spirit of a mass rite.

Kurt Eisner, the leader of the Bavarian Revolution of 1918–19, was one of the most enthusiastic supporters of May Day. Writing at the beginning of the century, he believed that those hitherto deprived of festivals had finally won their own festival—the spirit of history and humanity of the festivals of the French Revolution had lived on. So did the festival of Hambach, where the people themselves attempted to proclaim their longing for unity. May Day was the inheritor of those traditions which, Eisner believed, had emanated from the people themselves.[23]

The time of May was symbolic. Spring, the creator and recreator of the world, had proclaimed itself the leader of the working-class movement. The unfettered drive of nature had become the driving force of the proletariat.[24] Eisner rightly criticized Wilhelminian festivals as having lost the spirit of joy and dedication: they had simply become long exchanges of homage.[25] He had a sense of the importance of festivals, though his own "Festival of the Revolution" (November 17, 1918), celebrated at the Munich Royal Theatre, was held in dark business suits, with a symphony orchestra and a speech.[26] Eisner was closer to the style of Lasalle than to modern political liturgy. Nor was May Day really comparable to the festivals of the French Revolution.

The "sacred silence" of the May Day parades was meant not only to impress the bourgeois spectators, but also to induce a feeling of unity among the marchers themselves. The massed flags presented the only startling color and symbol. To heighten the uniform effect, the workers were eventually asked to wear their Sunday best.[27] The sheer mass counted, and one Socialist paper suggested that artificial mounds be built at the sides of the streets so that the individual could leave the procession for a moment and look at the thousands who marched behind and in front of him.[28] The tradition of the mass, of the monumental, which we saw developing in brick and mortar through the national monument, now came alive in this conquest of the streets. The mass formed itself into a unit, something which the earlier nationalists had attempted but which now reached its fulfillment through the disciplined May Day parades in which hundreds of thousands took part.

The parade was the high point of May Day. But this was soon supplemented by other forms of agitation. Leaflets were passed out, posters put up, and eventually "May Day Papers" published for the occasion, proclaiming the motto for the day, based on the worker's class struggle and his coming victory. As Kurt Eisner wrote: "The strong light of May must accompany the upright proletarian through all days of the year, and on no occasion must he forget the festive enthusiasm which he owes to his cause."[29]

The French workers at their first May Day in 1893 were disconcerted not to find themselves at a traditional popular fête with Japanese lanterns and gay flags.[30] There is no evidence that ritual silence remained the case in Germany, for by the end of the First World War some silent parades moved toward accepting the trappings of traditional festival processions. Thus in Stuttgart four bands marched in the procession, and workers' choral societies also took part.[31] In France, the demands of the workers themselves transformed the demonstration into a festival;[32] this happened in Germany, too, to some extent. The Communists, in 1920, accused the Social Democrats of having started to reduce May Day to "morning and evening meetings" long before the First World War. These had then become "comfortable affairs of the party family."[33] In Austria, also, Communists held that the Social Democratic May Day was really a "Volksfest," a frivolous occasion.[34] These were gross exaggerations. "Rebel Sunday," as May Day was sometimes called, did have a tendency to become a Volksfest, but strenuous efforts were made by all Socialists to prevent this. For example, May Day usually ended with the signing of petitions for a workers' cause. After this, the workers were supposed to go home and no light entertainment was offered.[35]

May Day was not the only workers' festival. We have seen how their choir societies furthered a more elaborate liturgy; the workers' gymnastic organization attempted to do the same. Both these groups may have taken their ideal of festive and liturgical form from their bourgeois parent organizations. The forms were derived from a tradition which had practiced rites of national worship, and when the workers split from the traditional associations they took this tradition with them, directing it toward the class struggle in counterpoint to the silent marches of May Day.

The gymnasts, with their strong nationalism, made life difficult for those workers in their ranks who joined the Social Democratic Party. And Socialists, for their part, attempted unsuccessfully to steer gymnasts away from their national concerns, demanding, for example, that the association ignore the Sedanstag. The workers' own gymnastic organization was founded in 1893 with some four thousand members. Membership soon increased dramatically, while the association accused bourgeois gymnasts of "subservience to authority" (see Plate 15).[36]

The Social Democratic Party showed just the same reluctance in recognizing the usefulness of gymnasts as it had the workers' choral association. The party leadership feared that such an organization might distract from its educational efforts, aware, no doubt, of the intense nationalism which had become traditional among gymnasts. Though the new Gymnastic Association grew rapidly, even by 1924 most workers who were gymnasts seemed to have remained within the original Deutsche Turnerbund.[37]

The workers' gymnasts attempted to justify their existence through their usefulness at festivals, and they did so in a language taken directly from the national liturgy: "We want to create enthusiasm in the masses and use more forms than exist today such as: choirs, pillars of fire, flags, short inspirational speeches."[38] Had their suggestions been accepted, Socialists would have fallen in line with nationalist worship and liturgy. As it was, they certainly helped to further the new political style of the movement.

Their "Festspiele" were rites not dissimilar to what the "Theatre of the Future" demanded. For example, at their second national meeting after the First World War in 1929 the workers' gymnasts presented a festival play called *Free Thyself*. It began with the entry of the "storm troops" to the tune of the *"Marseillaise"*; this *Aufmarsch* adopted the form of the "choir of movement" we have discussed earlier.[39] Slaves and enslaved workers crossed the stage as the choir of youth attempted to rouse them to action. Instead, they wasted their time in frivolities to the rhythm of jazz. But youth kept on trying. Finally, in a dance (adopting this form as well) to the sound of the "International," youth itself stormed the prison which kept the workers captive. A short speech followed and then a solemn oath was sworn by all to the ideals of committed youth. Finally, the program listed the "Apotheosis" of the play. Through choirs of movement, youth descended into the audience picking up flaming torches on the way. All around the auditorium fires were lit. While the choruses marched along the swimming basin (a part of the auditorium), competitions took place, and when these had finished a torchlight parade through town ended the festival play.[40]

It is worth describing this festivity in detail. For here we have a fully developed liturgy, using past traditions as well as the newer chorus and the modern dance. New artistic forms which had sprung up in the 1920's were integrated with traditional secular liturgy, demonstrating that to the same extent as the right, the left was capable of this new style of politics. The leader of the Workers' Gymnastic Association himself believed that a movement that wanted to conquer the world could not be guided by material forces alone; great thoughts must come alive to penetrate every aspect of human action.[41] But the Social Democratic leadership could not be expected to follow him here. Marxist concepts of human consciousness had long given way to Karl Kautsky's materialist interpretation of history and, in any case, the Social Democrats felt, consciousness should not be raised through a liturgical approach but rather through didactic workers' education. Yet the Austrian Social Democrats, deeply concerned with the political education of their youth during the crisis year of 1931, praised the German Workers' Gymnastic Association for its efforts at indoctrinating its followers. These gymnasts knew how to use the sports arena in order to further a political world view. "We must create a similar association."[42] Austrian Marxists showed a greater awareness of the usefulness of the liturgical forms inherent in sports organizations then did their German brothers.

Nevertheless, so-called red sports organizations became increasingly popular, especially during the Weimar Republic. Then the "workers' sports movement" encompassed not only gymnastics but many other sports as well. The "red cyclists" had formed an association as early as 1896 and had found favor in the eyes of the party, for they acted as messengers during elections. Even a "free sharpshooting society" was founded by workers in 1920, but this always remained one of the smallest of their sports associations. As a matter of fact, the "workers' sports movement" was one of the largest Socialist organizations during the 1920's, with around two million members.

This movement resisted the breakup of Socialism into Communist and Social Democratic parties and indeed remained the only united workers' organization. By 1929, however, the tensions between Social Democrats and Communists having become unbearable within the association, the Social Democrats staged a takeover. The Communists then attempted to found their own gymnastics and sports society, but this always remained a small splinter group.[43] Yet all Socialists remained united in believing that the "thousands who express the power of the proletariat through the harmonic play of their bodies in games, fuse with the mass of spectators into one whole—into a totality which characterizes true festivals of the people."[44]

The "worker youth" (*Arbeiter-Jugend*), .which had a membership of between seventy and ninety thousand during the Weimar Republic, also stressed ritual and symbol. This was a Social Democratic organization; thus the staid parliamentary party was able to obtain, despite its leadership, a sense of liturgical form at least among some of its youth. The symbols, of course, were adapted from the national tradition, just as singers had adapted familiar symbols in their festivals. The torches carried at Whitsuntide and the flames lit on the hills proclaimed the new Reich of the proletariat, "just as 2000 years ago these symbols had served to proclaim the German Reich."[45] The worker youth celebrated the summer solstice with flags and fire while putting great emphasis on roaming through the German countryside (where the Kyffhäuser provided them with a goal).[46] The worker youth were similar to the German Youth Movement; they, too, performed rhythmic dances and lay plays. Here Schiller's *Robbers* or *Wilhelm Tell* (though not medieval plays) were popular because of their appeal to freedom.[47]

Clearly, the urge toward political liturgy and symbolic form had also found a foothold in the workers' movement. That movement added its own impressive contribution to the new politics, but the usual workers' festivals still had an old-fashioned air. They stressed the formation and disciplining of the masses, yet wordy speeches were still the central part of such demonstrations. The Berlin demonstration in 1928 in memory of Bismarck's repressive socialist legislation carefully combined organizational skill with speechmaking, but the liturgical elements were lost. Local groups were coordinated to march into the park where the festival was held and there were assigned to six or seven various speakers' platforms where speeches were being made simultaneously. To be sure, flags provided color and choirs a mood, but the festival tended to fall into individual groups. The liturgical unity was missing.[48]

From the 1880's onwards the *tableau vivant* was especially popular among the workers' movement, and it was no accident that the workers' gymnastic organization made so much use of it. The *tableaux* were usually explained by a commentator and interspersed with the reading of epic-dramatic poetry. As one of the last acts before his death, Wilhelm Liebknecht himself designed such a *tableau vivant* for the Mainz Party Congress of 1900, entitled the "Reunion of German Social Democracy." It first presented the Marxist and the Lasallian groups separately. They then united, each still carrying its own flag, under a red flag which Marx, rising out of his grave, shows to Lasalle. Finally, Marx lifts up a laughing Lasalle while the orchestra plays the *"Marseillaise."* Liebknecht's commentary deserves to be cited: "[The Congress members] will not forget the hidden treasure of the *Nibelungen* which is rescued from the Rhine."[49]

Did Liebknecht believe this German myth had made so great an impact that a Socialist theme had to build upon it in order to be effective? That Socialist unity was a new *Nibelungen Hort*? His comment would lead us to think so. Here Socialist unity was anchored in Germanic myth, just as later the workers' choral societies would anchor the Weimar Republic in a blond Germania. The cultic elements of the workers' movement were easily linked to the historical tradition of the national cult. After all, the middle class celebrated its festivals in a similar manner; *tableaux vivants* and poetry reading were common at birthdays, anniversaries, and public festivals such as the Schiller celebrations of 1859. It proved difficult for the workers' movement to find its own liturgical form, and though the movement never really succeeded, it still made an important contribution to the more general development of the national cult.

After the war, when the revolutionary dynamic seemed at its height, a new departure was indeed tried out, though this, too, reached back to earlier cultic experience. An attempt was made in the period from 1920 to 1924 to create workers' mass festivals at Leipzig which tried to present the historical dimensions of Socialist revolution. These mass festivals were, in reality, like the *Thing* theatres mentioned earlier—plays acted out by a large body of workers (up to three hundred men and women)[50] while others watched. But this new theatre was conceived as a festival and given this name, "festival" here meaning a cultic rite, as it had for the earlier open-air theatres on which these ceremonies were based. The themes presented within such a setting were the Spartacus revolt in ancient Rome (1920), the peasant war (1921), and the French Revolution (1923); or more general topics such as *War and Peace* (1923), which ended in the triumph of world brotherhood; and *Awake!* (1924), in which sailors of warring nations swear brotherhood and proclaim peace on earth. Simplicity of action was essential. Thus in *Spartakus*, slaves were flogged, patricians celebrated victory feasts, and debauchery prevailed; slaves refused to fight "brother gladiators" and were tied to the cross.[51]

Music was used to create the proper atmosphere. In the *Peasants' War*, choirs of movement descended into the audience in order to draw the onlookers into the play. Ernst Toller wrote the fifteen scenes of the *French Revolution*; indeed, these dramas were written by professionals and directed by those familiar with the theatre. But by 1924 the workers' mass festivals had failed. The reason for this failure lay in the fact that the spoken word was the artistic medium of intellectuals such as Toller. But the predominance of the spoken word over the choirs and the massed movements of the actors destroyed the simple effect which such drama was originally meant to convey. One observer wrote that in Toller's play the individual actor could no longer be recognized or his words understood: "Only the call of the masses rises toward heaven like distant thunder."[52] The play lost its effectiveness when language moved into the foreground, bringing with it more complex characterization. The festival which had been defined as a call to action and involvement through the drama tended to become a conventional play.

As soon as this happened, workers went home or stayed away, for they could no longer participate easily or grasp the complexity of the drama in such a vast auditorium. The plays became a bore, since their success really depended upon song and movement; increased emphasis on the spoken word destroyed the visual and musical harmony of the action. Nationalists recognized that speeches must be short on such occasions and the speaker nothing more than a fully integrated symbol.

The mass workers' festivals failed, but speaking choruses continued to thrive and become increasingly popular among all shades of Socialists in the second half of the 1920's. We are told that in 1929, as soon as speaking choruses managed to compete with the novelty of the microphone, they were regarded by Socialists as cells of the communal Theatre of the Future and were compared to Athenian democracy in action.[53] These choirs also depended upon a dialogue with the audience, and were therefore useful instruments in encouraging mass participation. We have seen that they were adopted by a part of the national cult, and later by National Socialism. But the Socialists made the greatest use of them in the 1920's. Here, again, however, there were few speaking choruses available, and the workers actually had to borrow many of them from that organization which had already used them before the war, the German Youth Movement.[54] At Socialist festivals these choruses were often combined with the dance, sometimes staged by von Laban himself. This led to some criticism, as such performances were said to be closer to oratorios than to proletarian mass agitation. Sometimes the Revolution made an appearance not as a fighting workers' movement but as a tall young lady.[55] It was difficult to remove from the consciousness of the workers the old personalized symbolism, whether it was the young female Revolution or the Germania of the Bavarian Singers' Festival. Such personification had always been opposed by those who wanted to form a national liturgy and who had been against national monuments of this nature.

Still, one Nazi, writing about the great popularity of such speaking choruses among the Hitler youth, mentioned that the Communists had developed this art form as an especially effective means of propaganda.[56] For the KPD itself speaking choruses became ever more elaborate, and between 1923 and 1925 their performances tended to become revues, choruses of movement, and even plays. Gustav von Wagenheim's *Choir of Work* (1923), for example, used dialogue instead of recitations and scenic effects. The characters were symbolic: peasants, Social Democrats, priests, and Communists. The form was that of a morality play done by large numbers of players, though single speakers were also used at times (i.e., the industrialist). Simplicity of scenery became the watchword. There was no stage, and the chorus, according to Wagenheim, should wear working clothes and not their Sunday best.[57]

Both Socialist parties published special editions of such speaking choruses for their own use, emphasizing the drawing together of chorus and audience: "the masses of men become as one person."[58] Yet even such choruses did not manage to form the kind of liturgical rite which we have seen operative in the workers' mass festivals or in the workers' gymnastic association meetings.

The speaking choruses sometimes developed into "political-satirical evenings of the proletariat," in which the KPD presented its ideology through film, satirical couplets, choruses, and even gymnastics. But this art form was borrowed directly from the bourgeois revue, and the workers still wanted to find an *Agitprop* (agitation and propaganda) form of their own. The inspiration for this came from the Soviet Union. The "living newspaper" performed by the Soviet "Blue Shirts" (*Blaue Blusen*) who visited Germany in 1927 gave Communist youth the impetus to train their speaking choruses in a new direction. First, the *Aufmarsch*: actors march into the hall; second, a short lecture giving the theme of the performance. This could be done in the form of a parade as well, the "Blue Shirts" dressed as Roman gladiators carrying placards with the names and themes of various Soviet newspapers. After this, the various themes are acted out: for example, the Blue Shirts performed a skit called *A New Way of Life*. In these sketches, interspersed with gymnastics, dances, and placards, town and village were united and a new life was born.[59]

This was one way of bringing the myth to the people. Not Wagner's way, but certainly similar, by the objectification of ideology and the creation of a common mood. But here there was no scenery at all; "no longing for beauty, no naturalism," as the Communist paper, *Red Flag*, put it.[60] Moreover, humor and satire were supposed to play a large role in the sketches. The common mood was to be one of distance toward the play, not empathy. Unlike Wagner, and indeed unlike the national cult, the Blue Shirts were supposed to induce critical thought. In this aim they also differed greatly from other workers' rituals, as we have seen earlier.

Erwin Piscator, the famous director of the workers' "political theatre," defined his intention as an appeal to reason. The workers' drama should transmit enlightenment, knowledge, and recognition rather than excitement, enthusiasm, and passion. But in reality, the tempo and the involvement of the audience in the action, as well as the oversimplifications, were clearly irrational. In fact, as a recent analysis of Piscator's theatre has shown us, he wanted to transform the random crowds into an ordered mass, not unlike the May Day parades and the Nuremberg rallies.[61] Piscator apparently shared this aim of the national cult. But the connection between his theatre and the development of the cultic elements we have traced seems closer still. Studying Piscator's political theatre, C. D. Innes quotes a Nazi writer who stressed that "the emotions, thoughts and hopes of a people [were brought] to the most palpable expression" in such a drama, creating an immediate communal experience. This Nazi view, we are then told, is almost a precis of Piscator's theatre.[62] The Nazis, however, did not have to borrow this drama from the Marxist theatre; they had no need of that, for such theatrical form had already involved the "Theatre of the Future" long before the First World War.

What the Nazis did borrow from the left, in addition to speaking choruses, was the idea of a "popular theatre" (Volksbühne) where plays supposedly opposed to bourgeois taste were performed at cheap prices. Such a Volksbühne was founded in 1890, performing plays by writers like Ibsen, Zola, and Schiller, stressing a critique of the ruling classes. This popular theatre was imitated by the Christian and nationalist right in 1930, but the Nazis did not join in that effort. They founded a Volksbühne of their own in 1931, which presented such plays as Schiller's *Robbers* and a Bismarck drama by Walter Flex, a hero of the Youth Movement who had fallen in the First World War.[63] This Nazi theatre apparently tried to balance opposition to the bourgeoisie as symbolized by Schiller's play with an attempt to claim the Bismarck tradition for the party. However, the Nazi Volksbühne degenerated into a theatre guild rather than becoming a dynamic *Agitprop* organization.

However, even apart from such a Volksbühne Nazi theatre troupes (*Spieltruppen*) had come into being, performing in rented or donated halls. The plays presented had nothing to do with Schiller or even Walter Flex, but were a crude type of street theatre emphasizing a blatant message. Thus in 1932, using the veteran association's Hall in Berlin, a Nazi troupe presented the murder of an S.A. comrade for which a Jew was blamed. The "Jew" was then dragged upon the stage "whining in his jargon" (i.e., mock-Yiddish) and sentenced to be shot immediately. Such play acting seems to have been especially popular among the Hitler Youth.[64]

Piscator's theatre continued its cutting edge, though in continual trouble with the Communist Party, which was uneasy with a theatre that attempted at least to appeal to reason and the critical spirit. Perhaps they also feared the emotionalism involved, which could easily escape party orthodoxy. Just as such art forms fell to the ax of Stalinism in Russia, so in Germany they proved but an episode surrounded by a much more didactic approach.

The "collective speech" (*Kollektivreferat*) was typical of the didactic development. It, too, arose out of the speaking choruses and was in general use by 1927–28. But it avoided the lyricism of the speaking choruses, expressing rather slogans, facts, and commands in short didactic form. The groups that performed them did move and act out their slogans and commands, accompanied by music, always an important part of the proletarian stage.[65] Wilhelm Pieck, the Communist Party leader, summed up the nature of all this *Agitprop* as embodying "simplicity of representation, empathy with its purpose, thorough preparation, and the strictest discipline in the common effort."[66]

Such *Agitprop* was one form of and had the same purpose as the "Theatre of the Future," to liquidate traditional theatrical forms on behalf of a direct relationship with the audience. The performances did, at one point, induce greater critical distance than the cultic stage. Nevertheless, the workers' theatre was a cultic theatre: symbolic, mythological, utilizing the popular song, dance, and gymnastics. Even the Nazis were interested in it as a technique capable of involving the people in an ideology. It was neither as new or as revolutionary as its propagators seem to have thought, but part of the whole thrust of the new politics.

The Socialist movement in general felt the urge toward theological and liturgical form. In France, for example, a "Society for People's Festivals" was created in 1918 after the First World War. It gave festivals for the Communist Party and the trade unions, but also for the Socialists. This association stressed the importance of an emotional commitment to the workers' struggle, similar to the ideas embodied in the German workers' gymnastic association. The celebration had to be based on the particular theme of the occasion and form an artistic whole with it. Symbolic figures as well as speaking choruses were used; but music was central in such events, and the association tended to become a choir society. The society used the classics, Bach, Beethoven, and Wagner, but also attempted to revive the music played at the festivals of the French Revolution.[67]

The urge toward liturgy, however, remained only an urge and certainly never dominated the workers' movement. The French "Society for People's Festivals" produced a "hymn to reason,"[68] but it was, naturally, the rational component of Socialism which proved hostile to such festivals. It may well be significant that in 1927 some five hundred rank-and-file members of the Social Democratic and Communist parties rejected all religious liturgy, though some had remained members of a Christian Church. None of these Socialists showed any sensitivity toward the psychological structure of liturgy, a fact which those who sent out the questionnaires on Socialism and religion and then evaluated them were careful to note.[69] Though these five hundred Socialists are a tiny sample, almost totally confined to the Berlin working-class suburb of Neuköln, they may well represent one trend among party members, while others obviously appreciated the liturgy of the workers' movement. Still, on the right we find a general appreciation of liturgical forms and no segment would have lacked sensitivity toward its psychological application. They did not suffer from such a handicap.

The rationalism basic to all forms of Socialism could, then, act as a barrier to liturgical development. It could also lead to an excessive didacticism. The didacticism of the Socialists is well illustrated by the plays which the workers were supposed to perform at the end of their local meetings. These plays had existed ever since the 1870's and were written, not by the workers themselves, but by their leaders or professional writers. Their titles are promising and present much of that historical past which the workers' mass meetings also used. But the plots are often interrupted by object lessons on topics like the labor theory of value.[70] Socialists always attempted to educate through an appeal to reason and logic rather than through a commitment to faith. That is why didactic speeches played a much more central part at their meetings than at those of their nationalist and rightist opponents.

Nevertheless, the Nazis were impressed by the example provided by proletarian demonstrations and festivals. Hitler pays explicit tribute to them in *Mein Kampf*. He had gazed at a mass demonstration of Viennese workers as they marched by four abreast. "For nearly two hours I stood there watching the gigantic human dragon slowly winding by."[71] He was impressed by Social Democratic discipline and likened the party to an army of officers and soldiers.[72] And he partly defined his own concept of organization against that of his Socialist opponents, which overawed him by its very success.[73]

Finally, the influence of the Socialists upon National Socialist liturgy must not be exaggerated. It did indeed contribute through its own examples, but in the last analysis National Socialist liturgy was the culmination of the development of a cult that spanned a century and a half of German history.

# CHAPTER EIGHT

# Hitler's Taste

ADOLF HITLER told the Nuremberg rally of 1935 that history finds no nation really worth while except when it builds its own monuments.[1] By monuments he meant not only the deeds of his own régime, but also the political liturgy of nationalism as the only viable mass politics. National Socialism built upon the development of the national cult which had taken place for over a century before the movement was founded. This development is vital for an understanding of the Nazi political style; without it, National Socialism as a mass movement cannot be properly analyzed.

Adolf Hitler was well aware of both the pragmatic and the ideological side of this liturgy, and succeeded in combining concrete political considerations with his own instinctual faith. No cynicism was involved in this mixture, though he was careful to strike a balance between political necessity and the final aim of secular religion. Hitler himself did not create the liturgy of the national cult, not even the immediate application of it to the ceremonial of his movement. He delegated this job to others, and made criticisms only after he had observed the *mis-en-scène*,[2] though his criticism did, of course, determine the future form of the cult. But even here he let liturgical forms run their course, which he himself thought ridiculous. For example, he despised the resurrection of supposedly ancient Germanic custom;[3] nevertheless, houses were built in that style, Germanic dress was worn, and the *Thing* theatre became a reality for several years. The reason that

Hitler despised these archaisms lay in his own taste, which is of obvious importance in understanding the Nazi political style.

The Vienna he had known in his youth determined his artistic and architectural preferences for the rest of his life. He was not one of those whose tastes grew and changed with the passage of time. The famous Ringstrasse remained for Hitler the true *via triumphalis*, as he called it. He had studied it carefully and it always sent him "into ecstasy."[4] The representational buildings which had dominated Vienna in his youth continued for him to typify architectural excellence. Theophilos Eduard von Hansen had constructed many of these from 1870 onwards; he was influential in determining the style of official Viennese architecture. Such buildings as his Reichsratsgebäude (Palace for the Council of the Empire) clearly showed his preference for ancient forms, the "classic simplicity" which contemporaries praised. But here the classical also became monumental, and the interior hall especially of the Reichsratsgebäude expressed such monumentality through its use of space. The pillared hall had as its model the baths of Rome. Hansen was by no means the only architect in Vienna who followed these examples. Heinrich von Fenstel, too, translated the sketches he had made in Rome into the buildings of the university. Gottfried Semper, whom Hansen greatly admired, had been one of the inspirers of the Ringstrasse and the monumental buildings which flanked it.[5]

Thus it was in Vienna that Hitler was imbued with the classical tastes which became so much a part of the national cult. Eventually he was to remark that humanity was never nearer to antiquity in its appearance and sensibilities than "today."[6] The classical style represented a form of self-expression which was simultaneously monumental and simple. Hitler's friendship with the architect Paul Ludwig Troost in the late 1920's deepened his classicism. Troost led him to appreciate Klenze's Munich, which Hitler had not liked before. Perhaps it was the pseudo-Renaissance buildings which caused

Hitler concern. The buildings that Troost designed for the party were classical yet simple, like the House of Art in Munich and the administrative buildings of the Nazi Party — all of which still stand today.

Vienna and Troost both influenced Hitler's discovery of the Prussian architectural Renaissance of the late eighteenth century. A book on Friedrich Gilly written during the Third Reich may also have had an effect upon him, according to one witness. This maintained that the monumental, the combination of Rome and the Acropolis, seemed to "transcend daily life."[7] Gilly's own design for an Arch of Triumph certainly impressed Hitler. He copied it carefully in his sketchbook of 1925 and wanted to have the names of those fallen in the First World War inscribed upon it. Later, he planned to incorporate this Arch of Triumph in the replanning of Berlin. But the design for the tomb of Frederick the Great also caught his fancy, and he was delighted when Albert Speer produced a model of this monument.[8]

These classical influences typified a banal taste. The foundations laid in Vienna were not changed by the influence of Troost and Gilly, and Hitler's conservatism always remained intact. When he sketched model streets or buildings they always resembled the public architecture common in Central Europe since the 1870's. There is no hint of originality or of the influence of the architectural schools that had become prominent after the First World War. To be sure, Hitler liked simplicity of form and the use of simple building materials. But this preference had nothing to do with the Bauhaus, which also advocated a new *Sachlichkeit* (relevance), but rather was based upon the neo-classic revival. Toward the end of the nineteenth century, the precepts for which this revival stood were deepened by the arts and crafts movement, whose journal, *Der Kunstwart* (*The Artistic Guardian*), from 1887 to the outbreak of the First World War attained great popularity among the cultured middle classes. The *Kunstwart* believed that art must clearly express the purpose it is supposed to serve, without surrogate decorations or playfulness of style. Such a concept was close to the *"architecture parlante"* which had set this trend ever since the eighteenth century. But the arts and crafts movement was also devoted to the German Volk; its traditional arts and crafts must be updated without the admixture of foreign influence.[9] The purpose of art and architecture was expressed through the simplicity of the native style.

Gottfried Semper and Wilhelm Kreis, whose architectural ideas we have discussed already, were members of this movement. More immediately, Heinrich Tessenow, the teacher of Albert Speer, was in the council of the Dürerbund, which had been founded in 1901 to spread the *Kunstwart's* message.[10] Tessenow exemplified and transmitted the precepts of the arts and crafts movement. He stressed simplicity and usefulness in architecture. "Simple industriousness, straightforward thinking and living," were connected to the use of simple materials. Ornamentation was considered feminine and playful. Such simplicity meant a love for order and symmetry which Tessenow ascribed to bourgeois society. For all this theory, the end product was neo-classical.[11] Tessenow illustrates in his architecture and writings the linking of the neo-classical as well as the arts and crafts movement with manliness, seriousness of purpose, and bourgeois life. Hitler would have agreed. Tessenow had written a handbook which was used in most German architectural schools even before the war, and Hitler in his architectural training may well have been familiar with it.

Admittedly, under the Third Reich, many factories, private dwellings, and even army barracks reflected the Bauhaus style; but Hitler was interested only in representational buildings within the neo-classical tradition and paid scant attention to any other architectural design even when it was submitted to him.

Such conservatism of taste is particularly clear in Hitler's designs for opera houses. This was always one of his obsessions and as such is closely related to the acceptance of the national cult. There are several sketches of opera interiors in Hitler's sketchbook of 1925, and they are all conventional. The "Theatre of the Future" is not reflected in these designs. Once more Hitler held to a concept which had impressed him in his youth: the opera in Vienna. And Bayreuth's festival hall seems to have represented the limit of what Hitler could accept in the way of theatrical innovation.[12]

Hitler's sketches for opera houses contain several features which point to his continuous preoccupation with ceremonial. The halls and official staircase take up much more room than the auditorium or the stage. No architect could ever have actually built an opera according to these plans, for the emphasis falls on the ascent to the auditorium and the great halls where the spectators would promenade during the intermissions. But even here, the stairway takes up more room than the halls themselves. Surely it is significant for Hitler's preoccupation with such staircases that the buildings along his beloved Ringstrasse (including the Opera) for the most part contained huge stair wells. Such staircases were an integral part of the concept of monumentality as architects like Semper, Hansen, or Festel conceived it.

Hitler loved huge ornamental staircases, not only in his theatrical design, but also when it came to planning official buildings for the new Berlin. Göring's palace was originally to contain the largest staircase, but Hitler promptly changed this in favor of his own monumental edifice. The designs brought to him for buildings and interiors during the Third Reich often show an extension of the principal staircase in the Führer's own bold strokes.

Without attempting to make a psychological interpretation of this predilection, it does point to an important trend in Hitler's taste. For Hitler, the impression which a building should make was as important as its function, and this impression had to be conveyed by a grandeur of space which set the mood immediately upon the entry and ascent into the building, and in the surroundings of the auditorium which, functionally, should dominate such a construction. The ceremonial atmosphere was, as it were, more important than the performance itself. This principle which Hitler applied to his theatrical sketches became reality in the Führerbau (House of the Führer) in Munich; here too the huge ornamental staircase predominates. One can well imagine the intimidating effect when Hitler stood at the top and Neville Chamberlain had to ascend it, during the Munich Conference of 1938.

Space meant monumentality and grandeur; it exemplified power and power relationships. Mussolini's office in the Palazzo Venezia, with the huge space that the visitor had to cross before he stood at the desk of the dictator, provides another example of such a setting. But for Hitler the ceremonial, the "monumental and astounding" which would create the proper mood, existed as part of his artistic taste even before it became a functional necessity for mass meetings and cultic rites. Then he asserted that buildings must keep the needs of the people in mind, and that this meant providing space for 150,000 to 200,000 men and women.[13]

The shift from classical to monumental is obvious in Hitler's designs, and it was to become accentuated with the passage of time. Paul Bonatz, the architect with whom he entrusted the construction of several party buildings, eventually fled Germany to escape such commissions. Hitler, he wrote, had lost all feeling for the handling of massiveness, an artistic instinct sacred to the Greeks.[14] This loss is already obvious in his theatrical designs with their halls and staircases, but it was no doubt enhanced by the need to contain huge masses of people; a need which became confused, in turn, with ideas of grandeur and power. But even this kind of space based itself on past models, and his conservatism still received full play. This time it was not the opera that dominated his fantasies but the Church.

Already in Hitler's sketchbook a hall for the practice of cults resembles a church with its huge dome and apse. But he

also featured church towers in his sketches, and a huge tower
of this sort is part of the dome. Moreover, Hitler's town halls,
which he designed often, took the shape of churches whose
towers had to be taller than those of all the churches in town.
Perhaps such town halls typify his attempt to beat the
churches at their own game through the use of a secular
symbol. His opposition to the Church becomes manifest even
here, long before he achieved power, an enmity which led him
to distinguish sharply between the secular and the Christian
cult. Hitler's conservatism, on the other hand, prevented a
clear separation, however much he desired it, and this almost
involuntary linkage placed him once again within the development of the secular cult as we have tried to analyze it. The
Germanic flame and altar continued to form a unity now, as
they had in 1815, even if within a much more elaborate and
fully formed liturgy.

During the Third Reich Hitler no longer designed town
halls. But the plans for party forums at Linz and Augsburg
contained, once more, churchlike towers which dominated
those of the local churches.[15] For if the traditional towers had
remained the most prominent, they would have rung in the
National Socialist festivals as they had rung in the festivals of
an earlier age, and still rang at times for such festivities during
the Third Reich. But this would have meant the intrusion of
the Christian into what were basically Volkish ceremonies.
Even here the parallel was by no means entirely abandoned,
though. The Nuremberg Hall of Congresses, modeled on the
Colosseum, was to contain a huge organ.[16] And the smaller
Volkish cult halls in factories, for example, retained the full
appearance of a church—apse, benches, and even the space
around the altar.

Hitler's conservative taste determined all his attitudes toward life. This fact helps to explain his attachment to social
traditions and the Volkish mystique. Middle-class morality
and the ancient personal bonds of family and tribe had to be
restored, not to that morality which the ancient Germans had

practiced in their forests, but to the bourgeois morality of the nineteenth century—the sanctity of family, of marriage, and of the unostentatious, dedicated life. The same period which determined his architectural taste also fixed his views of morality. Albert Speer has written that Hitler's intellectual formation stopped with the world between 1880 and 1910.[17] He believed that the rifles he had used during the First World War were good enough for soldiers two decades later. Gerdy Troost, widow of the architect, thought that as far as painting was concerned Hitler had stopped at 1890.[18] This was also true. The painters he liked and protected belonged to the school of sentimental realism, and the official art journal of the Reich pointed to the romantic painters Caspar David Friedrich, Hans Makart, and Hans von Marés as exemplary German artists.[19]

These models, then, were not those of the ancient Germans whose valor was so often invoked by the party. For Hitler, German art was the art and architecture which combined classical and romantic forms. Small wonder that he despised imitations of supposed ancient Germanic traditions. Hitler's definition of what was truly German meant an acceptance of the artistic forms that had also informed the national cult in the nineteenth century. The synthesis of the classical and the romantic which we have discussed earlier conformed to his definition. He was delighted when he found out that Wilhelm Kreis was still alive,[20] and a few years later he entrusted him with the building of cemeteries and memorials to the fallen of the Second World War. Kreis's ideal of the romantic landscape and his retention of classical models must have appealed to him, apparently even before he met the architect. Hitler also showed respect for architects like Gottfried Semper and Bruno Schmitz, that prolific builder of national monuments that were classical, pyramidal, and included sacred spaces.[21]

The romantic and the classic determined the traditional self-representation of the nation. Modernity was rejected; "beauty" was defined, once more, against industrial and bour-

geois civilization. Vischer's aesthetic principles remained intact, for which the worship of the landscape in Nazi art is a
good example. Such a landscape had to be "immediate" for the
beholder, had to bring out in him the unchanging ideal of
beauty. Man must, through such contemplation, revive the
wellsprings of his being, which had been obscured by the
degeneration of modern art. Beauty was "genuine," but it
could not be chaos. A principle of order was an essential part
of the beautiful: "Our time requires a monumental heightening" of such contemplation, "which derives from a will to
order." Once more, as in the past, such a will means "restfulness."[22] The unrest of the spirit must be calmed by architectural and artistic form, by the combination of materials such
as stone, wood, and metal. Hitler and the Nazis never objected
to the use of the most modern technology, but it had to be
harnessed in the service of a concept of beauty which, in
Winckelmann's words (already quoted earlier), was like the
still surface of the ocean, smooth as a mirror although constantly in motion.[23]

Beauty also provided a principle of order. As Hitler put it:
"The nervous nineteenth century has come to an end."[24] For
Nazis, nervousness was a sign of "degeneration," a term which
they took from Max Nordau's famous book. His *Degeneration*
(*Entartung*, 1892) had also emphasized restfulness and clarity
as opposed to modernity as the principle of art. The style
which found Hitler's favor embodied this ideal of beauty and
order. Romanticism was tamed in this manner, as it had been
integrated with classical forms throughout the development of
the national cult.

Further, the modern and the industrial were not to intrude.
The paintings at the first exhibition of German art in Munich
in 1937, which Hitler had personally approved, were, for the
most part, landscapes or peasant scenes,[25] while the sculptures
exemplified the "ideal German type," of classical extraction.
The film *Youth Goes to the Führer* (1939), depicting Hitler
youth from all over Germany marching to Nuremberg, is a

remarkable document; the camera follows Hitler youth groups throughout their march from every part of the Reich. The Germany pictured is one of landscapes, villages, and small towns. Not a factory is seen, not a housing project, no modern machinery. The film portrays a Germany free of industrialization and modernity, as underdeveloped as the most backward regions of the Third World. Nevertheless, it is a Germany where order and immaculate cleanliness reign. Warm family scenes exhibit the proper morality, and the place of women in the Nazi world is clearly reproduced throughout the film; girls appear only once for a few seconds as partners in a folk dance.

This film typified a world of illusion made real through the national cult and its liturgy. In Hitler's own mind this perception of reality co-existed with pragmatic political attitudes. He believed, for example, that national rites should take place in the center of the otherwise despised city, and not on its periphery. He may have had the example of the Roman Forum in mind.[26] That is partly why he had a low opinion of *Thing* theatres, being set off by themselves, far from the concentration of the population. The party forums planned for Munich, Augsburg, or Linz were to be in the center of the city. Moreover, Hitler showed great interest in town planning. The monumental rebuilding of Berlin destined for the post war period was to take place within the city confines. No special party town was planned or even considered. Surely there is a contradiction between this preoccupation with city planning and the rural Germany shown through the eyes of the Hitler youth.

Politics dictated that party ceremonial be easily accessible to all, which meant the necessity of staging it in town rather than in the countryside. The very physiognomy of a city was created by the needs of the party. Hitler accepted urbanism and tried to bend it to his own ends; even here he was both consummate politician and conservative. Cult and liturgy were anchored in an existent reality, however degenerate the city was considered to be.

Conservative attitudes, combined with appreciation of political realities, did not exclude a very strong appeal to the senses. Hitler admired Bayreuth's festival hall, and shared Wagner's theory of the theatre. Illusion, for Hitler too, led to a higher reality springing from the inspiration of myth and symbol. The *Mythos* had to be carried to the people in this manner. Benno von Arendt, Hitler's official stage designer for the Reich, has explained what was involved here: stage design can never have a purpose of its own and must not be used for experimentation. The public would dislike such manipulation, which would get in the way of the illusions created and the dreams fulfilled.[27] Richard Wagner had held similar ideas about the staging of his operas, and indeed Hitler actually designed two settings for *Tristan und Isolde* which exemplified these principles.[28] A further experience of Hitler's Viennese youth, this time the stage settings of Alfred Roller, whom he continued to praise even during the Second World War, was basic to these designs.

Alfred Roller (1864–1935) had been Gustav Mahler's stage designer at the Viennese opera, but had also worked for the Burgtheater, as he was later to design scenery for Max Reinhardt. He was a sworn enemy of surplus decoration; his scenery conveyed pure mood and came close to Impressionism. Roller attempted to create a "frame" for the action: "Decoration must never be a purpose in itself . . . it exists to convey a mood as soon as the curtain rises."[29] In 1903, Roller designed the scenery for a performance of *Tristan und Isolde*, thus giving Hitler a model for his own later sketch. Roller's emphasis utilized the concept of illusion which Benno von Arendt described. He also liked to work with thick fog, fragments of cloud, rain, and sighing winds.[30] A romantic mood was combined with simplicity of design; once more, harmony of form was linked to emotion. Hans Severus Ziegler, who

directed Hitler's favorite theatre at Weimar, called such stage
designing "poetically transformed realism,"[31] a description
that could in fact fit the entire national cult. The function of
theatre, the Nazis' leading playwright, Hanns Johst, tells us in
*Ich Glaube!* (*I Believe!*, 1928) is to renew a community of
faith. This community is formed through an ethos which contains the irrationality of the masses within a tangible form.[32]
Hitler saw the theatre and its function in a similar light, and so
the impressiveness of the general *mis-en-scène* as he tried to
convey it in his sketches included careful stage design.

Roller also made new use of lighting. He understood how
"lighting changed forms, heightened them, dissolved them and
turned them into fairy tale magic."[33] Did Hitler get his ideas
about the use of light in his ceremonies from this source? We
cannot know. But, as we have seen, the effect of light on space
was also a principle of the modern dance. Here, increasingly,
popular stage effects were used in conjunction with that new
art form to illustrate the importance of the uses of light in the
formation of space.[34] It was only logical to co-opt this form
for mass meetings and rites. Hitler himself believed that festivals ideally should take place only with the arrival of darkness,
for then men's senses were wide open to influence.[35] But this
statement, both romantic and pragmatic, also left room for the
startling use of lighting effects as we witness them in most
Nazi ceremonials.

For Hitler the opera was *the* great spectacle—the illusion of
the stage and the magic of the music, but also the ceremonial
which surrounded it and which was captured in his own designs: ". . . never shall I forget the gracious spectacle of the
Vienna Opera, the women sparkling with diadems and fine
clothes."[36] This was the theatre of his youth, just as for him
the architecture of his youth symbolized true self-representation, and the art of 1890 proper artistic creativity. Such taste
was directly transferred to the liturgy of the Third Reich and
made to symbolize romanticism and order, classical harmony
and worship. Quite naturally, Hitler's taste coincided with the

development of the national cult. To be sure, he adopted new features which had become prevalent in the 1920's: speaking choruses, massed flags, lighting effects. But the basic conservatism remained.

This was a great advantage. It made Hitler appreciate the permanence of liturgical forms with which, as a Catholic (even though a nonpracticing one), he was familiar. Changes in liturgy are always dangerous, for they may lead to disorientation and thus to lessened effectiveness. Martin Luther had already understood this fact clearly, and was therefore agonizingly slow in changing any liturgical form. We have already discussed the failure to impose festivals from above during the Second Reich and the Weimar Republic. The traditional world of myth and symbol cannot be manipulated except with great care, for it involves the ways in which men objectify their world. The myth has to symbolize an eternal, healthy, and moral universe.

Nazi art and literature was generally popular, for the reasons just discussed. We know that the paintings at exhibitions of German art sold rapidly and without any party pressure;[37] people liked what they stood for. Similarly, the literature produced under the Third Reich was widely popular because it, too, symbolized a healthy world which offered the illusion of permanence. Hitler's tastes have been called primitive, and so they were from the point of view of sophisticated intellectuals, but they were singularly in tune with longstanding popular ideals. He was himself a part of his own definition of artistic creativity: "And therefore, speaking of German art, I shall see the standard for that art in the German people, in its character and life, in its feeling, its emotion, and its development."[38] When Josef Goebbels abolished art criticism and left the people themselves to pass judgment, he did not have a great deal to fear. Hitler's own conservatism was perfectly suited to popular taste. As this conservatism also determined the national cult, we can understand its widespread popularity. Nazi ceremonial was built upon a tradition which had made such a form possible in the first place, but it also captured the taste of a population living in a complex industrial society.

Popular taste had remained largely unchanged, certainly from the 1870's onwards. The novels read by the millions are a good example of this, and their basic content hardly varies from Marlitt at the end of the nineteenth century to Hedwig Courths-Mahler in the twentieth. Such works always presented a healthy world of sentiment and order. The virtuous won all battles, rejecting external riches and power for the proper working of a "golden heart." Wish fulfillment always operated within the confines of such a romantic yet ordered universe, "where everything is in its proper place and one is immediately at home."[39] This was Hitler's world as well—the private universe which Albert Speer in his memoirs has described so well, and the public universe of ritual and symbol.

Hitler once said that the writer Karl May had opened his eyes to the world. May, whose novels sold seven and a half million copies between 1892 and 1938, wrote adventure stories which all took place either among the American Indians or in the Orient. His heroes were dedicated to law and order, yet were open to a world of beauty and respected the dignity of man. Hitler was attracted to the bourgeois morality which pervaded Wilhelminian Germany. He praised Karl May's heroes for their ability to attain decency through the mastery of their own drives.[40] The virtues that May's—and Hitler's—heroes wanted to protect and defend were those associated with a healthy bourgeois world: order, morality, and the "pure heart." But Hitler never lost his Manichaean world view, and omitted from his acceptance of Karl May the hero's distaste for violence. May and other popular novelists such as Marlitt or Courths-Mahler had deplored a ruthless use of power, which seemed to them generally opposed to sentimentality and a danger to a moral, ordered universe. But Hitler thought otherwise, influenced by the kind of racism he had learned in his Viennese youth.

This racism was violent and brutal, the racism associated with a small sect around Lanz von Liebenfels and Guido List. These men had no job or position, but devoted themselves exclusively to advocating a mixture of racism and theosophy. Through their "philosophy," the Aryan became a manifestation of the cosmos, whose soul could read the book of nature. For List, Christianity had wiped out the true "nature wisdom" of the ancient Germans, thus destroying the genuine life force which descended from the cosmos to the Volk. This life force, then, was not transmitted by a plastic ether, as the theosophists thought, but instead by the Aryan life force. Moreover, as the sun was the center of the universe, the Aryans were sun people. Lanz von Liebenfels published a journal, *Ostara* (named after a German goddess), subtitled "Library of Those Who Are Blond and Defend the Rights of the Male," and it is most likely that Hitler read this production.[41] *Ostara*, List, and their circle advocated war between the blond and dark-haired peoples, between the Aryan and, particularly, the Jew. According to this group, subhuman racial elements were tyrannizing the world and preventing "true wisdom" from breaking through. St. Paul, the Jew, had perverted Christianity, for Christ Himself spoke the secret language of Aryans.[42] The Aryans were the only race who could fathom the mysteries of the universe.

Here in Vienna Hitler received an important part of his political education, and he combined it with his admiration for the morality and aesthetic of the bourgeois world of the *fin de siècle*. The rite of national worship was part of that public world. The occult and racial became Hitler's private, intimate world, which he took good care to hide from the public eye, or at least kept respectable in public. His Manichaeanism centered on Aryan versus Jew, but this did not penetrate into the liturgy except as the worship of the Aryan stereotype and the attacks upon Jews in the speeches. The stereotype was always present, in the sculptures and paintings, and in the use of lighting to get rid of the fat stomachs of the leaders taking part in meetings and processions.[43] It was part of the "positive," which had to be stressed in liturgical rites and in all self-representation. The "negative," the Jewish stereotype, was never represented in the ceremonial and its symbols, but was spread outside the cult in newspapers and pamphlets. The Jewish stereotype which was thought to typify ugliness could not be allowed to disturb the beauty which informed national worship.

Hitler's belief in occult forces no doubt deepened his view of the world as a battlefield between virtue and vice. There seems little doubt that he saw his National Socialist revolution in these terms. Activism was needed to overthrow the evil existing order, but it had to be in the name of restoring the healthy past. Hitler's revolution was a "displaced revolution": no fundamental social and economic change was involved; rather, it was to create a world restored, reviving true morality, the traditional force which bound men together. The enemy was not a class, but the Jew, who symbolized the evil principle of modernity. Hitler's anti-Jewish revolution was supposed to produce the "positive" world which the national liturgy exemplified. This is why he constantly sought to restrain the activism which he needed to accomplish his purposes. But the tension between activism and the principle of harmony and order was implicit, not only in the problems faced by the party, but in Hitler's own personality as well. The Jew as the enemy was an occult force which had to be fought by all means possible, culminating in open war, though always in the name of order.

Hitler saw the need for such activism in terms of a "fanatic faith." For, "the greatest revolutions in the world would have been impossible if, instead of fanatical, even hysterical, passions, their moving force had been the bourgeois virtues of law and order."[44] These words of 1924 might contradict what we have said about Hitler's admiration for the law-and-order architecture of the *fin de siècle* and his belief in Wilhelminian morality. But he did not strive merely for one or the other ideal; he wanted rather to infuse bourgeois virtues and taste with the fire of a chauvinistic faith. This was that "depth of belief" to which he referred so often. Both the conventional and the occult were necessary correlates in the formation of Hitler's thought.

His most private thought often turned to a nature mysticism close to theosophy. In the late 1920's, he discussed at some length the supposed fact that the magical forces of nature break through in man's dreams, though his culture has falsely sublimated them. Knowledge must, once again, take on the characteristics of a "secret science." As he said during the years of crisis in 1932 to 1934, "Only when knowledge assumes once again the character of a secret science, and is not [the property] of everyone, will it assume once more its usual function, namely, as an instrument of domination, of human nature as well as that which stands outside man."[45] Hitler kept this "secret science" to himself or, at most, discussed it with his intimates. It penetrates his public utterances only in characterizing the demonical force of the Jew, and by no means disturbs the restfulness of the positive symbols of faith.

Such ideas may represent his continued longing for tradition, for the "genuine" as symbolized by the landscape and by the Volk. But this concept of the Volk seems related to the myths of German antiquity and racism, rather than to the classics which informed Hitler's taste. Yet even here he fused these divergent traditions. For example, Hitler believed that Hermann, who defeated the Roman Legions, foreshadowed the unification of Germany though he was, in reality, a disciple of Rome. Indeed, German pre-history was based on Greece and Rome.[46] Thus the myth was kept intact, and with it Hitler's faith both racist and occult, while neo-classicism remained basic and determined the outward form.

Hitler preferred music drama to word drama, and there is ample evidence to sustain this preference. He also preferred the spoken to the written word. What, then, was the relationship between the speeches and the liturgical drama? In any fully formed cult the speech is merely an integral part of the proceedings, a part of the ritual. Hitler's speeches, on the other hand, contained more than just slogans or repetitions; they were very often progammatical. While local leaders were directed to speak no longer than fifteen minutes at their meetings so as not to interfere with the ceremonial,[47] Hitler's own speeches went on for a much longer period of time. They were, in fact, the focal point of the meeting, around which much of the popular participation took place. Nevertheless, they integrated themselves with the total setting and the liturgical rhythm much in the same way as famous preachers functioned in the churches of the Baroque.

This integration was formalized in one ceremony where Hitler marched as part of the masses and emerged only to give his speech.[48] During one of Hitler's most important speeches in February 1933, the film made of the event concentrated, with few exceptions, upon the crowds rather than upon the leader.[49] Albert Speer, who should know, tells us that it was Hitler's aim to restrict the impact of a single personality upon the ritual, be it the head of state or any other leader (Plate 16). The ceremony itself had to have an independent life. Hitler, in his vanity, could not conceive that his successor might possess his own magic. Therefore, the ritual had to predominate, for in this case it would matter little if the future Führer was a "small scoundrel." He would still be carried along by the national rite.[50] Hitler implied that the liturgy, together with its setting, would be able to continue the political system. That is why he designated certain rites as "final," the ceremony for fallen heroes, or the march of the Hitler youth at Nuremberg, and others as merely "provisional."[51] This principle of liturgical autonomy did not always work in practice. Nevertheless, in Hitler's own mind, the confrontation of leader and Volk must never degenerate into a personality cult.

The integration of the leader's function with the ceremonial as a whole can also be observed through the very rhythm and construction of the speeches. Hitler always insisted on "clarity," and expressed his delight at having condensed his own world view into twenty-five theses.[52] Clarity, however, also meant a strictness of form which rejected all compromise. His political axiom that "People don't understand handshakes" was translated into his words.[53] He would have fully agreed with D'Annunzio's saying that words are feminine, deeds masculine, and that words must therefore be deeds.[54] His speeches were in fact such deeds, through the words he used, the rhetorical questions, the unambiguous statements. Moreover, they had an undeviating rhythm in which the people could join through exclamations.

These rhythms were militant, aggressive, and, particularly, required a very impressive tone of voice. Hitler himself had written that speeches open the gates to the heart of the Volk like blows from a hammer.[55] The speeches were often logically constructed, but the inner logic was disguised by the rhythm and activity of the voice. The audience thus experienced the logic in the speeches emotionally; they felt only the militancy and the faith, without grasping the real content or reflecting on its meaning. The crowd was captured by the prose itself, they "lived" the speeches rather than examining their content. Structure played an integral part in the entire experience of living the ideology; because of its powerful effects, it was difficult for the audience to establish any critical distance.[56] Though we can now grasp the effect of such speeches through a structural analysis, Hitler himself was not deliberate or even conscious of their structure. He dictated them under great stress, spontaneously and with great rapidity (two secretaries were always needed for the dictation).[57] This manner of working must have heightened their ritualistic effect, for here Hitler was himself and clearly demonstrated the faith he shared with his audience. His public speeches took on much the same form as those of Mussolini, if in a different liturgical setting.

Hitler's speeches were thus actions, an integral part of the dramatization of the rite of national self-representation; they were not didactic, as were those of so many liberals and Socialists. Moreover, they were clear expressions of a shared faith. Hitler was greatly influenced by Gustave Le Bon,[58] and followed the dictum in *La Psychologie des Foules* that the leader must be an integral part of a shared faith, that he cannot experiment or innovate. His own experimentation and innovation consisted only in heightening the meaning of what was already widely accepted, in introducing a Manicheanism which transformed his words into deeds.

The speech as a mere symbol among other symbols is best illustrated by the local Nazi rites. There the emphasis was on short appeals and confessions of faith rather than upon formal speeches by the leader. Within such ceremonies the leader was merely giving voice to the feeling of community. Though Hitler performed this function as well, his own role was of greater importance. For he was himself a living symbol who could commune with other symbols as when, in lonely eminence, he walked to the eternal flame at the Nuremberg rallies. But as a symbol, he formed part of an ensemble, and did not stand in lonely eminence outside it, as earlier leaders like Ferdinand Lasalle or Karl Lueger had done. The *Aufmarsch*, the studied movements of the crowd, the flame, the lighting effects, and Hitler's speeches formed one dramatic totality (see Plate 17). Hitler, indeed, arranged his public and even his private life around himself as a living symbol.

His very uniform, unambiguous and plain, characterized the simplicity and clarity that any symbol must have, even when realized in a human being. The decorations he wore were straightforward: the brown shirt, the swastika, and, when he made himself commander-in-chief of the army, the cluster of oak leaves. He was not supposed to have a private life at all, nor would it do for a symbol to appear as a paterfamilias. This would have been frivolous in terms of the national cult, reminiscent of the mixture of socializing and ceremonial of Wilhelminian times. Seriousness was demanded of any cult; Rousseau had already advocated public festivals as necessary to draw people away from spectacles and light amusement.[59] The morality of the bourgeois was advocated, but in public life no embourgeoisement could be shown, for it could be easily confused with *Gemütlichkeit*. Moreover, a Führer living an ordinary life, surrounded by his family, would have run counter to the party's image as a society of men (*Männerbund*), an image which had been present ever since its founding.[60] The maintenance of virility and masculinity was a crucial element in the positivism of the symbols. Hitler had naturally read Otto Weininger's *Geschlecht und Charakter* (*Sex and Character*, 1903), in which the sun is exalted as masculine, while the feminine is merely its pale reflection.[61] The transformation of a human being into a symbol was very effective. At times, popular imagination changed the swarthy, dark Hitler into the ideal type, and we find an astounding number of assertions that the Führer was blond and blue-eyed.[62] The dream had, in this case, become the reality.

The world of dream and illusion could capture millions through its objectification by the liturgy, but it did not stand in isolation. The pragmatic side came to the fore in *Mein Kampf* which was, after all, devoted half to ideology and half to organization. Nazi liturgy was based upon the total organization of life: everyone was supposed to belong to one of the innumerable groups controlled by the party. These provided a framework for directed activity, not excluding social life. To be sure, "*Weihestunden*" ("hours of worship") were a part of these groups, especially those concerned with youth. But other kinds of activity dominated. When Hitler talked about the realization of his world view, he meant by this not only ceremonial or meetings, but also the organization of the "whole man" under party auspices. Such thoroughness was possible only once the Nazis assumed power, though on the road to power it had already been applied to party members.

This underpinning was crucial when the revolutionary National Socialists became the Establishment and faced problems similar to those of the Second Reich. Perhaps these were even more acute in a movement which depended on a dynamic. Weariness with the liturgy had already expressed itself before 1933, and it was certainly present after that date. We have evidence for this from Protestant Hannover and the Catholic Rhineland. Officials complained of "tiredness and passivity" as early as 1933. All the meetings, the ceremonial, the cultural evenings, the Christmas festivals of the party, had been "too much of a good thing."[63] The party had been tempted to fall into a "Hurrapatriotismus"—a blatant patriotism in the Wilhelminian manner, a formalism which ignored the potential impetus of the cult. Nevertheless when, as late as 1943, the party started a major political action to reactivate popular enthusiasm, the devices which we have analyzed were again given first place. In Trier alone there were two mass meetings with 9,200 participants, seventy-one public meetings with 20,000 people, hours of worship, and an *Aufmarsch* of the Hitler youth.[64]

Organization and liturgy became part of the seasonal rhythm which filled the year. Hitler promulgated a law of festivals which fixed the dates of their celebration. The Nazi reckoning of time was supposed to displace the Christian year, but the Christian rhythm was kept intact. The festival of fallen heroes, summer solstice, the Day of Work, and others were in some Nazi calendars mixed in with the traditional Christian festivities of Pentecost and the ascension of the Virgin Mary.[65] But by and large the Nazi year received its own rhythm in which everyone was supposed to participate, attending hours of worship or flagging their homes. The chronicler of the City of Herne during National Socialism described this calendar well: a cycle of festivities was arranged which was always being repeated. And the racial experts of the party spoke reverently about renewing the myth. The traditional festivals had to take a back seat. Christmas developed into the feast of the winter solstice. The Hitler youth no longer sang Christmas carols, but "High Night of Clear Skies."[66]

There was an attempt, especially in schools and party organizations, to build festivals into the daily routine, hoisting the flag as well as morning and evening devotions. Classes in a Düsseldorf high school during 1935–36 were interrupted nineteen times by Nazi festivals and ceremonial.[67] Festivals as cultic rites were, in this manner, built into the organizations and daily life. Hitler did not make any clear distinction between the pragmatic needs for organization and the rites of worship. The national cult had penetrated his thought as a political necessity which would serve to make the world whole again. When Mussolini said that politics must be like art, he meant that political decisions must be informed by the creativity of the artist, and did not have a political liturgy in mind.[68] But Hitler considered himself an artist; his mind was visual rather than literary. Mussolini was not interested in so-called degenerate art, nor was he opposed to artistic experimentation. Hitler, as his speeches on culture show, considered art as symbolic of life and politics. That is why his taste is so important—indeed, decisive in Nazi politics. Political style was identical with a secular religion, founded on a particular concept of beauty and expressed through liturgical form.

The cult of nationalism had found a committed supporter. Nazi liturgy repeated in essence all the various forms that we have discussed: processions comparable to those which the various associations had practiced at their festivals, such as the one which paraded in front of Hitler with its floats at the opening of the House of Art; *Aufmärsche*, speaking choruses, silent marches, confessions of faith, choruses of movement. The *mis-en-scène* remained familiar—the sacred space, the buildings surrounding it, lighting effects, and flags as well as flames. The slogan, "No spectators, only actors," was put into practice both through the creation of an atmosphere of shared worship and through active participation. At times such worship was reminiscent of the popular excesses of medieval Christianity. In 1933, for example, the City of Düsseldorf created a veritable cult of relics around Albert Leo Schlageter, who had been executed for supposed sabotage by the French during their occupation of the Ruhr Valley. The bed in which he had slept was reconstructed and Hitler was presented with a silver reliquary which contained the bullet said to have pierced his heart.[69] The veneration of relics was not to last, however, for the ever-present "flag of martyrs" offered a more acceptable symbol.

But even the "hours of worship" became ever more elaborate in their symbolism, at times reaching an exaggerated form similar to the worship of relics. The Nazi substitute for baptism, "consecrating the name," was held in a special room in the center of which stood an altar. Hitler's picture replaced that of Christ on the altar, and three SS men stood behind it, symbolizing by their very presence the new type of man the régime was supposed to produce. The altar was flanked by vessels holding fires and "trees of life."[70] This ceremony summarizes much of the symbolism whose development we have covered—the ideal type of beauty objectified in the human form, the sacred flame, and the symbol of the tree.[71] Hitler's picture was an integral part of this symbolism, as was his person throughout the Third Reich. Only a reliquary is missing to complete the analogy between the Christian and the secular religion. The ceremony shows how far the party had moved from earlier times when, at some meetings, a simple band playing marches had sufficed to keep the crowd in the proper mood.

The rhythm of national worship served to define politics as a democratic faith meant to penetrate all human activity. Hitler's taste not only heightened every aspect of the national cult; it also, through his conservatism, integrated itself with this historical development as it had grown for nearly a century before his birth.

# CHAPTER NINE

# The Political Cult

IT WAS Hitler's strongest belief that the education of the masses to nationalism could only take place through "social uplift," meaning that the people would partake of the cultural benefits of the nation, and that a new human type would be created through the correct cultural environment based upon the Aryan race.[1] The political cult exemplified this environment, and called itself the true self-representation of the people. But the Nazi mass meetings as we see them in films or pictures today have lost their force: the flames on the sides of the Nuremberg stadium, the huge overwhelming flags, the marches and speaking choruses, present a spectacle to modern audiences not unlike those American musicals of the 1920's and 1930's which Hitler himself was so fond of watching each evening. It was not always so. For participants, it was the symbolic content which took priority, the ritual expression of a shared worship that was so crucial to their sense of belonging. A written description or even a view of these ceremonials cannot capture the uplift which came from actual participation. Mass ceremonial, public festivals, and the "hours of worship" provided by the party were the concise realization of a new political religion.

This "new" politics, as we have called it, did adapt much of the traditional Christian liturgy, and it also went back into pagan times for some of its associations. Moreover, classical influence was of crucial importance; indeed, the ideals of beauty and form were dominated by it.

We return again to the Christian liturgical forms—of prime importance in determining the whole secular cult—for the concept and use of space. The idea of the "sacred space," a place which could be filled only with symbolic activity, dates back to primitive times and pagan worship, later taken over by Christians. Such space was considered, throughout history, as a necessary prerequisite to liturgical action. The new politics can be regarded as one successful way in which this sacred space was filled: with parades, marches, gymnastic exercises, and dances, as well as ritual speeches. Adopted and used in Germany from the celebration of the Battle of Leipzig in 1815 to the Nuremberg party rallies, this kind of space had to be clearly defined and distinct from its surroundings. The attempt to provide this runs from the "festival meadow" on which the gymnasts first performed outside Berlin, through the siting of national monuments, to Hitler's Great Hall (Plate 19). Whatever the change in content or differing conceptions of politics, we are confronted with a consistent development of the whole nationalist liturgy which makes the new politics basic to modern history.

But the form and content of the new politics only partially explain its success. The longing for national unity, for the kind of community this politics represented, was linked to the social factors of the age. Too little is known about them. However, it seems clear that the perimeter of the new politics cannot be confined to those fringe classes which at the grassroots level are sometimes said to provide the dynamic of the European right: marginal farmers, small shopkeepers, self-employed artisans, underemployed professionals, white-collar workers, and underpaid civil servants. Nor was it limited to those who depended for survival and advancement upon government subsidies, tariffs, and contrasts.[2] Indeed, the formation of a right transcended these classes in most parts of Europe. France, for example, contained at the turn of the nineteenth and twentieth centuries a large working-class movement which was directed by the political right.[3] We cannot accept the presupposition that the very alienation of the proletariat kept it from meaningful involvement with the counterrevolution. From this point of view, a great many European workers showed a misguided consciousness. The dynamics of the right were never as marginal as those classes upon which it was wrongly said to be based.

We have shown that the workers were also drawn into the new politics; that these politics were in fact largely (but not always) cross-class, and the ideal of national unification was spread downward, the lower classes being drawn into it, for example, through their sports organizations and male choirs. Just how many were drawn in is impossible to say. We do know that their numbers were not small, though they did not encompass the majority of the working class. Eventually, to be sure, workers were underrepresented in the Nazi Party. In 1930 they comprised some 21 per cent of the membership.[4] But of greater significance than electoral statistics is the fact that toward the end of the Weimar Republic the Socialist parties themselves were forced to take the nationalist atmosphere into account.

The Communists now actively competed with the right for nationalist votes, and even the Social Democratic Party saw itself forced to make concessions to the prevailing nationalist and anti-Semitic atmosphere. The key factor in this situation was the ability of the National Socialists to force even their enemies to argue from within a framework which they themselves had created.[5] That the Nazis so successfully defined the terrain of political debate shows not only their own success in making themselves felt but also the magnetism of a nationalist appeal. Surely, the tradition behind the new politics had contributed to this depth; we have seen how in their own ceremonial the workers, in 1925, anchored the Republic which they supported in the blond Germanic past.

For all that, we can still hold that the masses "remained mute, uncomprehending witnesses to the great achievements of the age of élite politics,"[6] especially during the process of

German unification. Such a statement, however, need not imply a denial that the new politics provided a meaningful involvement for many of these "mute" masses. They did not affect the immediate course of German politics; that was directed by men like Bismarck or Hitler. But they also simply could not be ignored. As such, the new politics did crystallize what is sometimes vaguely called public opinion, usually conveyed only through discussion of what the newspapers printed, though these of course were always controlled by individuals or small groups. Through the new politics many people were formed in this way into an organized political force which certainly expressed their shared longings for order, happiness, and national unity.

In the search for social origins we must not forget the attraction of the spiritual dimension. Men's isolation was heightened by industrial society, but this did not mean that its outlets had to be logically determined by the social and economic factors which produced it. The formalization of emotions was as important for the nineteenth and twentieth centuries as it was for the fifteenth century when, according to Huizinga, "having attributed a real existence to an idea the mind wants to see it alive, and can effect this only by personalizing it."[7] Throughout history, the mere presence of a visible image of things holy has served to establish its truth to believers. The apparently cross-class attraction of the new politics, though it varied in content, might be explained by such permanent and timeless longings. "Mythical symbolism leads to an objectification of feelings; myth objectifies and organizes human hopes and fears and metamorphosizes them into persistent and durable works."[8]

Such works were the essence of the new political style. Anthropology can be useful here; in a sense, national monuments were the totem poles of the nineteenth and twentieth centuries. Claude Lévi-Strauss was no doubt correct when he asserted that the great manifestations of society originate at the level of unconscious existence.[9] Men do form such manifestations—which are themselves only a further, though physical, abstraction of an idea—into a system which explains the world and promises to solve its dilemmas. Form is imposed upon and informs content. Myth and symbol become an explanation for social life, a fact which functionally does not, however, rob life itself of importance. The "objective reality," as Marx would have called it, provides the setting and defines the limitations within which myth and symbols can operate. The actual political situation of Germany was in fact crucial in determining the content of myth and symbol and its linkage to nationalism. The workers' movement, while accepting much of the form of the new politics and even some of the nationalism involved, infused it with concepts of freedom which were directly relevant to the condition of the proletariat.

But in spite of the changing content, the form and the basic presuppositions remained intact: the longing for a healthy and happy world, and for a true community exemplified by the aesthetics of politics in which all could join. What Lévi-Strauss calls the "cosmic rhythm," which possesses mankind from the earliest times onward,[10] we would define in a more pedestrian manner as the desire for permanence and fixed reference points in a changing world.

In the age of growing mass movements, the new politics became one way of organizing the masses, of turning a chaotic crowd into a mass movement. This was not just a movement of protest reacting to specific grievances, such as the bread and food riots during the French Revolution—though some of these did become political demonstrations with far-reaching aims[11]—but was rather a form of mass politics which appealed to more permanent longings, and which tried to hypostatize these through myth, symbol, and aesthetic politics. The new political style attempted to take the place of mediating institutions such as representative parliamentary government which link governors and governed.

It is no coincidence that Benito Mussolini spoke of the

myths and rites which every revolution needs, and in the same breath likened the crowd to a herd of sheep until it is organized.[12] But this urge to organize the crowd was a product not only of the reality of mass politics, but also of a preoccupation with history. Friedrich Ludwig Jahn and many others believed that festivals must be spontaneous and not enforced, by which they meant that they must be connected to history and tradition, necessary for expressing permanent and timeless desires in an equally eternal symbolic form. Why did this preoccupation with the historical dimension become so urgent just at the beginning of the nineteenth century?

Time does not move with the same speed in every epoch of history. It speeds up with the improvement of communications and the faster pace of life in an industrializing world. This was the case at the beginning of the nineteenth century. We all have a vague notion that time passes quicker in the city than in the "restful" countryside. How can such a step-up of time avoid chaos? How can permanent forms of art and beauty survive? Goethe considered this problem in the preface to his *Faust*. How can true and lasting poetry, indeed the human imagination, survive when an audience comes into the theatre fresh from reading the fleeting news of the day in their newspapers? Men hurry about absentmindedly; there is no longer any time for concentrated thought.[13] What Goethe castigated between 1790 and 1808 was the new rate of time, of which the newspaper became the symbol throughout the nineteenth century. Those who looked for roots and permanence condemned the newspaper as an evil force opposed to true culture.

Calling to history was one way of organizing time, of coping with its speed. Thus the emphasis upon history was not only necessary for myth and symbol, but also served to preserve order within an ever faster flow of time. The Greek ideal of beauty which Winckelmann had put forward, embedded in history as it was, exemplified the noble simplicity and quiet greatness which contrasted so sharply with the speed and unrest of the present. The new politics reflected the age of mass politics, the new preoccupation with history and with time.

But we must keep our perspective here as well. The age which witnessed the development of the new politics also believed in representative government. Benedetto Croce, as late as 1931, saw the nineteenth century as the great liberal age, and the very period when the new political style received its first trials (1815–30) as the victory of parliamentary government over absolutism.[14] This is, no doubt, how many perceived the age in which they lived.

Moreover, not all Germans desired national unity. There was a considerable body of opinion which believed in the sovereign existence of each separate German state and which condemned the Prussian efforts at national unity. Such men and women have also stood outside the scope of our analysis. German history as a whole cannot be viewed as taken up solely with the quest for national unity; many liberals, conservatives, and even Socialists were preoccupied with other concerns—the economy, social structure, or regional independence. We have here been concerned with only one strand in the history of modern Germany, something which should have been obvious all along but which needs restating because of a tendency to make "absolute" claims by those who attempt to investigate the origins of things.

Liberals, Socialists, Positivists, all had different perceptions of the politics of their time. The perception within the reality which has concerned us seems especially important because of its association with nationalism, mass movements, and eventually National Socialism. The men and movements we have analyzed placed themselves in this nationalist context, regardless of what their social base might have been. Historians have been told lately that they should show less concern with culture and more with the economic aims of individual groups and the actual demands and achievements of movements like nationalism.[15] This is a legitimate approach. But as we hope to have shown, the reality of nationalism and of National Socialism represented itself to many, perhaps most people, through a highly stylized politics, and in this way managed to form them into a movement.

It must also be remembered that cultural experience was a political reality in Central Europe. Hegel's assertion that the universal spirit constitutes the culture of a nation[16] stands within a specific tradition not shared widely in England or in the United States. The spirit, he said, forms the culture, and culture forms the nation. No doubt in Germany this thought reflects the depth of the Pietistic tradition to which we have referred so often, that the "fatherland is within you." This assertion was put forward by men like Arndt and Jahn at the beginning of the nineteenth century and repeated by the playwright Hanns Johst, in his evolution toward National Socialism (1922): "Germany? . . . No one knows where it begins, where it ends. It has no border, O Lord, in this world . . . it exists in one's heart . . . or it will never be found anywhere."[17] Robert Minder has defined this as the German penchant to look behind the scenery and not to appear in front of the curtain.[18] And the Nazi leaders (and Hitler) understood that only through such an attitude could ideas of beauty and of the soul lead to political objectification.

We have been concerned with a cultural phenomenon which cannot be subsumed under the traditional canons of political theory. For it was not constructed as a logical or coherent system that could be understood through a rational analysis of philosophical writings. The phenomenon which has been our concern was a secular religion, the continuation from primitive and Christian times of viewing the world through myth and symbol, acting out one's hopes and fears within ceremonial and liturgical forms.

The new politics filled Germany with national monuments and public festivals, the objectifications of conscious and unconscious wishes in which millions found a home. Again, we are not claiming that the Third Reich could have succeeded without tangible results in ending unemployment and in foreign policy. The liturgy is one crucial factor among others, though in this case, one which can help us see Nazi politics as it saw itself. Whether a liturgy can be regarded as still more basic than social forces depends upon our view of human nature. A belief in man's inherent goodness and rationality, for instance, would view the new politics as mere propaganda and manipulation.

We have tried to demonstrate that certain very profound currents informed the concept of politics in which so many saw an expression of true democracy. Whether many people in and outside Germany continued to attempt this after the end of the Second World War is difficult to ascertain.[19]

To be sure, many of the national monuments and festivals we have discussed eventually lost their appeal. It is doubtful whether most men still associate timeless beauty with any of the national monuments they may visit. We no longer share many of their political and even aesthetic presuppositions. Particular manifestations of the new politics seem to us timebound and out of date.

Despite all of these facts, however, large numbers of people today may still share those basic longings for wholeness and the need to objectify which seem an integral part of humanity. There is, even in our own time, a longing for the totality of life which is closely related to myth and symbol. Politics and life must penetrate each other, and this means that all forms of life become politicized. Literature, art, architecture, and even our environment are seen as symbolic of political attitudes. At times when parliamentary government does not seem to be working well, men are apt to return to the idea of culture as a totality which encompasses politics. Under such circumstances, men do not mind that the pressure of the world may grow heavy upon the literary imagination,[20] stifling artistic creativity and transforming it into political documentation. But what is often condemned as the politicization of all aspects of life is in reality a deep stream of history, which has always condemned pluralism, the division of politics from other aspects of life. When representative government, which symbolizes this division, threatens to break down, men again wish for a fully furnished home where what is beautiful and gives pleasure should not be separated from the useful and the necessary.[21] However removed from a true humanism, the new politics provided one such home.

Past history is always contemporary. The grand spectacle which we have analyzed is not so far removed from our own dilemmas. This book deals with a past which, for most men, seemed to have ended with the Second World War. In reality it is still contemporary history.

# Notes

# Notes

Chapter One. *The New Politics*

1. *Mussolinis Gespräche mit Emil Ludwig* (Berlin, 1932), 72.
2. Karlheinz Schmeer, *Die Regie des Öffentlichen Lebens im Dritten Reich* (Munich, 1956), 16, 62–63, 48ff.
3. *Oeuvres Complètes de J. J. Rousseau* (Paris, 1907), Vol. 5, 43.
4. George L. Mosse, "The Heritage of Socialist Humanism," *The Legacy of the German Refugee Intellectuals*, ed. Robert Boyers (New York, 1972), 127–128.
5. Alfred Kantorowicz, *Exil in Frankreich* (Bremen, 1971), 67.
6. George L. Mosse, "Three Faces of Fascism by Ernst Nolte," *Journal of the History of Ideas* (October–December 1966), Vol. XXVII, 621–626.
7. Georg Gottfried Gervinus, *Einleitung in die Geschichte des Neunzehnten Jahrhunderts* (Frankfurt am Main, 1967), 162; first published 1855. Michael D. Biddiss, *Father of Racist Ideology* (London, 1970), 171.
8. George Rudé, *The Crowd in History; A Study of Popular Disturbances in France and England, 1730–1848* (New York, 1964).
9. Friedrich Nietzsche, "Die Geburt der Tragödie aus dem Geiste der Musik," *Nietzsche's Werke* (Leipzig, 1899), Vol. I, 159–165; Theodore Ziolkowski, "Der Hunger nach dem Mythos," *Die Sogennannten Zwanziger Jahre*, ed. Reinhold Grimm and Johst Hermand (Bad Homburg, V.D.H., 1970), 169–201.
10. J. Huizinga, *The Waning of the Middle Ages* (London, 1924), 186.
11. *Ibid.*, 165.
12. Gershom Scholem, *The Messianic Idea in Judaism* (New York, 1971), 257.
13. Quoted in René Gérard, *L'Orient et la Pensée romantique allemande* (Nancy, 1963), 170.
14. Scholem, *op. cit.*, 279.

15. *The Complete Works of Friedrich Nietzsche*, ed. Oscar Levy (Edinburgh and London, 1910), Vol. V, 51–52.

16. Theodor Heuss, *Hitlers Weg* (Stuttgart, 1932), 130.

17. *Ibid.*, 132.

18. See, e.g., Dietrich Strothmann, *Nationalsozialistische Literaturpolitik* (Bonn, 1963), 384; Hildegard Brenner, *Die Kunstpolitik des Nationalsozialismus* (Hamburg, 1963), 112–113.

19. Renzo De Felice, *Le interpretazioni del fascismo* (Bari, 1971), 51ff.

20. Gustave Le Bon, *The Crowd* (New York, 1960), 3.

21. Georges Sorel, *Reflections on Violence* (New York, 1950), 78.

22. Erik H. Erikson, *Young Man Luther* (New York, 1962), 186.

23. See Albert Mathiez, *Les Origines des Cultes Révolutionnaires* (Paris, 1904), 79.

24. *Ibid.*, 61.

25. David Dowd, *Pageant-Master of the Republic; Jacques-Louis David and the French Revolution* (Lincoln, Nebr., 1948), iii.

26. Gerhard Kaiser, *Pietismus und Patriotismus im Literarischen Deutschland* (Wiesbaden, 1961), 41.

27. *Ibid.*, 43.

28. *Ibid.*, 40, 49.

29. E. M. Arndt, *Entwurf einer Teutschen Gesellschaft* (Frankfurt, 1814), 36; Nikolaus Ludwig von Zinzendorf, *Ergänzungsband zu den Hauptschriften*, ed. Erich Beyreuther and Gerhard Meyer (Hildesheim, 1963), Vol. III, 74–75, 266. (The year for these statements is 1738.)

30. William McDougall, *The Group Mind* (New York, 1920), 33, 247.

31. See, e.g., Philippe de Félice, *Foules en Délire, Extases Collectives* (Paris, 1947), passim.

32. Ernst Toller, "Masse-Mensch," *Deutsche Revolutionsdramen*, ed. Reinhold Grimm and Johst Hermand (Hamburg, n.d.), 427.

33. Hans Rothfels, *Bismarck und der Staat* (Stuttgart, 1953), xxxix.

## Chapter Two. *The Aesthetics of Politics*

1. Jacques Laurent, *Les Bêtises* (Paris, 1971), 65.

2. Ursula Kirchhoff, *Die Darstellung des Festes in Roman um 1900* (Münster, 1965), 13ff.

3. George L. Mosse, "Was Sie Wirklich Lasen: Marlitt, Gang-

hofer, May," *Popularität und Trivialität* (Bad Bomburg, V..D.H., 1974), 101–120.

4. Friedrich Schiller, *On the Aesthetic Education of Man* (London, 1954), 138. First published in 1795.

5. *Ibid.*, 106.

6. Willi Oelmüller, *Friedrich Theodor Vischer und das Problem der Nachhegelschen Ästhetik* (Stuttgart, 1959), 104–201.

7. *Ibid.*, 175.

8. *Ibid.*, 107.

9. E. Marlitt, *Im Hause des Kommerzienrates* (Leipzig, 1877), 41.

10. J. J. Winckelmann, *Gedanken über die Nachahmung der Griechischen Werke etc.* (Stuttgart, 1885, first published 1755), 7. Albert Speer remarks that this quote guided him as architect. Memorandum to George L. Mosse, April 9, 1973.

11. *Winckelmanns Werke*, ed. Heinrich Meyer and Johann Schulze (Dresden, 1811), Vol. IV, 53, 57.

12. *Ibid.*, 37.

13. Winckelmann, *Gedanken etc.*, 24.

14. *Ibid.*, 24.

15. *Ibid.*, 25.

16. Schiller, *op. cit.*, 81, 106.

17. Winckelmann, *Gedanken etc.*, 21.

18. *The Aesthetic and Miscellaneous Works of Friedrich Schlegel* (London, 1860), 414, 424.

19. *Winckelmanns Werke*, IV, 182–183.

20. *Ibid.*, 39–40, 46, 49.

21. See George L. Mosse, "Racismo," *Encyclopedia del Novocento* (Rome, 1975).

22. Friedrich Ludwig Jahn and Ernst Eiselen, *Die Deutsche Turnkunst* (Berlin, 1816), xvii, 236. Jahn believed that the Germans were the Volk closest to the Greeks, *Deutsches Volkstum* (Leipzig, n.d.), 106.

23. Conversation with Albert Speer, March 16, 1972.

24. *Ibid.*; "Albert Speer spricht über Architektur und Dramaturgie der nationalsozialistischen Selbstdarstellung," Script, Institut für den Wissenschaftlichen Film, Göttingen, 1970, 27.

25. Goethe, *Italienische Reise* (Munich, 1961), 27.

26. Arthur Moeller van den Bruck, *Der Preussische Stil* (Munich, 1916), 130, 131.

27. *Die Kunst im Dritten Reich* (March 1939), 82, 83.

28. Quoted in Armand Dehlinger, *Architektur der Superlative* (unpublished MS, Institut für Zeitgeschichte, Munich), 38.

29. E. M. Arndt, *Entwurf einer Teutschen Gesellschaft* (Frankfurt, 1814), 39; Carl Euler, *Friedrich Ludwig Jahn* (Stuttgart, 1881), 44.

30. *Deutsche Bauzeitung*, Vol. XXIV (1890), 498–499, 496.

31. *Bayreuther Blätter*, Vol. 9 (1886), 369.

32. *Der Kyffhäuser als Nationalfeststätte* (Sondershausen, 1897?), 2, 15.

33. Emil Kaufmann, *Von Ledoux bis Corbusier* (Vienna, 1933), 26.

34. *Kunst und Volk* (July 1936), 240. *Kunst in Dritten Reich* (February 1939), 76.

35. Elisabeth Frenzel, *Stoffe der Weltliteratur* (Stuttgart, 1970), 151–154.

36. Hubert Schrade, *Das Deutsche Nationaldenkmal* (Munich, 1934), 93. Heinrich Himmler thought Theodoric's tomb one of the earliest monuments in stone of German history. Josef Ackermann, *Heinrich Himmler als Ideologe* (Göttingen, 1970), 255.

37. Hans Stephan, *Wilhelm Kreis* (Oldenburg, 1944), II, 53.

38. *Ibid.*, 18.

39. Wilhelm Kreis, in *Der Cicerone*, Vol. 3 (1911), 218.

40. *Deutsche Bauzeitung*, Vol. XXXVIII (1903), 198.

41. *Ibid.*, 199.

42. Hitler was delighted to find that Kreis was still alive. Conversation with Albert Speer, March 16, 1972.

43. Ragna Enking, *Der Apis-Altar Johannes Melchior Dinglinger. Ein Beitrag zur Auseinandersetzung des Abendlandes mit dem alten Egypten* (Glückstadt, 1939), 57, 62.

44. Hans Vogel, "Ägyptisierende Baukunst des Klassizismus," *Zeitschrift für Bildende Kunst*, Vol. 62 (1928–29), 164.

45. *Ibid.*, 162, 161.

46. Adolf Max Vogt, *Boullée's Newton Denkmal: Sakralbau und Kugelidee* (Basel and Stuttgart, 1969), 161.

47. Quoted in *ibid.*; 12, Herder, *Werke*, I (Munich, 1953), 827.

48. Jacques Solé, "Un Exemple d'archéologie des Sciences humaines: L'étude de l'Egyptomanie du XVIe au XVIIIe siècle," *Annales*, Vol. 27, No. 2 (March–April 1972), 477.

49. *Schlegel, op. cit.*, 505.

50. Vogel, *op. cit.*, 161.

51. Kaufmann, *op. cit.*, 27; Euler, *op. cit.*, 44.

52. Karl Hoffmann, *Des Teutschen Volkes Feuriger Dank und Ehrentempel* (Offenbach, 1815), 93.

53. *Handwörterbuch des Deutschen Aberglaubens*, ed. Hanns Bachtold-Stäubli (Berlin and Leipzig, 1929–30), 1390–1397.

54. See, e.g., Karl Hoffmann, *op. cit.*, 28.

55. *Handwörterbuch des Deutschen Aberglaubens*, 646, 647. The oak figures already as the *"Wunderbaum"* (the magic tree) in the *Edda*. "Nothing larger, nothing older exists than the oak"— Werner Hahn, *Edda; Lieder germanischer Göttersage* (Berlin, 1872), 57.

56. Georg Sammler, "Mittsommerfeuer," *Der Schulungsbrief*, Vol. III (June 1936), 211, 212.

57. Hans Schemm, "Deutsche Sonnenwende," *Der Schulungsbrief*, Vol. VI (June 1937), passim.

58. Percy Schramm, *Herrschaftszeichen und Staatssymbolik*, Vol. II (Stuttgart, 1955), 642, 646.

59. *Ibid.*, 652.

60. *dtv-Lexicon politischer Symbole* (Munich, 1970), 218. The flag also provided a point of orientation in battle. If soldiers faced defeat, they had to turn back to their flag. Hans-Jochen Gamm, *Der braune Kult* (Hamburg, 1962), 43.

61. Willi Schröder, *Burschenschaftsturner in Kampf um Einheit und Freiheit* (Berlin, 1967), 188.

62. Jahn and Eiselen, *op. cit.*, 244.

63. Karl Hoffmann, *op. cit.*, 982.

64. C. G. Carus, *Über die Ungleichheit verschiedener Menschen-stämme für höhere geistige Entwicklung* (n.p., 1849), n.p.

65. *Winckelmanns Werke*, IV, 449.

66. *Cosima Wagner und Houston Stewart Chamberlain im Brief-wechsel, 1888–1908* (Leipzig, 1934), 312.

### Chapter Three. National Monuments

1. Paul Clemen, *Der Denkmalbegriff und seine Symbolik* (Bonn, 1933), 8–9.

2. Thomas Nipperdey, "Nationalidee und Nationaldenkmal in Deutschland im 19. Jahrhundert," *Historische Zeitschrift*, Heft 206/3 (June 1968), 559.

3. Franz Schnabel, "Die Denkmalskunst und Der Geist des 19. Jahrhunderts," Franz Schnabel, *Abhandlungen und Vorträge, 1914–1965* (Freiburg, 1970), 134ff.

4. See *Die Kunst in Deutschen Reich*, Vol. 6, Folge 3, Edition A (March 1942), 60–71.

5. Hubert Schrade, *Bauten des Dritten Reichs* (Leipzig, 1937), 15. Schrade, an art historian, was professor in Heidelberg and Hamburg during the Third Reich, and after the war in Freiburg.

6. Alfred Rietdorf, *Gilly, Wiedergeburt der Architektur* (Berlin, 1940), 128. He believed that Gilly was closer to us today than

ever before, *Die Kunst im Dritten Reich* (October 1940), 172.

7. Emil Kaufmann, *Von Ledoux bis Corbusier* (Vienna, 1933), 30, 33.

8. *Ibid.*, 30.

9. Yvan Christ, *Projets et Divagations de Claude-Nicolas Ledoux* (Paris, 1961), 14–23, 105–107.

10. Adolf Max Vogt, *Boullée's Newton Denkmal: Sakralbau und Kugelidee* (Basel and Stuttgart, 1969), 155.

11. *Ibid.*, 144.

12. See pages 188–189.

13. See page 189.

14. Conversation with Albert Speer, March 16, 1972.

15. Christ, *op. cit.*, 24.

16. Gerhard Kaiser, *Pietismus und Patriotismus im Literarischen Deutschland* (Wiesbaden, 1961), 49.

17. Hubert Schrade, *Das Deutsche Nationaldenkmal* (Munich, 1934), 47.

18. Oswald Herderer, *Leo von Klenze* (Munich, 1964), 246; Ludwig Volkmann, *Egypten-Romantik in der Europäischen Kunst* (Leipzig, 1942), 69, 135.

19. At the Hambach Festival. Egon Caesar Conti, *Ludwig I von Bayern* (Munich, 1960), 188.

20. Vogt, *op. cit.*, 159.

21. Herderer, *op. cit.*, 306.

22. *Geschichte und Beschreibung der Walhalla und des anliegenden Marktfleckens Donaustauf* (Regensburg, 1933), 2.

23. *Johann Winckelmanns sämtliche Werke* (Donauöschingen, 1825), Vol. 3, 69.

24. Herderer, *op. cit.*, 22–25.

25. *Ibid.*, 35.

26. *Ibid.*, 16.

27. Alfred Holder, *Die Aeltere Edda* (Leipzig, 1875), 149; Gustav Neckel, *Walhalla* (Dortmund, 1913), 30.

28. *Geschichte und Beschreibung der Walhalla*, 3ff.

29. Paul Herre, *Deutsche Walhall: Eine Auseinandersetzung und ein Programm* (Potsdam, 1930), 35, 36.

30. *Hakenkreuzbanner* (June 7, 1937), Wiener Library Clipping Collection. Most recently, in July 1973, Jean Paul and Richard Strauss were admitted to *Walhalla*. In his speech the Bavarian Minister of Culture stressed the Bavarian rather than the German nature of their accomplishment. *Süddeutsche-Zeitung*, No. 166 (July 21/22, 1973), "SZ am Wochenende," I.

31. Herre, *op. cit.*, 16.

32. *Ibid.*, 41, 59.

33. Herderer, *op. cit.*, 336–341, 377, 246.

34. Alfred Kuhn, *Peter Cornelius und die Geistigen Strömungen seiner Zeit* (Berlin, 1921), 271, 151. Cornelius also painted the ceiling of the Ludwigskirche which still stands.

35. Ludwig Dehio, *Friedrich Wilhelm IV von Preussen, Ein Baukünstler der Romantik* (Munich, 1961), 82.

36. Heinz Quitsch, *Die Ästhetischen Anschauungen Gottfried Sempers* (Berlin, 1962), 31; Gottfried Semper, *Wissenschaft, Industrie und Kunst*, ed. Hans M. Winger (Mainz and Berlin, 1966), 107.

37. Quitsch, *op. cit.*, 73.

38. *Ibid.*, 31.

39. Hermann Hettner, "Gottfried Semper," *Kleine Schriften* (Braunschweig, 1884), 97, 99.

40. Robert W. Gutman, *Richard Wagner* (New York, 1968), 295.

41. Hermann Schmidt, *Ernst von Bandel, ein deutscher Mann und Künstler* (Hannover, 1892), 29.

42. *Ibid.*, 144, 213, 37, 43.

43. *Ibid.*, 160.

44. Karl Meier-Lengo, "Das Hermannsdenkmal und sein Schöpfer," *Monatsblätter der Bergstadt* (1924–25), 353.

45. Adolf Hitler, "Speech of September 6, 1938," *The Speeches of Adolf Hitler, April 1922–August 1939*, ed. Norman H. Baynes (New York, 1969), Vol. I, 394.

46. Schmidt, *op. cit.*, 349–350.

47. Albert Speer to George L. Mosse, 11. January 1972, 4.

48. Schmidt, *op. cit.*, 126.

49. *Ibid.*, 131–132, 196–197.

50. Karl Hoffmann, *Des Teutschen Volkes Feuriger Dank und Ehrentempel* (Offenbach, 1815), 8, 9.

51. Ferdinand Heyl, *Das Nationaldenkmal auf den Niederwald* (Frankfurt, n.d.), passim.

52. *Ibid.*, passim.

53. *Die Deutschen Kriegervereine in Sonderburg von 1872–1928* (n.p., n.d.), 2; during Weimar they staged some impressive pageantry and march-pasts. See Francis Cathnath, "The Kriegervereine and the Weimar Republic," *Journal of Contemporary History* (forthcoming).

54. *Krieger-Vereins-Zeitung* (September 30, 1924), 57.

55. *Deutsche Bauzeitung* (1898), Vol. XXII, 27.

56. *Ibid.*

57. *Der Kyffäuser als Nationalfeststätte*, ed. Verband der Orts-ausschüsse für Nationalfeste am Kyffhäuser (Sonderhausen, n.d.), 1–3, 10.

58. Alfred Gotthold Meyer, *Reinhold Begas* (Bielefeld and Leipzig, 1897), 105.

59. *Ibid.*, 106–107, 111. The Nazis disapproved of Begas's neo-Baroque, *Die Kunst im Deutschen Reich* (December 1940), 368.

60. Max Dessoir and Herman Mutesius, *Das Bismarck National-denkmal* (Jena, 1912), 10, 22, 25, 27, 24.

61. Eduard Bachman, *Die Völkerschlacht, Das Völkerschlacht-denkmal, und sein Erbauer Clemens Thieme* (Leipzig, 1938), 42. For the influence of Theodoric's tomb, see Albert Hofmann, *Handbuch der Architektur; Denkmäler*, Vol. II (Stuttgart, 1906), 648. Bruno Schmitz's first commission was to build a victory monument in Indianapolis (1888), Hans Schliepmann, *Bruno Schmitz* (Berlin, 1913), iv.

62. Alfred Spitzner, *Deutschlands Denkmal der Völkerschlacht* (Leipzig, 1913), 107.

63. *Ibid.*, 66ff., 74.

64. Bachmann, *op. cit.*, 69.

65. *Ibid.*, 70, 72.

66. *Ibid.*, 94, 95.

67. Friedrich Ludwig Jahn, "Deutsches Volkstum," *Friedrich Ludwig Jahns Werke*, ed. Carl Euler (Hof, 1884), Vol. I, 320.

68. *Deutscher Patriotenbund zur Einrichtung eines Völker-schlachtdenkmals bei Leipzig*, "Gedenkfeier der Völkerschlacht, Sonntag, den 17. Oktober 1915, mittags 12 Uhr" (a program).

69. *Der Cicerone* (1911), Vol. 3, 218–220.

70. Carl Meissner, *Wilhelm Kreis* (Essen, 1925), 13.

71. Quoted in Paul Bonatz, *Leben und Bauen* (Stuttgart, 1950), 50.

72. *Die Kunst im Deutschen Reich* (January 1940), 55: Hanns Johst, quoted (1931) in Karl Ernst Bemer, "Deutsche Literatur im Urteil des 'Völkischen Beobachters' 1922–1932" (Inaugural Disser-tation, Munich, 1954), 34.

73. Hubert Schrade, *Bauten des Dritten Reiches*, 10, 11.

74. Hubert Schrade, *Das Deutsche Nationaldenkmal* (Munich, 1934), 106.

75. *Tannenberg*, ed. Kuratorium für das Reichsehrenmal Tan-nenberg (Oldenburg, 1939?), 227, 228.

76. *Ibid.*, 227.

77. *Das Tannenberg-Nationaldenkmal* (Berlin, n.d.).

78. *Tannenberg*, *op. cit.*, 202, 204, 203.

79. *Ibid.*, 210, 211, 205.

80. But others also realized that this was an "independent and new design for National Monuments," *Zentralblatt der Bauverwaltung* (1925), Vol. 45, 291.

81. *Tannenberg, op. cit.*, 218.

82. Wolfgang Ribbe, "Flaggenstreit und Heiliger Hain," *Aus Theorie und Praxis der Geschichtswissenschaft: Festschrift für Hans Herzfeld zum 80. Geburtstag.* ed. Dietrich Kurze (Berlin, 1972), 183, 187.

83. *Ibid.*, 175–188.

84. Kurt Junghans, *Bruno Taut* (Berlin, 1970), 51–52; Hermann Schmitz, *Revolution der Gesinnung!* (Neubabelsberg, 1931), 205.

85. *Deutscher Ehrenhain für die Helden von 1914/18* (Leipzig, 1931); Werner Lindner, *Ehrenmäle: Grundsätze und Beispiele ihrer Gestaltung* (Kassel and Basel, 1952), ii.

86. Schrade, *Das Deutsche Nationaldenkmal*, 7–8.

## Chapter Four. Public Festivals: Foundations and Development

1. Hitler himself was apt to connect Nazi meetings with the mass meetings of the left, such as the Spartacists, Speech of November 8, 1935. *The Speeches of Adolf Hitler, April 1922–August 1939*, ed. Norman H. Baynes (New York, 1969), Vol. I, 130.

2. *Oeuvres Complètes de J. J. Rousseau* (Paris, 1907), Vol. 5, 245, 246.

3. *Ibid.*, Vol. I, 230.

4. *Ibid.*, Vol. I, 269.

5. *Ibid.*, Vol. I, 187, 188.

6. Gerhard Kaiser, *Pietismus und Patriotismus im Literarischen Deutschland* (Wiesbaden, 1961), 76.

7. *Ibid.*, 67.

8. *Ibid.*, 69.

9. Friedrich Ludwig Jahn, "Deutsches Volkstum," *Friedrich Ludwig Jahns Werke*, ed. Carl Euler (Hof, 1884), Vol. I, 321.

10. E. M. Arndt, *Entwurf einer Teutschen Gesellschaft* (Frankfurt, 1814), 35, 34.

11. *Ibid.*, 36.

12. Christoph Albrecht, *Schleiermachers Liturgik* (Göttingen, 1963), 64, 104.

13. Arndt, *op. cit.*, 40.

14. See Karl Hoffmann, *Des Teutschen Volkes Feuriger Dank und Ehrentempel* (Offenbach, 1815), 86, 153, 1099.

15. *Beschreibung des Festes auf der Wartburg. Ein Sendschreiben an die gutgesinnten* (n.p., 1818), 18.

16. Hoffmann, *op. cit.*, 980, 1099, 259, 153, Introduction (by E. M. Arndt).

17. Albrecht, *op. cit.*, 60, 98.

18. *Ibid.*, 142.

19. *Ibid.*, 10, 36, 39.

20. *Ibid.*, 23, 24.

21. See page 147.

22. *Beschreibung des Festes auf der Wartburg*, passim; Heinrich Ferdinand Massmann, *Kurze und Wahrhaftige Beschreibung des grossen Burschenfestes auf der Wartburg bei Eisenach* (n.p., 1817), 23–24, 28.

23. Hans Werner von Meyenn, *Die politische Feier* (Hamburg, 1938), 21, 22.

24. Klaus Vondung, *Magie und Manipulation, Idelogischer Kult und Politische Religion des Nationalsozialismus* (Göttingen, 1971), 148.

25. *Ibid.*, 42–43.

26. Oskar Söhngen, *Sekularisierter Kultus* (Gütersloh, 1950), 17.

27. Karlheinz Schmeer, *Die Regie des Öffentlichen Lebens im Dritten Reich* (Munich, 1956), 58.

28. Friedrich Ludwig Jahn, "Deutsches Volkstum," *Werke, op. cit.*, Vol. I, 315–316, 323.

29. Jahn, *ibid.*, 310ff. E. M. Arndt, *Ueber Sitte, Mode und Kleidertracht* (Frankfurt, 1814), 50–51.

30. See page 40.

31. See page 65.

32. Friedrich Ludwig Jahn and Ernst Eiselen, *Die Deutsche Turnkunst* (Berlin, 1816), 252, 203; i.e., Gymnastic Festival, October 18, 1817, Jahn, *Werke, op. cit.*, Vol. 2, 878.

33. Veit Valentin, *Das Hambacher Nationalfest* (Berlin, 1932), 31, 39–50.

34. *Ibid.*, 49–50.

35. J. G. A. Wirth, *Das National Fest der Deutschen Zu Hambach* (Neustadt a/h, 1832), 11–14; Valentin, *op. cit.*, 34.

36. Valentin, *op. cit.*, 39–40; Wirth, *op. cit.*, 55–74.

37. Valentin, *op. cit.*, 74, 59, 61.

38. *Ibid.*, 31.

39. Saint-René Taillandier, *Études sur la Révolution en Allemagne* (Paris, 1953), Vol. II, 108, 110.

40. Karl Griewank, *Deutsche Studenten und Universitäten in der Revolution von 1848* (Weimar, 1949), 32.

41. *Ibid.*, 36–37.
42. Bernhard Endrulat, *Das Schillerfest in Hamburg* (Hamburg, 1860), 12.
43. *Courier an der Weser* (November 13, 1859), No. 310, Vol. XIV. (These and most other references to the "Schillerfeiern" will be found as clippings in the Niedersächsische Staatsbibliothek, Göttingen, H. Lit. biogr. V. 1057.)
44. *Instruktionen für die Handhabung der Ordnung beim Schiller Fest 9, 10, 11 November 1859* (Stuttgart, n.d.), 9; Endrulat, *op. cit.*, 8, 11, 14.
45. *Festprogramm des Leipziger Buchhandels* (November 10, 1859), passim.
46. *Augsburger Abendzeitung* (November 10, 1859), No. 312, 256.
47. *Programm der Schiller-Jubel-Feier zu Frankfurt am Main 9 und 10 November, 1859*, passim; Ferdinand Naumann, *Die Schiller-Feier in Hameln* (Hannover, 1859), 29.
48. Endrulat, *op. cit.*, 128.
49. *Dresdner Journal* (October 26,1859 ), 248, 997.
50. Endrulat, *op. cit.*, 128.
51. G. V. Bodelschwingh, *Friedrich V. Bodelschwingh* (Bethel, 1922), 307.
52. Georg Müller, "Friedrich von Bodelschwingh und das Sedansfest," *Geschichte in Wissenschaft und Unterricht* (1963), Vol. 14, 85.
53. *Ibid.*, 86.
54. *Ibid.*, 83, 86.
55. *Ibid.*, 83.
56. *100 Jahre Vereinsgeschichte des Männergesangvereins "Liederkranz" Oldenburg-OLD* (n.p., 1956), 53.
57. Müller, *op. cit.*, 87.
58. *Ibid.*, 77.
59. *Ibid.*, 88.
60. See, e.g., *Deutsche Nationalfeste, Schriften und Mitteilungen des Ausschusses 1897–1898*, (n.p., n.d.), 169.
61. Friedrich Ludwig Jahn, "Deutsches Volkstum," *Werke*, Vol. I, 320.
62. Schmeer, *op. cit.*, 75ff.
63. Müller, *op. cit.*, 77.
64. Jahn and Eiselen, *op. cit.*, xvii.
65. *Jahrbuch für Volks und Jugendspiele* (1901), Vol. 10, 299–303; *ibid.* (1898), Vol. 7, 52.
66. *Ibid.*, Vol. 7 (1898), 46; *ibid.* (1900), Vol. 9, 34; *Deutsche*

*Nationalfeste, op. cit.*, 221–222, 70–72; Fritz Schmidt, *Emil von Schenckendorffs verdienste um die koerperliche Erziehung der deutschen Jugend* (Leipzig, 1919), passim.

67. *Jahrbuch für Volks und Jugendspiele* (1898), Vol. 7, 159.
68. "Leitsätze," *Deutsche Nationalfeste, op. cit.*, n.p.
69. *Jahrbuch für Volks und Jugendspiel* (1900), Vol. 9, 15.
70. *Deutsche Nationalfeste, op. cit.*, 15.
71. *Jahrbuch für Volks und Jugendspiele* (1900), Vol. 9, 90.
72. *Deutsche Bauzeitung* (1898), Vol. XXII, 27, 44, 60, 168.
73. *Deutsche Nationalfeste, op. cit.*, 169.
74. *Jahrbuch für Volks und Jugendspiele* (1901), Vol. 10, 257–258, 263–269.
75. A. Soboul, *Paysans, Sansculottes et Jacobins* (Paris, 1966), 183–202.
76. Here we also hear complaints that there was no real popular participation, apart from dancing, *Le Petit Journal du Soir* (July 15, 1880), n.p.
77. *Jahrbuch für Volks und Jugendspiele* (1898), Vol. 7, 56; *ibid.* (1901), Vol. 10, 281.
78. *The Complete Diaries of Theodor Herzl*, ed. Raphael Patai, tr. Harry Zohn (New York, 1960), Vol. I, 43, 39, 27.
79. *Ibid.*, 67, 33.
80. *Deutsche Bauzeitung* (1898), Vol. XXII, 190.
81. *Ibid.*, 114.
82. *Ibid.*, 64.
83. *Deutsche Bauzeitung* (1889), Vol. II, 515.
84. See pages 170ff.

### Chapter Five. Public Festivals:
### The Theatre and Mass Movements

1. George L. Mosse, "Was Sie Wirklich Lasen: Marlitt, Ganghofer, May," *Popularität und Trivialität* (Bad Homburg, V.D.H., 1974), 101–120.
2. Richard Wagner, quoted in Leopold von Schröder, *Die Vollendung des arischen Mysteriums in Bayreuth* (Munich, 1911), 102–103.
3. George L. Mosse, *The Culture of Western Europe: The Nineteenth and Twentieth Centuries* (Chicago, 1961), 21ff.
4. *Richard Wagner in Selbstzeugnissen und Bilddokumenten*, ed. Hans Mayer (Hamburg, 1959), 142.
5. Quoted in Klaus Vondung, *Magie und Manipulation, Ideologischer Kult und Politische Religion des Nationalsozialismus* (Göttingen, 1971), 173.

6. *Bayreuther Blätter* (1882), Vol. V, 8.

7. Julius Petersen, *Geschichtsdrama und nationaler Mythos* (Stuttgart, 1940), 49, 50.

8. *Ibid.*, 49.

9. Mayer, *op. cit.*, 143.

10. See page 75.

11. Mayer, *op. cit.*, 161; George L. Mosse, *The Crisis of German Ideology* (New York, 1964), 203–209.

12. *Bayreuther Blätter* (1881), Vol. IV, 10.

13. *Bayreuther Blätter* (1884), Vol. VII, 123.

14. Hermann L. Strack, *Das Blut; Glauben und Aberglauben der Menschheit* (Leipzig, 1911). For the later literary history of the "Holy Grail," see Johst Hermand, *Von Mainz nach Weimar* (Stuttgart, 1969), 269–298.

15. Vondung, *op. cit.*, 174.

16. *Bayreuther Blätter* (1884), Vol. VII, 124; von Schröder, quoted in Winfried Schuler, *Der Bayreuther Kreis von Seiner Entstehung Bis Zum Ausgang der Wilhelminischen Ära* (Münster, 1971), 219.

17. *Bayreuther Blätter* (1884), Vol. VII, 168.

18. *Bayreuther Blätter* (1885), Vol. VIII, 148, 149.

19. *Bayreuther Blätter* (1886), Vol. IX, 59.

20. *Cosima Wagner und Houston Stewart Chamberlain im Briefwechsel 1888–1908* (Leipzig, 1934), 187, 312.

21. *Ibid.*, 362.

22. *Ibid.*, 564; see also George L. Mosse, "Introduction," Houston Stewart Chamberlain, *Foundations of the Nineteenth Century* (New York, 1968), v–lxiii. Cosima also disliked Chamberlain's general attitude toward Christianity, which rejected the Protestant orthodoxy of Wagner's wife. Moreover, Bayreuth resented his omission of references to Wagner in the book. Schuler, *op. cit.*, 121ff.

23. See *Hitler's Secret Conversations 1941–1944* (New York, 1953), 198.

24. Gabriele D'Annunzio, *The Flame of Life* (New York, 1900), 124; for D'Annunzio and the new politics, see George L. Mosse, "The Poet and the Exercise of Political Power: Gabriele D'Annunzio," *Yearbook of Comparative and General Literature*, No. 22 (1973), 32–41.

25. Petersen, *op. cit.*, 39, 41. Petersen believed that such a theatre was an integral part of the longing for the "Third Reich," Julius Petersen, *Die Sehnsucht nach dem Dritten Reich* (Stuttgart, 1934),

57. Petersen was a National Socialist professor of German Literature and Philology.

26. Ernst Wachler, "Das Deutsche Theater der Zukunft," *IDUNA Taschenbuch auf 1903* (Berlin, 1903), 173.

27. *Ibid.*, 175.

28. *Ibid.*, 173; Petersen, *op. cit.*, 29.

29. For Wachler, see George L. Mosse, *The Crisis of German Ideology* (New York, 1964), 80–82.

30. Wachler, *op. cit.*, 172.

31. Friedrich Albert Meyer, *Die Zoppoter Waldoper, ein neuer Weg des Festspielgedankens* (Berlin, 1934), 61, 12, 13, 16ff.

32. Petersen, *op. cit.*, 41–43.

33. Wachler, *op. cit.*, 174.

34. *Deutsche Bauzeitung* (1890), Vol. XXIV, 84.

35. Wachler, for example, had high praise for the Bayreuth theatre, which lacked loges and where the auditorium was not divided by corridors. Wachler, *op. cit.*, 174.

36. Rudolf Mirbt, *Laienspiel und Laientheater* (Kassel, 1960), 73.

37. Vondung, *op. cit.*, 19.

38. See Gottfried Haas-Berkow and Max Gumbel-Seiling, *Totentanz* (Leipzig, 1920). Haas-Berkow was an important instigator of lay plays before the First World War.

39. Mirbt, *op. cit.*, 29, 15, 16.

40. *Deutsche Bauzeitung* (1890), Vol. XXIV, 83; *Bayreuther Blätter* (1884), Vol. 7, 18; Vondung, *op. cit.*, 25, 26. The dramatist was Thomas Westerich.

41. Hans Herrig, *Luxustheater und Volksbühne* (Berlin, 1887), 79, 400.

42. *Ich Glaube! Bekenntnisse von Hanns Johst* (*Munich*, 1928), 36.

43. *Ibid.*, 56.

44. Rainer Schlösser, *Das Volk und seine Bühne* (Berlin, 1936), 39.

45. *Hitlerjungens im Kampf*, ed. Rudolf Mirbt (Munich, 1934), passim.

46. Schlösser, *op. cit.*, 51, 45ff.

47. *Ibid.*, 53; Karl-August Götz, "Der Grundsatz des Thingdienstes," *Der Deutsche Student* (December 1935), 45ff., 693.

48. Wilhelm von Schramm, *Neubau des deutschen Theaters* (Berlin, 1934), 55, 39–40, 41, 42. Schramm was for a time the spokesman of the "Deutsche Bühne," as well as novelist, dramatist, and poet.

49. Götz, "Der Grundsatz des Thingdienstes," *Der Deutsche Student*, 691. Wolfgang Neuschaefer, *Thing am Heiligen Berg* (Mühlhausen, 1935), 25; von Schramm, *op. cit.*, 46, 48.

50. *Ibid.*, 5.

51. See pages 186–187.

52. Benno von Arendt, in *Die Kunst im Dritten Reich* (February 1939), 43.

53. Adolf Hitler, *Mein Kampf* (Munich, 1934), 133.

54. *Ibid.*, 119, 133.

55. Rudolf Kuppe, *Karl Lueger und seine Zeit* (Vienna, 1933), 284, 285, 295, 343.

56. Hitler, *op. cit.*, 131.

57. See page 200.

58. Hitler, *op. cit.*, 115.

59. See Walter Frank, director of the Institute for the History of the New Germany, in his *Hofprediger Stoecker und die christlichsoziale Bewegung* (Hamburg, 1935), 238.

60. Eugen Schmahl, *Die antisemitische Bauernbewegung in Hessen von der Boeckelzeit bis zum Nationalsozialismus*, Wilhelm Seipel, *Entwicklung der Nationalsozialistischen Bauernbewegung in Hessen* (Giessen, 1933), 74, 86, 100.

61. *Ibid.*, 89ff, 128, 121; the best general discussion of the Boeckel movement is Rüdiger Mack, "Antisemitische Bauernbewegung in Hessen," *Wetterauer Geschichtsblätter* (1967), Vol. 16, 3–37.

62. Paul W. Massing, *Rehearsal for Destruction* (New York, 1967), 91.

63. *Mitteilungen des Vereins zur Abwehr des Antisemitismus* (August 13, 1893), No. 33, Vol. 3, 313.

64. *Mitteilungen* (January 29, 1893), No. 5, Vol. 3, 34.

65. Schmahl, *op. cit.*, 101.

66. Hitler, *op. cit.*, 43.

67. *Gott, Freiheit, Vaterland; Sprech-chöre der Hitler-jugend* (Stuttgart, n.d.), 7.

68. G. Bonet-Maury, *De la Signification morale et réligieuse des Fêtes Républiques dans les Républiques modernes* (Dole, 1896), 25. He was also concerned with the inefficacy of the Fourteenth of July, *op. cit.*, 3.

69. *Ibid.*, 25.

70. George L. Mosse, "Caesarism, Circuses, and Monuments," *Journal of Contemporary History* (1971), No. 2, Vol. 6, 176–177.

71. French National Archives, BN 4⁰ G. 1279; G. Bessonet-Faure complained that Republican festivals amounted merely to a

"défile" by a delegation in front of the president. *Les Fêtes Républicaines depuis 1789 jusqu'à nos Jours* (Paris, n.d., written between 1900 and 1914), 274.

72. See page 90.

73. *Zum Verfassungstag* (Berlin, 1931), 5, 7.

74. Theodor Heuss, *Erinnerungen 1905–1933* (Frankfurt, 1965), 167.

75. Hans Grimm, *Warum-Woher-Aber Wohinn* (Lippoldsberg, 1954), 120–121. *Festschrift zur republikanischen Kundgebung mit Banner-Enthüllung, 30 August mit 1 September 1929* (Burghausen A.S.), n.p.; Karl Rohe, *Das Reichsbanner Schwarz-Rot-Gold* (Düsseldorf, 1966), 404, 406, 409, 414.

*Chapter Six. Organizations Take a Hand*

1. Thomas Nipperdey, "Verein als Soziale Struktur in Deutschland im Späten 18 und Frühen 19 Jahrhundert," *Geschichtswissenschaft und Vereinswesen Im 19 Jahrhundert* (Göttingen, 1972), 36 n. 100. Other professional organizations also encouraged a "national German consciousness." Irmline Veit-Brause mentions the philologists and natural scientists. *Die deutsch-französische Krise von 1840* (Inaugural Dissertation, Cologne, 1970), 124.

2. Friedrich Ludwig Jahn and Ernst Eiselen, *Die Deutsche Turnkunst* (Berlin, 1816), 236, 253.

3. *Ibid.*, xvii.

4. *Ibid.*, 203.

5. For instance, at the "Turntag" to celebrate the anniversary of the Battle of Leipzig, *Friedrich Ludwig Jahns Werke*, ed. Carl Euler (Hof, 1887), Vol. 2, 878.

6. Jahn and Eiselen, *op. cit.*, 252.

7. Willi Schröder, *Burschenschaftsturner in Kampf um Einheit und Freiheit* (Berlin, 1967), 183, 185.

8. *Ibid.*, 286; Edmund Neuendorf, *Die Deutsche Turnerschaft 1860–1936* (Berlin, 1936), 7.

9. Schröder, *op. cit.*, 287.

10. Neuendorf, *op. cit.*, 52. (Some give 529,000 members in Germany and Austria in 1896.)

11. *Ibid.*, 37.

12. Jahn himself suggested the book burning, Schröder, *op. cit.*, 197.

13. Neuendorf, *op. cit.*, 144, 23.

14. *Ibid.*, 14.

15. *Ibid.*, 23.

16. *Ibid.*, 46.

17. *Deutsche Bauzeitung* (1889), Vol. II, 444.
18. Paul Bonatz, in *Kunst der Nation* (May 1, 1933), 1.
19. See page 000.
20. Conversation with Albert Speer, March 16, 1972.
21. Neuendorf, *op. cit.*, 162.
22. Karl Seidelmann, *Bund und Gruppe als Lebensformen Deutscher Jugend* (Munich, 1954), 294.
23. Neuendorf, *op. cit.*, 176.
24. Jurgen Dieckert, *Die Turnerjugendbewegung* (Stuttgart, 1968), 22.
25. *Ibid.*, 26, 29.
26. Neuendorf, *op. cit.*, 139, 146.
27. Dieckert, *op. cit.*, 21.
28. Neuendorf, *op. cit.*, 215.
29. Dieckert, *op. cit.*, 49.
30. *Ibid.*, 49.
31. Neuendorf, *op. cit.*, 218.
32. Dieckert, *op. cit.*, 94.
33. See Neuendorf, *op. cit.*, 247ff. Neuendorf did not write this last chapter of his book; it was written for him by the Nazis, Dieckert, *op. cit.*, 94.
34. Konrad Henlein, *Reden und Aufsätze zur Völkischen Turnbewegung, 1928–1933* (Karlsbad, 1934), 112.
35. *Jüdisches Vereins-Liederbuch*, edited Ausschuss der Jüdischen Turnerschaft (Berlin, 1911), 29.
36. *Ibid.*, 38, 99 (Yiddish songs were brought in German).
37. Christoph Albrecht, *Schleiermachers Liturgik* (Göttingen, 1963), 79, 100.
38. Eberhard Preussner, *Die bürgerliche Musikkultur* (Kassel and Basel, 1935), 126.
39. *Ibid.*, 128, 129.
40. *Hundert Jahre Männergesangverein "Arion" v. 1829* (New Brandenburg, 1929), 19–20, 22.
41. Hans Staudinger, *Individuum und Gemeinschaft in der Kulturorganisation des Vereins* (Jena, 1913), 62.
42. Preussner, *op. cit.*, 141.
43. Veit-Brause, *op. cit.*, 125–127.
44. Rudolf Haase, *Geschichte des Solinger Chorwesens* (Cologne, 1956), 9.
45. *Der Männerchor* (1926), Vol. II, Heft 2, n.p.; *Festbuch des Männer-Gesangverein Ettenheim 1862–1912* (Ettenheim, n.d.), 5.
46. *Festbuch . . . Ettenheim*, 4, 6, 8; see also "Festprogramm 1912."

47. Hildegard von Radzibor, *Untersuchungen zur Musikgeschichte der Stadt Düren* (Cologne, 1969), 63.

48. Preussner, *op. cit.*, 134.

49. Cited in *Jahrbuch des Deutschen Sängerbundes* (Dresden, 1926), 2.

50. Staudinger, *op. cit.*, 92, 94–95.

51. *Deutsche Sängerbundeszeitung* (April 7, 1909), Vol. I, 250.

52. Staudinger, *op. cit.*, 102.

53. *Deutsche Sängerbundeszeitung* (April 7, 1909), Vol. I, 251.

54. Staudinger, *op. cit.*, 97.

55. *Die Sängerhalle* (January 17, 1895), 25; even when some associations like the *Concordia* of Mannheim became increasingly working-class in membership, they still formed a committee composed of royalty, nobility, and haute bourgeoisie to judge their competitions. Staudinger, *op. cit.*, 105.

56. For example, *100 Jahre Vereinsgeschichte des Männergesangvereins "Liederkranz" Oldenburg-OLD* (n.p., 1956), 14, 18, 20.

57. *Deutsche Sängerbundeszeitung* (January 27, 1909), Vol. I, 651.

58. *Ibid.*, 67.

59. *Deutsche Sängerbundeszeitung* (January 5, 1910), Vol. II, 4.

60. *Ibid.* (February 22, 1910), Vol. II, 156.

61. *Ibid.* (January 4, 1911), Vol. III, 3.

62. *Hundert Jahre Männergesangverein "Arion" v. 1829* (New Brandenburg, 1929), 80.

63. *Jahrbuch des Deutschen Sängerbundes* (Dresden, 1926), 19.

64. *Ibid.*, 20, 83.

65. *100 Jahre Vereinsgeschichte . . . "Liederkranz" Oldenburg*, 89.

66. *Jahrbuch des Deutschen Sängerbundes* (Dresden, 1933), 44.

67. *Jahrbuch des Deutschen Sängerbundes* (1926), 102.

68. Erich Streubel interviewed in *Kunst der Nation* (December 1, 1933), 1.

69. *Ibid.*, 2; see, for instance, Will Reeg, *Tag deutscher Stämme, Chorisches Spiel für die deutsche Jugend* (Mühlhausen, i. Thur., n.d.), 3, 12, 16. For *Thing*, see pages 115–116.

70. *Gott, Freiheit, Vaterland, Sprech-Chöre der Hitler-Jugend* (Stuttgart, n.d.), 7.

71. Hans Severus Ziegler, *Adolf Hitler aus dem Erleben dargestellt* (Göttingen, 1964), 60–61.

72. Klaus Vondung, *Magie und Manipulation, Ideologischer Kult und Politische Religion des Nationalsozialismus* (Göttingen, 1971), 146.

73. *Fränkische Sängerzeitung* (May 15, 1936), Vol. II, 106–110.
74. Georg Götsch and Ludwig Klebetz, *Männerchor oder Singende Mannschaft* (Hamburg, 1934), 12, 16.
75. *Jahrbuch des Deutschen Sängerbundes* (Dresden, 1933), 44.
76. *Jahrbuch des Deutschen Sängerbundes* (1934), 79, 80, 81.
77. *Ibid.*, 81.
78. Götsch and Klebetz, *op. cit.*, 21 n.
79. *Fränkische Sängerzeitung* (May 15, 1936), Vol. II, 106.
80. *Jüdische Rundschau* (January 9, 1934), 3.
81. *Singkamerad, Liederbuch der Deutschen Jugend*, edited by the Reichsamtleitung des Nationalsozialistischen Lehrerbundes (Munich, 1934), 23, 24.
82. *Nationalsozialistisches Volks-Liederbuch mit Noten*, ed. Bernhard Priewe (Berlin-Schöneberg, 1932), 33–34.
83. *Jahrbuch des Deutschen Sängerbundes* (Dresden, 1926), 52.
84. They participated and performed at *Schützenfeste*, for example, *Festblatt des Bundesschiessens 1865* (Bremen, July 23, 1865), n.p.
85. Quoted in Wilhelm Ewald, *Die Rheinischen Schützengesellschaften* (Zeitschrift des Rheinischen Vereins für Denkmalspflege und Heimatschutz, Heft I, September 1933), 70.
86. *Ibid.*, 66.
87. *Wir Schützen*, ed. Wilhelm Ewald (Duisburg, 1938), 296.
88. See *Bayrische-Schützenberbands Zeitung* (April 15, 1933), No. 16, n.p.
89. Ewald, *op. cit.*, 76.
90. *Ibid.*, 210.
91. *Ibid.*, 71.
92. *Fest-Blatt des Zweiten Deutschen Bundesschiessens* (Bremen, June 25, 1865), 10.
93. Friedrich Theodor Vischer, *Kritische Gänge, Neue Folge* (Stuttgart, 1863), Heft 4, 20, 30ff.
94. *Ibid.*, 36.
95. See Hans Mayer, "Rhetorik und Propaganda," *Festschrift zum achzigsten Geburtstage von Georg Lukacz* (Neuwied, 1965), 122–124.
96. *Fest-Blatt des Zweiten Deutschen Bundesschiessens* (June 18, 1865), 13.
97. Festplatz für das X Deutsche Bundesschiessen, *Deutsche Bauzeitung* (1890), Vol. 24, 339, 362.
98. *Bayrische Schützenzeitung* (January 6, 1922), No. 1, 2; *ibid.* (January 27, 1922), No. 4, 1; *ibid.*, (March 10, 1922), passim.

99. *Vereinigte Deutsche Schützen-Zeitung* (July 6, 1923), No. 27, 5.

100. *Bayrische Schützen-Verbands Zeitung* (October 21, 1933), No. 43, 1.

101. *Vereinigte Deutsche Schützen-Zeitung* (July 27, 1923), 1.

102. *Bayrische Schützen-Verbands Zeitung* (January 2, 1932), No. 1, 2.

103. Ludwig Thoma, *Gesammelte Werke* (Munich, 1922), 536, 537. (For a general critique of Schützevereine before 1914, see 536–540.)

104. *Bayrische Schützen-Verbands Zeitung* (April 15, 1933), No. 16, 1.

105. *Ibid.* (October 14, 1933), 1; *ibid.*, (April 29, 1933), No. 18,. 1.

106. *Ibid.* (September 30, 1933), 2.

107. *Ibid.* (April 29, 1933), 1.

108. In 1923 there were three thousand such organizations, *Bayrische Schützenzeitung-Vereinigte Deutsche Schützen-Zeitung* (July 6, 1923), Vol. XXXI, 2. I have not been able to obtain membership figures for later dates.

109. Oskar Söhngen, *Säkularisierter Kultus* (Gütersloh, 1950), 53.

110. Adam Ritzhaupt, *Die "Neue Schaar" in Tübingen* (Jena, 1921), 28.

111. Albert Speer to George L. Mosse, II. January 1972, 2.

112. Mary Wigman, *Die Sprache des Tanzes* (Stuttgart, 1964), 12, 13.

113. *Ibid.*, 17, 22, 23.

114. *Ibid.*, 89.

115. Jacques-Dalcroze, *Rythmische Gymnastik* (Neuchatel, 1906), Vol. I, xiii.

116. Karl Storck, E. *Jacques-Dalcroze, Seine Stellung und Aufgabe in unserer Zeit* (Stuttgart, 1912), 81; E. Jacques-Dalcroze, in *Der Rythmus: Ein Jahrbuch* (Jena, 1911), 49.

117. Storck, *op. cit.*, 85; *Der Rythmus*, 50.

118. Wigman, *op. cit.*, 23.

119. Max von Boehm, *Der Tanz* (Berlin, 1925), 128.

120. Wigman, *op. cit.*, 93; Mary Wigman, "Tänzerisches Schaffen der Gegenwart," *Tanz in dieser Zeit*, ed. Paul Stefan (Vienna and New York, n.d.), 5.

121. Rudolf von Laban, *Ein Leben für den Tanz* (Dresden, 1935), 191, 52.

122. *Ibid.*, 194.

123. *Ibid.*, 108–109.
124. *Ibid.*
125. *Ibid.*, 191, 188.
126. *Ibid.*, 213; Wigman, *Die Sprache des Tanzes*, 87. She continued to create dance dramas until 1961.
127. *Kunst der Nation* (November 1, 1934), 1.
128. *Jahrbuch für Volks und Jugendspiele* (1902), Vol. II, 86, 87, 91.
129. *Ibid.*, 91, 113.
130. *Jahrbuch Deutscher Tanz 1937* (Berlin, 1937), 19.
131. *Jahrbuch für Volks und Jugendspiele* (1902), 55, 57.
132. Albert Speer to George L. Mosse, II. January 1972, 2. Unfortunately it was impossible to find out more about the attraction of jazz for the Nazi leadership.
133. Albert Speer, *Erinnerungen* (Frankfurt, 1969), 40; conversation with Albert Speer, March 16, 1972.

### Chapter Seven. The Workers' Contribution

1. Ferdinand Lasalle, *Ausgewählte Reden und Schriften* (Leipzig, n.d.), Vol. I, 139.
2. Ferdinand Lasalle, *Gesammelte Reden und Schriften*, ed. Eduard Bernstein (Berlin, 1919), Vol. IV, 230–242.
3. *Ibid.*, 236.
4. Shlomo Na'aman, *Lasalle* (Hannover, 1970), 664.
5. *Festschrift, I. Südbayrisches Arbeiter-Sängerbundesfest* (Augsburg, 1926), 15; the precursor to the Arbeiter-Sängerbund, the *Verband der Freien Sänger*, had 12,000 members in 1894. *Die Sängerhalle* (February 22, 1894), 93.
6. Victor Noack, *Der Deutsche Arbeiter-Sängerbund* (Berlin, 1911), 16, 3.
7. *Ibid.*, 19.
8. *Ibid.*, 5, 6.
9. *10 Jahre Volkschor Harmonie Charlottenburg* (n.p., 1929), 5.
10. Siegfried Günther, *Kunst und Weltanschauung: Wege und Ziele des Arbeiter-Sängerbundes* (Berlin, 1925), 18.
11. Erich Mühsam, *Revolution, Kampf-Marsch und Spottlieder* (Berlin, 1925), 7, 8. (I owe this reference to Lawrence Baron.)
12. *Ibid.*, 8.
13. *Festschrift*, IX. Bayrisches Arbeiter-Sängerbundesfest (Munich, 1914), 80.
14. *Ibid.*, 89.
15. *Festschrift*, X. Bayrisches Arbeiter-Sängerbundesfest (Nuremberg, 1925), 85.

16. *Ibid.*, 86, 87, 89, 93.
17. *Vorwärts* (April 11, 1910), 4.
18. *Ibid.*, 1.
19. *Ibid.*, 1.
20. Maurice Dommanget, *Histoire du Premier Mai* (Paris, 1953), 330, 332.
21. Friedrich Giovanoli, *Die Maifeierbewegung* (Karlsruhe, 1925), 101.
22. *Ibid.*, 115; Dommanget, *op. cit*, 396: in France May Day was sometimes called "Pâques ouvrier" (Workers' Easter).
23. Kurt Eisner, *Feste der Festlosen* (Dresden, 1905?), 20–21.
24. *Ibid.*, 44.
25. Kurt Eisner, *Taggeist* (Berlin, 1901), 142.
26. Allan Mitchell, *Revolution in Bavaria 1918–1919* (Princeton, N.J., 1965), 113.
27. Giovanoli, *op. cit.*, 106 n. 35.
28. From *Der Kampf* (1908); *ibid.*, 99.
29. Kurt Eisner, *Gesammelte Schriften* (Berlin, 1919), Vol. II, 93.
30. Dommanget, *op. cit.*, 176.
31. *Maifestschrift des geeinigten Proletariats Würtembergs* (May 1, 1919), n.p.
32. Dommanget, *op. cit.*, 361, 363.
33. *Welten-Mai; Maizeitung 1920 KPD (Spartakusbund)* (n.p., n.d.), 7.
34. *Der Erste Mai der Kommunistischen Internationale* (KPD, Vienna, n.d.), 11.
35. Giovanoli, *op. cit.*, 93, 111–112.
36. Edmund Neuendorf, *Die Deutsche Turnerschaft 1860–1936* (Berlin, 1936), 146.
37. Oskar Drees, in *Reichsjugendpflege Konferenz der Zentralkomission für Arbeitersport und Körperpflege e.v.* (Berlin, 1927), 9, 6.
38. *Ibid.*, 32.
39. See page 144.
40. Erich Grisas, *Nürnberg wir kommen* (n.p., 1929), 78.
41. Oskar Dress, in *Reichsjugendpflege*, 32.
42. *Der Vertrauensmann*, No. 1, Vol. VII (January 1931), 2.
43. Heinz Timmermann, *Geschichte und Struktur der Arbeitersportsbewegung 1893–1933* (Marburg, 1969), 15, 62, 56, 83, 89, 90, 121.
44. *Ibid.*, 7.
45. *Arbeiter-Jugend*, (June 1922), 162.

46. *Ibid.* (February 1933), 47; *ibid.* (October 1924), 287.

47. *Ibid.* (July 1922), 198.

48. *Vorwärts* (October 20, 1928), 1.

49. Friedrich Knilli and Ursula Münchow, *Frühes Deutsches Arbeitertheater 1847–1918, Eine Dokumentation* (Munich, 1970), 343, 351.

50. Klaus Pfutzner, *Die Massenfestspiele der Arbeiter in Leipzig, 1920–1924* (Leipzig, 1960), 10.

51. *Ibid.*, 11, 13–14.

52. *Ibid.*, 20, 24; Eugen Kurt Fischer, *Die Laienbühne als Gesinnungstheater* (Munich, 1926), 29.

53. *Die Literarische Welt,* Sondernummer "Arbeiterdichtung" (July 12, 1929), Vol. 5, 1.

54. *Ibid.*, 2.

55. *Ibid.*, 5.

56. *Gott, Freiheit, Vaterland, Sprech-Chöre der Hitler-Jugend* (Stuttgart, n.d.), 7.

57. Ludwig Hoffmann and Daniel Hoffmann-Ostwald, *Deutsches Arbeitertheater 1918–1933* (Berlin, 1961), 100, 128.

58. See *Arbeiter Fest-Tage* (Vienna, 1927), 134.

59. Hoffmann and Hoffman-Ostwald, *op. cit.*, 226–228.

60. *Ibid.*, 225.

61. C. D. Innes, *Erwin Piscator's Political Theatre* (Cambridge, 1972), 29, 31, 144.

62. *Ibid.*, 92.

63. On the "left" Volksbühne, see *Wesen und Weg der Berliner Volksbühnenbewegung,* ed. Julius Bab (Berlin, 1919); for the "Nationalsozialistische Volksbühne," see *Die Volksbühne,* Vol. 5, No. 11 (February 1931), 482; *Der Aufmarsch,* No. 2 (February 1931), 8; *ibid.,* No. 3 (March 1931), 8. This is the newspaper of the NS Schülerbund (Nazi high-school student organization).

64. "Die Stellung der Nationalsozialistischen Deutschen Arbeiterpartei zur Judenfrage," *Eine Materialsammlung vorgelegt vom Centralverein deutscher Staatsbürger Jüdischen Glaubens* (Berlin, 1932). This was a large collection of documents which was submitted to the president of the German Republic, Von Hindenburg, as part of the defense activities of the chief German Jewish organization—Arnold Paucker, *Der jüdische Abwehrkampf gegen Antisemitismus und Nationalsozialismus in den letzten Jahren der Weimarer Republik* (Hamburg, 1968), 137, n. 40; the best sources for Nazi theatre before 1933 are the journals *Das Junge Deutschland* and *Aufmarsch.*

65. Hoffmann and Hoffman-Oswald, *op. cit.*, 45.

242 Notes

66. *Ibid.*, 230, 231.
67. Jean Marguerite, "Les Fêtes du Peuple," *Les Cahiers du Travail* (June 2, 1921), serie 1, cahier 7, 43, 48, 7.
68. *Ibid.*, 5.
69. Paul Piechowski, *Proletarischer Glaube* (Berlin, 1928), 91, 93. This is the sixth edition of the book.
70. See Ursula Münchow, *Aus den Anfängen der Sozialistischen Dramatik I* (Berlin, 1964), 3ff. (Jean Baptiste von Schweitzer, "Ein Schlingel").
71. Adolf Hitler, *Mein Kampf*, tr. Ralph Mannheim (Boston, 1943), 41.
72. *Ibid.*, 457.
73. *Ibid.*, 171.

*Chapter Eight. Hitler's Taste*

1. Quoted in Hamilton T. Burden, *The Nuremberg Party Rallies: 1923–1939* (New York, 1967), 103.
2. "Albert Speer spricht über Architektur und Dramaturgie der nationalsozialistischen Selbstdarstellung," script, Institut für den Wissenschaftlichen Film, Göttingen, 1970, 13.
3. Albert Speer, *Erinnerungen* (Berlin, 1969), 108; P. Villard, "Antiquité et *Weltanschauung* Hitlérienne," *Revue d'histoire de la deuxième guerre mondiale*, Jahrg. 22, No. 88 (October 1972), 12, 13.
4. Friedrich Heer, *Der Glaube des Adolf Hitler* (Munich, 1968), 153.
5. *Wiener Monumental-Bauten* (Vienna, 1892), Vol. II, passim. Klaus Eggert, *Die Ringstrasse* (Vienna and Hamburg, 1971), 34ff.
6. Quoted in Armand Dehlinger, *Architektur der Superlative* (unpublished MS, Institut für Zeitgeschichte, Munich), 33.
7. Alfred Rietdorf, *Gilly, Wiedergeburt der Architektur* (Berlin, 1940).
8. Adolf Hitler, *Skizzenbuch* (unpublished MS in the possession of Albert Speer, deposited at The Kunstgeschichtliches Seminar, Göttingen); Speer, *op. cit.*, 149, 150.
9. Gerhard Kratsch, *Kunstwart und Dürerbund* (Göttingen, 1969), 202, 203: "Volkkräftige Kunst stärkt das Volk," *Der Kunstwart* (October 1887), Vol. I, 4.
10. *Ibid.*, 466, 464.
11. Heinrich Tessenow, *Hausbau und dergleichen* (Munich, 1916), 3, 8.
12. Conversation with Albert Speer, March 16, 1972; for Hit-

ler's fixation on representative buildings, see "Albert Speer spricht," 15.

13.  Dehlinger, *op. cit.*, 38.
14.  Paul Bonatz, *Leben und Bauen* (Stuttgart, 1950), 181.
15.  Designs in the possession of Albert Speer.
16.  Dehlinger, *op. cit.*, 65.
17.  Speer, *op. cit.*, 55.
18.  Dehlinger, *op. cit.*, 30.
19.  See articles throughout *Kunst im Deutschen Reich.*
20.  Conversation with Albert Speer, March 16, 1972.
21.  Albert Speer to George L. Mosse, II. January 1972.
22.  *Kunst und Volk* (April 1937), 118, 120.
23.  J. J. Winckelmann, *The History of Ancient Art*, tr. G. Henry Lodge (Boston, 1973), 44.
24.  Burden, *op. cit.*, 81.
25.  Hildegard Brenner, *Die Kunstpolitik des Nationalsozialismus* (Hamburg, 1963), 112.
26.  Conversation with Albert Speer, March 16, 1972.
27.  *Die Kunst im Dritten Reich* (February 1939), 43.
28.  Hitler, *Skizzenbuch.*
29.  Quoted in Heinz Kindermann, *Theatergeschichte Europas* (Salzburg, 1968), Vol. 8, 242.
30.  *Ibid.*, 241, 243.
31.  *Die Kunst im Dritten Reich* (February 1939), 52.
32.  *Ich Glaube! Bekenntnisse von Hanns Johst* (Munich, 1928), 45, 23.
33.  Kindermann, *op. cit.*, 242.
34.  See page 155.
35.  Adolf Hitler, *Mein Kampf* (Munich, 1942), 530ff.
36.  Quoted in William A. Jenks, *Vienna and the Young Hitler* (New York, 1960), 195.
37.  Brenner, *op. cit.*, 113.
38.  *The Speeches of Adolf Hitler, April 1922–August 1939*, ed. Norman H. Baynes (New York, 1969), Vol. I, 587.
39.  George L. Mosse, "Literature and Society in Germany," *Literature and Civilization*, ed. David Daiches and Anthony Thorlby (London, 1972), Vol. II, 284–288.
40.  Hans Severus Ziegler, *Adolf Hitler aus dem Erleben dargestellt* (Göttingen, 1964), 76.
41.  George L. Mosse, "The Mystical Origins of National Socialism," *Journal of the History of Ideas* (January–March 1961), Vol. XII, 83–96.
42.  Guido List, *Der Uebergang vom Wuotanismus zum Chris-*

*tentum* (Leipzig and Zurich, 1911), 101–103, Lanz von Lie-benfels, *Bibeldokumente I, Der Mensch der Bibel* (n.p., n.d.), 53; Joachim Besser, "Die Vorgeschichte des Nationalsozialismus im neuen Licht," *Die Pforte*, Vol. 2, Heft 21–22 (November 1950), 775.

43. Speer, *op. cit.*, 71.

44. Quoted in Alfred Stein, "Adolf Hitler und Gustav Le Bon," *Geschichte in Wissenschaft und Unterricht* (1955), 367.

45. Hermann Rauschning, *Gespräche mit Hitler* (New York, 1940), 40.

46. Villard, *op. cit.*, 11. Michael H. Kater, *Das "Ahnenerbe" der SS* (Stuttgart, 1974), 23.

47. *Fest und Freizeitgestaltung im NSLB* (1936), Vol. I, 12.

48. At the transferring of the dead of the Hitler putsch of 1923 to their permanent resting place (1935).

49. K. F. Reimers, J. Bauer, W. Funke, M. Held, and H. Piont-kowitz, "Hitler's Aufruf an das deutsche Volk vom 10 February, 1933," *Publikationen zu Wissenschaftlichen Filmen*, Vol. II, Heft 2 (May 1971), 246.

50. "Albert Speer spricht über Architektur und Dramaturgie," 19.

51. *Ibid.*, 19.

52. Hitler, *Mein Kampf*, 423–424, 513–514.

53. *Ibid.*, 371.

54. Gabriele D'Annunzio, *The Flame of Life* (New York, 1900), 124–125.

55. Hitler, *Mein Kampf*, 116.

56. Cornelius Schnauber, *Wie Hitler Sprach und Schrieb* (Frankfurt, 1972), 37, 50, 51, 87.

57. *Ibid.*, 9.

58. See Stein, *op. cit.*, 362–368.

59. *Oeuvres Complètes de J. J. Rousseau* (Paris, 1907), Vol. I, 269.

60. George L. Mosse, *The Crisis of German Ideology* (New York, 1964), 216, 229.

61. Heer, *op. cit.*, 271; Otto Weininger, *Geschlecht und Charakter* (1903), had sold 26 editions and between 55,000 and 58,000 copies by 1927. *Mitteilungen des Vereins zur Abwehr des Antisemitismus*, Vol. 37 (October 1927), 126.

62. See, for instance, *Die Sonne*, Vol. 10, Heft 10 (October 1933), 517.

63. Franz Josef Heyen, *Nationalsozialismus im Alltag; Quellen zur Geschichte des Nationalsozialismus Vornehmlich in Raum Mainz-Koblenz-Trier* (Boppard a Rh., 1967), 290–291.

64. *Ibid.*, 309.

65. "Das Jahr 1940 in Chronologischer und Astronomischer Beziehung" (Wiener Library Clipping Collection).

66. George L. Mosse, *Nazi Culture* (New York, 1966), 375–577.

67. Hans-Peter Görgen, *Düsseldorf und der Nationalsozialismus* (Düsseldorf, 1969), 131.

68. Renzo De Felice, *Mussolini il fascista*, Vol. I, *L'Organisazione dello stato fascista 1925–1929* (Rome, 1968), 358, n. 2.

69. Görgen, *op. cit.*, 98.

70. Josef Ackermann, *Heinrich Himmler als Ideologe* (Göttingen, 1970), 85.

71. See Chapter Two.

## Chapter Nine. The Political Cult

1. George L. Mosse, *Nazi Culture* (New York, 1966), 8.

2. Arno J. Mayer, *Dynamics of Counterrevolution in Europe, 1870–1956* (New York, 1971), 119.

3. George L. Mosse, "The French Right and the Working Classes: Les Jaunes," *Journal of Contemporary History* (July–October 1972), 185–209.

4. Max H. Kele, *Nazis and Workers* (Chapel Hill, N.C., 1972), 164.

5. George L. Mosse, "German Socialists and the Jewish Question in the Weimar Republic," *Year Book of the Leo Baeck Institute* (1971), Vol. XVI, 123–151.

6. Theodore S. Hamerow, *The Social Foundations of German Unification; Ideas and Institutions* (Princeton, N.J., 1969), 398.

7. J. Huizinga, *The Waning of the Middle Ages* (London, 1924), 186.

8. David Bidney, "Myth, Symbolism and Truth," *Myth, A Symposium*, ed. Thomas A. Sebeok (Bloomington, Ind., and London, 1958), 14.

9. Claude Lévi-Strauss, *Tristes Tropiques* (New York, 1967), 127.

10. *Ibid.*, 126.

11. George Rudé, *The Crowd in History; A Study of Popular Disturbances in France and England, 1730–1848* (New York, 1964), 208.

12. *Mussolinis Gespräche mit Emil Ludwig* (Berlin, 1932), 123.

13. *Goethes Faust*, ed. Georg Witkowski (Leipzig, 1929), 7, 60; see George Steiner, *Language and Silence* (New York, 1970), 384. I am indebted to George Steiner for several insights about the nature of time discussed here.

14. Benedetto Croce, *History of Europe in the Nineteenth Century* (London, 1934), Chapter IV and passim.

15. See, for instance, Robert M. Berdahl, "New Thoughts on German Nationalism," *American Historical Review* (February 1972), Vol. 77, No. 1, 69ff.

16. G. W. F. Hegel, *Reason in History*, tr. Robert S. Hartman (Indianapolis, 1953), 63; (from Hegel's *Lectures on the Philosophy of History*, 1837).

17. Quoted in Helmut F. Pfanner, *Hanns Johst* (The Hague, 1970), 151.

18. Robert Minder, *Kultur und Literatur in Deutschland und Frankreich* (Frankfurt, 1962), 50.

19. For an analysis of United States politics in terms of the political style we have discussed, see Murray Edelman, *The Symbolic Uses of Politics* (Urbana, Ill., 1967).

20. Steiner, *op. cit.*, 389.

21. Herbert Marcuse, *Kultur und Gesellschaft I* (Frankfurt, 1965), 57.

# Index

## DATE DUE

| | | | |
|---|---|---|---|
| il: 3972042 | | | |
| 11-9-94 | | | |
| | | | |
| | | | |
| | | | |
| | | | |
| | | | |
| | | | |
| | | | |
| | | | |
| | | | |
| | | | |
| | | | |
| | | | |
| | | | |

HIGHSMITH 45-220